JAILHOU

JAILHOUSE ROCK

Valeri Barinov
with
Danny Smith

HODDER AND STOUGHTON
LONDON SYDNEY AUCKLAND TORONTO

The publishers would like to thank the following for permission to include their photographs in this book:

In Leningrad with Panthera, 1982 © Jubilee Campaign
January 1987, outside KGB headquarters, Leningrad © Jubilee Campaign
"Let me preach the gospel" © Jubilee Campaign
Arrival at Heathrow, November 1987 © Chris Gander, *Christian Family*
Press conference on arrival © Chris Gander, *Christian Family*
At Cobham Christian Fellowship © Rosie McLaughlin

British Library Cataloguing in Publication Data

Barinov, Valeri
  Jailhouse rock.
  1. Soviet Union. Political prisoners — Biographies
  I. Title II. Smith, Danny
  365.45092
  ISBN 0-340-52686-6

Published by Hodder and Stoughton, a division of Hodder and Stoughton Ltd, Mill Road, Dunton Green, Sevenoaks, Kent TN13 2YA. Editorial Office: 47 Bedford Square, London WC1B 3DP.

Photoset by Medcalf Type Ltd, Bicester.

Printed in Great Britain by Cox & Wyman Ltd, Reading.

ACKNOWLEDGMENTS AND THANKS

Playing postman in 1981, I "smuggled" a guitar into Leningrad for Valeri Barinov; later we sent him a synthesiser, enabling his band to record "The Trumpet Call". When Valeri was arrested, we released the secret recordings (in English) to raise prayer and action. In 1987, through the Foreign Office, I issued a personal invitation to the Barinov family, endorsed by the British Prime Minister on her visit to Moscow. With airline tickets provided by Campaign friends, we welcomed Valeri and Tanya, Zhanna and Marina, to Britain in 1987.

Perhaps there will be another moment to pay tribute to all those people who played a part in the campaign for Valeri Barinov. Here I would like to thank those who were an encouragement while I tried to record his story.

To my family who made space in the life we share: Joan, Jessica, Rachel and Luke; Mum and Clement.

To everyone at Jubilee Campaign who continued to patrol the tower: Richard Warnes, Howard Taylor, John Anderson, Alison Halls, Rosie McLaughlin, Mark Douglas and Bob "Slasher" Day who edited the final draft.

Thanks also to Dirk Jan Groot, Pete Fabian, Mike Rowe, Mike Morris, Mike Wakely, Bill Hampson, Sue Richards, Charlie Colchester, Lyndon Bowring, Emma Foa, Simon Thomas, John Quanrad, Pete and Karen Titchener, Ian and Rosemary Dick, Bob Hitchings, Mark and Carrie Teddor, Pat Harpole, Heartbeat, Kevin Hutson; to those who organised the "House Fund" — Andy Butcher, Clive Price, Gerald Coates, Brian Philips; to those who helped steer us on the final journey — Edward England, Carolyn Armitage,

David Wavre; to David Alton MP, for unwavering support; to George Verwer, who reminded me of the important things in life.

Danny Smith

CONTENTS

PART III: ANOTHER COUNTRY

PROLOGUE: Spring 1983

*The jailor's keys jangle against the steel door of my cell.
Footsteps along the prison corridor stop outside. Voices alert
me to visitors.*

*I cross the room, which seems like a dark, dirty toilet,
covering the distance in a couple of paces, trying to inhale
fresh air through the window. Toilet number 207 on the fifth
floor.*

*The window is a joke. It has a metal grid like a car radiator
with louvre-type partitions. Iron railings run vertical and
horizontal, both inside and outside, preventing sunlight from
invading your inner space. It's a brisk April afternoon, and
I search for a tiny patch of blue sky that might have escaped
the watchman's eye.*

*What is it to be this time? Am I going to be allowed to
contact Tanya at last? Are they coming to announce my
release? Or am I to face another barrage of endless
questions?*

*I am alone with my thoughts. My Jesus, how easy it is
to be with you. I know that you are here in this prison cell.
Thank you, Jesus, for your faithfulness to me. I can risk
anything with you in my life.*

*My cell is dark and silent like a tomb. The door swings
open, and light from the corridor fills the room with a
strange glow. My eyes focus on the familiar blue of the KGB
officer's uniform. I recognise one of the guards. It's Sasha,
who patrols our floor.*

*He shuffles forward and stands to attention inside the
room.*

Sasha is aged about twenty, married with a family. From

the prison grapevine I learn that he is troubled by the corruption he has witnessed within the prison system. He does not look at me.

Behind Sasha, several others march into my cell. Two military officers followed by a doctor and his assistant, who both carry black cases. The last one to enter is a middle-aged, almost mild-mannered man whom I recognise as one of the chiefs of the prison. Captain Starkov is short and well-built. He is known for his efficiency; others may say his ruthlessness.

The door slams shut, a weird metallic gong that echoes in my head. The dark walls of the cell add a sinister menace to our meeting. The naked bulb dangling from the middle of the ceiling creates an eerie atmosphere in an unreal midnight world.

"Mr Barinov, the rock singer," Captain Starkov says matter-of-factly. "We meet again."

With six adults closeted together between two beds, our bodies almost touch. I nod my head, acknowledging his introduction.

As though considering each word carefully, Captain Starkov speaks in a slow drawl. "Why are you giving us so much trouble? Don't you like our food?"

"No, no, I assure you, I have no complaints about the food. Not at all."

"Then why are you continuing this hunger strike?" the captain barks. Changing his tone almost to a whine, he continues, "I was surprised when I was told about this. I didn't think you would resort to such unchristian methods of provocation. Are you not a believer?"

Captain Starkov's questions are pitched in a serious, puzzled manner and seem to hang in the air between us.

"But surely this is not the kind of behaviour for a Christian?"

I look directly at him and reply in a clear, calm voice. "This is my prayer — fast to God. But you don't be-lieve in God. For you, this must seem very strange. So *maybe you will understand my action as a hunger strike.''*

Stroking his jaw, the KGB officer continues, "But why are you on hunger strike?''

"I was arrested even though there was never any evidence against me. I never broke any law. You know that I am an innocent man. Yet I have been held in this prison.''

I pause for breath. "I know that false documents are being prepared to frame me and that I will be sentenced to prison. But who can I turn to for justice? For this reason I am fasting to God.''

The KGB chief holds up his hand to warn me to stop speaking. Now his voice has an edge to it. "You must stop this hunger strike at once,'' he insists.

"If you refuse to eat, then you give us no choice but to force-feed you.'' The captain glances round at the officers cramped together in the tiny room. Their presence lends him tacit support. But I am not afraid of their schemes.

"Your hunger strike is now in its fifth day. You know that other troublemakers aren't allowed to continue their hunger strike for more than three days. This can be quite dangerous for your health. You know that Doctor Karenko, here from the prison hospital, is quite concerned for your health.''

Doctor Karenko, who until now has stood impassively by the door, confirms his assent. The captain continues to speak, now quicker than before. It seems that he is impatient to conclude our conversation. Perhaps other pressing duties await him elsewhere in the prison.

"So, Barinov, I have given you a final warning. Now the time has come for you to decide. What will you do? Will you stop this hunger strike?''

I am not afraid. I feel the inner peace of the Holy Spirit's presence. My God revealed to me in a vision that I should begin this fast so I am confident that I am in his will. He has never let me down. I must simply trust him and obey his command. I can't go back.

The Lord puts a boldness in my voice. "I know that you are wrong. I will continue this fast to my God."

Captain Starkov shrugs his shoulders, issues a command to the men and then moves behind them to lean against the far wall. He peers through the window grating. I wonder whether he can see the sky.

Two officers grasp my hands and place handcuffs on me. Until this moment, Doctor Karenko has remained a silent observer. Now he begins his work, removing tubes and medical apparatus from his black bag. His assistant also empties the bag he carries. The preparation is completed in silence.

The officers motion me towards the bed and I obey. Gripping my shoulders, they hold me down. From the bed I stare directly at each of the men in the room. No one will look at me.

Silently I pray to my Jesus.

Doctor Karenko stands above me and places his hand beneath my jaw. It is uncomfortable but I allow it. He expresses no emotion. In his right hand he holds a long colourless tube that snakes across the floor by his feet. He inserts the tube into my nose.

The sensation is excruciating. The pain is inside my head, a tingling all over my body. My nose leaks, tears stream from my eyes. I gasp for breath. I feel my whole body wrestle with this painful intruder.

The weight of the officers forces me down. The pain is all around and inside me. I can't identify its source.

Doctor Karenko forces the tube into my body. I can now feel it in my throat and every breath is a torment. I forget where I am or what is happening to me, and I cry out in agony without really knowing what sound is emerging. As the tube reaches down into my abdomen it seems to be ripping my insides apart. The torture seems too much to bear.

I grapple with the officers but their grip is like iron. The captain walks over and stares at me. Sounds appear distorted. Voices directed at me are coming from the ceiling but I can't hear any words. Perhaps they expect me to plead with them to stop this torture.

The tube in my stomach makes me feel nauseous and I retch continually. Perhaps five minutes have passed, it seems like fifty. Now the doctor brings what looks like a large injection. He attaches it to the tube and pumps a mixture of food into it. From the corner of my eye, it seems to be a special kind of meat. Eventually it hits my stomach with a weird sensation. The operation is repeated until my belly has been filled.

Doctor Karenko signals to his assistant. The KGB men relax their grip as he begins the humiliating task of pulling the tube from my body. The tissues inside my throat and nose are raw and I can see blood on the tube. He turns his back and the evil thing is removed from my sight. My handcuffs are unlocked.

Now I can see the captain clearly. He is enraged, not expecting me to endure the violence. "Did you enjoy that? Think about it, Barinov! No one knows about this hunger strike. No one cares what happens to you. You're making life miserable for yourself. We'll soon have you singing another song. Stop this hunger strike!"

He storms out of the cell, followed by the KGB officers and finally Doctor Karenko and his assistant.

And then I am alone. My head is spinning. My stomach feels bloated and bilious. My nose and throat are sore from the invasion.

"Thank you, Jesus. You give me the strength to endure this torture." I collapse backwards on to the bed, exhausted by the encounter.

Perhaps an hour had passed, maybe more. I lay on my prison bed as if in a trance. Starkov's words rang in my ears. No one knows. No one cares. Betrayal and despair lined the dark tunnel of sanity.

I had to get up off the bed. I had to resist the tide that was swamping me. The room was spinning and I felt the bile rise within me as I stood up.

The basin in my cell was cracked and filthy. I turned the rusty tap and felt the cold water gush out into my hand. For a moment the flow of the clear water pouring itself into the filthy basin catches my eye. The purity of the water as it glistens amidst the dirt seems strangely symbolic of the broken body of our Lord giving his life for us.

Scooping a handful of water into my palm I splash my face. The shock of the water to my senses is exactly what I need to revive myself. Instantly my mind is racing with questions.

How is Tanya coping? Has she found work to earn money for the family? What are Zhanna and Marina doing at the moment? Do they miss their dad?

These are the questions which the KGB exploit with vile rumours to gain the psychological advantage. But I am not afraid of the KGB or anything they can do to me. My Jesus watches over me. He protects me. My complete trust is in him.

The physical effort of raising my hands in the air focuses my mind as I pray aloud. "My Jesus, I praise you my Lord. This trumpet call will never be silenced!"

PART I

YOUNG DREAMS

1

CHILDHOOD ISLAND

Mama sat by the open window, her chin cradled in the curve of her arm, elbow in the breeze. A cold north wind brought a predawn chill to our room in the Pioneer Camp where we lived.

I rubbed the sleep out of my eyes, and tumbled out of bed. Mama stretched out her hand and drew me towards her. In one movement, I leapt forward and curled up in her lap.

Mama had turned her face away, but her eyes were red and I could tell she was upset.

"Mama!" I called out in surprise, "You're crying. Are you hurt?"

Although she shook her head, I noticed that her pink, neatly embroidered handkerchief was wet through.

"What's wrong Mama?" I asked again, with all the innocence of a six-year-old. "I won't let anything bad harm you."

"Oh Valeri, my son, you're everything I've got," she whispered, her voice weak and faltering. She gave me a gentle squeeze. With Mama's arm around me, I felt warm and protected.

Mama's tears didn't belong in my childhood world. She switched moods to protect me, and I was easily distracted.

Mama was the eldest daughter of a family of three. She was closest to her sister Tamara. Ura, the boy in the family, was the youngest by four years.

My grandfather was a hero in the Revolution, and served in the Chekka, the forerunner of the KGB. When Lenin died, grandfather became depressed and began to drink heavily. "With Lenin dead, I know what will come of the Revolution," he would comment wistfully. When Mama was sixteen he jumped from a moving tram, fell beneath the wheels, and died of his injuries in hospital.

Grandmother was a cultured lady who spoke four languages and impressed neighbours and friends with her dinner parties. She took the news of Grandfather's death badly. Soon after the tragic accident, she suffered a heart attack.

Within a few weeks of each other both parents had died, leaving Mama to raise the family. Tamara was fourteen and Ura was a handful at the age of ten. Mama sacrificed her teenage years to this responsibility and undertook any job she could find.

Conditions in Leningrad were critical during the war. Thousands of families mourned the million casualties who were buried in the Leningrad cemetery. Amidst the turbulence of the war, Mama met a dashing young figure in a Red Army uniform who was to be the love of her life.

Alexander Sardonikov and Mama married after a whirlwind romance. I was a winter "war baby" born on December 6, 1944 at Maternity Hospital No. 2 in Leningrad.

But the laughter soon faded. My father was unprepared for domesticity, and my mother was plunged into turmoil. Mama never got over the shock of coming home one day to find that my father had gone.

Mama sheltered me from everything and we became exceptionally close. I have only happy memories of sunny days strolling through the park with her, hand in hand.

I have no childhood recollections of my father and I never called anyone papa or dad.

My mind focuses on a tall figure standing beneath a streetlight. Somewhere in the distance a radio is playing. He turns and walks into the night casting long shadows in his path. I close my eyes and desperately try to remember my father. I feel as though I am walking down a long corridor and eventually stop outside a door. I knock and wait, but there is no reply. I continue to knock, now banging on the door. My hands are hurting, and my knuckles are red. But still, no one comes. The only sound I hear is the silence of loss.

My mother was attractive and took great pride in her appearance. I, too, was always dressed smartly, and Mama worked long hours, training as a professional book-keeper so that I could attend a local kindergarten as a toddler of three, and school at seven. I was oblivious to the many sacrifices that my mother was forced to make to keep us together.

Mama's sister Tamara proved a dependable stalwart in difficult circumstances, but Ura was reckless, and too much in need of discipline himself to offer any real assistance.

Mama was extremely popular, and I suspect she had many admirers, but remained infatuated by my father. Her photo album was a treasured possession, and she spent many hours staring at the visual memories of happy, carefree days.

I loved music, and at night I would sneak out of bed and sit on the steps outside our neighbour's flat and listen to music playing from their gramophone.

As a child I was very shy. When I entered a room for the first time, I would clutch Mama's skirt. But when music was played, I instinctively began dancing, swaying and moving to the rhythms. When I heard Russian choirs singing harmony, I would leap up and down, bob and weave until the music stopped. Then I would become shy and reserved once more.

I loved to sing and could quickly pick up a melody. At school concerts I was frequently given solo parts to perform. Music seemed to unlock something within myself.

Although I was a mischievous child and frequently needed discipline, I was also sensitive. As I grew older, I was aware that Mama was weary from a heavy burden. I found her crying helplessly on several occasions, a crumpled figure wounded from a broken heart.

Saddened by this unnamed sorrow, I was frequently alone

and turned to the radio for comfort and companionship. Many nights I fell asleep with the light on in the room, static blasting out of the set. Even the late night station had closed down.

But Mama loved me and I cherished her.

When I was eight years old I became seriously ill. I was delirious with a high fever but I know Mama sat up all night with me holding my hand and trying to comfort me.

Mama's friend came to visit me in hospital. His black hair was streaked with silver and he talked with a soft soothing voice. He took me in his arms and prayed with me.

I hadn't responded to the treatment but was then given some herbal tablets and recovered quickly. I think the prayers helped more than anyone realised at the time.

On most Sundays, Mama would dress me up and silently we would walk to the Orthodox Church. I especially liked it if we arrived as the bells were ringing. There was something pure and uplifting about the chimes of the church bells.

Inside the church I was engrossed by the chanting and the music. When Mama walked forward for communion, I followed and sat beside her on the steps of the altar. Calmly I waited for the priest with his flowing beard and long robes to bend down and pat my head.

The strong distinctive fragrance and the brightness of the candlelit sanctuary created an atmospheric experience for a young boy who was taught at school that this charade was covering a vile deception.

I wasn't aware of any contradiction, but I knew that Mama's views on God differed from those of our schoolteachers, who taught that the concept of God was a fairy tale, an invention of wicked people who used religious ideas to exploit the poor.

Mama arranged for my baptism as a child in the Orthodox tradition. Brother Piotr Tiyetich, a family friend who was also an engineer and a devout believer, conducted the brief ceremony.

Although it was not apparent at the time, Mama's

heartfelt prayer, offering her child to God, was to play a most dramatic role in my life.

As I grew wild and unruly on the streets of Leningrad, the problems increased for Mama. How could she contain the energy of such an active youth? Eventually she found a job in the accounts department of a Pioneer Youth Camp outside Leningrad.

This was to prove a popular decision. Situated by a beautiful lake surrounded by woods, the camp had numerous activities to occupy a growing lad.

Pioneer Camps are used by workers who pay monthly subscriptions entitling them to children's holidays. Each camp had an orphanage attached to it and I was permitted to stay there to continue my studies, while Mama had a room with the rest of the staff.

I had the run of the place and was given swimming lessons and learned to play several games. I was a skilful rower and won first prize in one of the competitions. I was also chosen to sing in some of the concerts organised at the camp. I grew into an enthusiastic young pioneer who wore his red scarf with pride.

Mama's room was in the attic of one of the residential blocks. She had decorated it tastefully and I would sneak in there late at night to eat biscuits or cake.

One afternoon I was with Mama in her room when she told me a secret. For some weeks she had been saving up to send me for singing lessons at the Rimsky-Korsakov Conservatoire in Leningrad. I was delighted. Mama talked avidly, plotting my future career and the different countries to which I would travel. That night I could hardly sleep for excitement.

A few days later Mama showed me a Russian doll that had been tucked out of sight, buried deep in her wardrobe. It was like those seen in tourist shops, but exceptionally large, and chipped in places with the paint peeling. Carefully I opened the doll, expecting to see a miniature doll inside.

But to my surprise, wrapped up inside the secret compartment was a roll of rouble notes.

Mama's eyes twinkled as she saw my response. I glided round the room on a rollercoaster of dreams.

"Oh Mama," I said, barely able to contain my joy. "I'll work hard and we'll always be together!" Mama rumpled my hair and smiled.

Over the next few weeks, I spent several fascinating hours lying on Mama's bed emptying the money out of the doll and neatly folding and caressing each note.

One sunny afternoon Mama was lying in the grass with two other ladies, catching the sun and reading *Pioneer Pravda*. Mama waved across to me and I strolled over and lay on the grass beside her.

The women were deep in discussion over an article featuring a phenomenon reported by Siberian peasants who had seen a cross appear through a reflection of light in the street. After some speculation, the article dismissed the image as a trick of the light.

I lay on my back and stared up at the sky, shielding the bright rays of the sun with my hand. The sky had no end. It just seemed to go on and on. But surely it must come to an end.

After some time the other two women left to prepare for their evening chores. I snuggled close to Mama and we cuddled in the sunlight. I was the only one who knew that her enchanting smile hid a secret heartache.

Mama never really got over my father. "He'll come back to us one day, you'll see. Everything will be alright," she would say. In her desperate search to find him she wrote to friends and relatives and made long journeys to visit anyone who may have remained in contact with him. If someone knew where he was, they weren't saying. But Mama never gave up hope.

At the Pioneer Camp someone suggested that she contact him through the army network. She wrote to the commanding officer of his unit, and to her surprise, this time she received a reply.

Mama seemed in shock for several days. She carried the letter around with her everywhere, reading and re-reading it.

Father had re-married but his second wife had died. The letter from the army bureau also included some startling information. An address! It was in Vyborg, an old town near the Finnish border. Ironically, he didn't live far away.

Unaware of the turmoil that Mama was experiencing, I waved her goodbye as she set off to Vyborg. Like the other kids at camp, my mind was on Sports Day, due to be held in a few days time.

I wasn't on the campsite the day Mama returned from this extraordinary journey. I had taken a boat out — without alerting its owner — on to the nearby river with my friend Alex, who was also eleven years old, but a little shorter than me with blond curly hair.

The day began peacefully. We tried fishing, but neither of us could sit still long enough to entice the fish.

Then, sometime during the afternoon, Alex called out in horror. Two angry-looking men were rowing furiously in our direction. At the camp we had all heard frightening tales of how some men had abducted children. The men's threats grew louder as they gained on us in spite of our frantic efforts to get away.

"Look Valeri, land!" Alex shouted. We hurried towards an island, with the men chasing us close behind. We couldn't understand what they said, but knew enough of life to recognise Finnish curses when we heard them.

We abandoned the boat and charged across the tiny beach. Without looking back, we scrambled into the undergrowth to hide from our assailants. As we lay on the cold earth my heart echoed so loudly in my ears that I thought anyone passing would discover us. Alex was as scared as I was, with his hands over his ears, and his eyes wide open.

We lay there for what seemed like hours. Protected by the bushes, the sounds of the wild became a source of comfort. Eventually we decided to step out of our hiding place and gingerly retrace our steps to the beach.

We gasped in surprise. Our boat had been taken by our pursuers. Trapped on the island, we considered all the ideas we could think of. Could we make a raft? Were there people living on the island, and would they be friendly? If we floated a message in a bottle would anyone find it? I knew how to swim, but Alex couldn't swim at all.

Gradually we grew daunted by the grim reality of the situation. Even if we finally managed to get back to the camp, what would they say about the boat we had stolen? Without knowing where the money would come from, we resolved to pay back the exact cost.

The cool, inviting water lapped at our feet as we lay on the beach considering our options.

Suddenly we heard a familiar noise in the distance. To our amazement, it was a motorboat. We were going to be rescued! We began to wave and shout, yelling and jumping up and down. They must see us! They must!

As the boat weaved through the water, heading in our direction I had a terrible thought. What if they were our attackers, returning to get us? But my fears were unfounded, dispelled by a friendly wave from the boat.

We had been rescued by a young Finnish couple who listened sympathetically to our story and agreed to take us back to the Pioneer Camp. "You've been very lucky," they said. "There are some nasty people around."

As we silently watched the boat glide through the greeny-blue water, my mind replayed the events of the last few hours. What a story I had to tell! Just wait till I saw Mama!

Alex and I arrived breathless back at the Pioneer Camp. Alex was hungry and went to scrounge some food in the kitchen. As I approached the wooden building where Mama lived, I noticed several people stop to stare at me. I knew I looked terrible in dirty, ripped clothes, but I ignored them and walked past.

"Valeri, where have you been?" a voice called out behind me. It was Schura, one of Mama's friends, a tall, slender lady with dark hair. She looked tired and worried and was carrying Mama's bag. Was something wrong?

"Schura, you'll never believe what happened to us," I blurted out. I had to get to Mama to tell her what had happened. "Is Mama in her room? I must see her!"

"Oh, Valeri," Schura replied despondently. Her eyes welled up with tears and she put her arm round me. I felt my body tense up at this sudden expression of affection, and wriggled free from Schura's grasp. I couldn't understand why Schura was upset. Or was she merely relieved to see me home safely? Grown-ups were always worrying needlessly. I shrugged my shoulders and tried to move away.

"Valeri, I've something to tell you. Your Mama's not well."

I stared at Schura without understanding what she was saying. Suddenly I felt tired, cold and alone, as the last rays of the sun enveloped the camp.

In the eerie twilight it seemed as though Schura was speaking from behind a thick pane of glass. I saw her lips move, but I couldn't hear the words. She explained that Mama had collapsed without meeting my father, that she was resting now and I could probably see her tomorrow if her condition improved.

Schura walked me back to my cabin, sensing my tiredness and shock. Suddenly, I turned to her and said, "We were chased by some bad people and trapped on an island for several hours and our boat was stolen!" It now seemed something that had happened a long time ago. "Where is Mama? Why can't I see her?"

Schura nodded and patted my arm. Everything seemed unreal. I was too tired to resist her gentle prodding and I followed her silently.

"Will you be OK, Valeri?" Schura asked as we reached the dormitory.

"Yes, I'll be fine. I just want to sleep." I eased my shoes off and plunged headlong on to the bed.

I awoke in a sweat, still dressed in yesterday's stained clothes. The dormitory was empty and I could hear a football match going on outside. That meant breakfast had been served and I had missed it. Boy, I was hungry!

As I changed my clothes hurriedly, yesterday's events seemed like a dream. I had to get to Mama. She would sort everything out.

Schura arrived just as I reached the door of the cabin. "You've been asleep a long time," Schura said. "I didn't want to wake you, you looked so tired. Mama wants to see you."

"How is she?" I asked. Schura tensed slightly as she nodded and mumbled, "She's tired, very tired."

As we walked across the playing field, a rowdy game of football was in progress. I saw Alex and we waved.

Schura knocked softly on Mama's door, and I followed her in. The curtains were half drawn and I could see Mama's form as she lay in the darkened room.

"Mama," I shouted, and raced over to her bed. As I leaned across my mother I was surprised that she didn't speak or embrace me. Her body seemed strangely crumpled. I had seen her just a few days ago and she had been bright and cheerful as ever. Just moving her head from side to side seemed to require an incredible effort.

Tears slipped down her cheeks when she saw me standing there. Schura moved round the bed and wiped the tears from her face. Mama indicated that she wanted to hold my hand so I eased my palm into hers. She tried to smile and squeeze my hand.

I wanted to tell Mama about the dramatic events of the last twenty-four hours. She stared at me and again made a valiant attempt to smile. I didn't want to leave Mama and clung to her hand. Mama signalled that she wanted me to stay with her. Schura left, and for a few moments we were alone.

I sensed Mama was trying to communicate with me. Perhaps she was praying for me . . .

Mama seemed to tire, and it was an effort for her to keep her eyes open. Schura returned and hovered in the background. Coming up behind me, she touched my shoulder and leant down to whisper, "She needs to rest. It'll be good for her."

I reached forward and kissed her gently. Her eyes flickered, followed by a momentary smile. And then she fell asleep again.

I walked slowly away and said goodbye to Schura. I had never seen Mama looking like that before, a pale reflection of her real self.

I found myself walking in the direction of the athletics field, where final preparations were being made for Sports Day at our Pioneer Camp. Decorations were going up everywhere for tomorrow's events. Rivalry among the campers was at fever pitch.

Misha, a thick-set Latvian youth, had spread the word: he was going to win the 200 metre sprint. Misha was a bully, and had already flattened another boy who insisted that he would contest the race. Rumour had it that Misha's father had promised him a brand-new foreign racing cycle if he won. Misha's father had connections and could pick up foreign goods quite easily.

I spotted Alex standing with a few other lads. He told me that he had reported the loss of the boat, but it hadn't been taken too seriously, overshadowed by preparations for Sports Day.

A skinny, gangly lad named Tomas stood beside us. He had already beaten Misha in the heats leading up to the finals. Alex saw me staring at a cut on Tomas' face, and said, "Misha's given him a black eye. He's warned him about the race." Tomas looked really nervous now.

Everyone was talking simultaneously, but for once, I remained silent, my mind by Mama's forlorn frame.

"What's the problem Valeri?" Alex asked.

"There's no problem," I snapped back sharply, surprised at myself. I watched Alex step back. I could tell he was hurt by my reply.

Yesterday I would have been one of the schemers, plotting Misha's demise, but now all I could do was trail after them.

Sports Day was held on June 26, 1956. We were awoken to the sound of a marching band, played through a special loudspeaker system rigged up throughout the camp. Events had been scheduled throughout the day. There was a treasure hunt in the morning, with a concert and a play (based on *Lenin Our Hero*) for the early evening. A band had been practising all summer and was due to play at several times throughout the day. A campfire sing-along would conclude the great day.

Dressed in blue silk shorts and blue cotton vest, ready for my rowing event, I ate a quick breakfast. There were still two hours to go before the games were to begin, so I decided to see how Mama was feeling.

Outside Mama's cabin I spotted Lara, a fair haired sweet-looking girl who was one of Mama's best friends.

"Hiya Lara," I called out and waved.

Lara looked at me and stopped for a moment. She hesitated and seemed to be on the verge of telling me something. She gave me a rueful smile and put her arm round my shoulder. Lara looked upset.

"What is it Lara?" I enquired.

Lara bit her lip nervously. I proceeded towards the staircase leading to Mama's room, but Lara was now blocking my path. She touched my arm, a gentle gesture that expressed sympathy more than restraint. I noticed some people at the top of the stairs. Schura was one of them.

"Hello Valeri," she said pensively. She gave Lara a questioning glance. I didn't see Lara's response, but I felt uncomfortable in the strained atmosphere. Something was going on, but I was being kept in the dark. I began to feel cross. When Mama recovered everything would be alright.

I walked away from Schura and Lara, planning to slip away from the Sports Day to see Mama later on.

The 200 metres was scheduled for 3 p.m. and I simply had to be there to cheer Tomas to victory. The band played as we ate lunch. There was a special menu which included chocolate ice cream. I relished every spoonful.

It was a brisk warm day, ideal for Sports Day. As we went to find Tomas and his gang, Mrs Avaloff, who worked at the medical station, came towards us, walking at a brisk pace. She looked serious and pointed at me. "Come with me, Valeri," she said.

I looked across at Alex and told him, "Keep a place for me next to you. I'll be back for Tomas' race."

As we headed in the direction of Mama's room, I realised that she must have got worse. Schura and Lara were still standing at the foot of the stairs, and talking to a man who looked like Uncle Ura.

It was Ura! He must have come from Leningrad. I went across to hug him. As he bent down to me he began weeping.

"I want to see Mama," I declared, climbing the stairs two at a time. Ura and the others followed close behind.

Mrs Avaloff stopped me at the door. Gently touching my shoulder, she said, "Valeri, do you realise that people don't live for ever?"

I hesitated. Mama was dead, I just knew it. I staggered a little as the shock ripped through my body. Mrs Avaloff realised that I understood.

I'm a man, I told myself, men don't cry.

Turning the handle of the door I entered the room. Mama lay on the bed. She looked peaceful, as though in a deep sleep. Her skin looked pale and translucent. I flung my arms around her neck.

"Mama, I love you, I love you," I cried, choking back the tears.

I lay on the bed beside her. My mind seemed empty and vacant. I was curiously aware of the silence in the room.

My precious Mama was dead. I stared at her face,

memorising every detail. And I never got to tell her about our narrow escape on the island, or the Sports Day. So many things I never got to say.

The room itself was darkened and all the familiar items stood in their place, untouched, as if in mournful respect. Every corner had a memory, now tinged with grief.

After some time I was aware of Schura's presence guiding me out of the room. I felt an overwhelming sense of helplessness as I looked back at Mama lying on the bed. Then the door was closed.

Several people were discussing the funeral arrangements in a nearby room. I hear Uncle Ura say, "I'll take the body back to Leningrad and finalise everything there."

"What will become of the little one?" I heard Mrs Avaloff say looking across at me.

"I'm not little," I wanted to reply. Uncle Ura spoke up, "He's not an orphan, he'll come to live with me in Leningrad." I didn't know why, but it was also decided that I would remain in camp and not travel to Leningrad for Mama's funeral. The details became complicated and someone suggested I should return to the Sports Day.

The athletics field was ablaze with colour and noise. Despite all the activity I felt little sense of sound. I seemed to be sleep-walking, but I could tell by the faces of the people I passed that the news had spread.

Suddenly, a shrill voice shattered my daydream. "Valeri's mother is dead! She's dead!" Claps and shouts accompanied the declaration. Other voices tried to restore the balance. "Quiet, shut up, you idiot!" I heard someone say.

I was caught by surprise. The words had some mystical, hypnotic power. Was this really happening to me? I heard a familiar voice call out. It was Alex.

"Valeri, where have you been? Why were you so long?"

I stared incomprehensibly at him. I started to speak but I could make no sound.

"Tomas won the race!" Alex cried out. "He won, Valeri. Tomas won the race!" Non-plussed by my reaction, he repeated himself. "Valeri, Tomas won. Misha came second, he's been beaten. Tomas came first."

I managed to mumble something in reply, nodding to confirm that I had understood. Alex stared at me, his eyes narrowed, "What's the matter?"

"My mother's dead," I heard myself say.

Alex opened his mouth and swallowed but could find nothing to say. He held up his hand, and then let it drop to his side.

Somehow the next few hours passed. When the camp band played a sad melody, I identified with the music. I felt as though my soul itself was weeping.

Later that evening, I returned to Mama's room for the last time. All the clothes, furniture, carpets and the little trinkets on her toilet table had been packed into boxes to be returned to Leningrad. I found the Russian doll, now empty, and caressed it gently. I would keep it. No one except me knew why Mama had saved money in the doll. It was our secret and it would remain that way, an eternal expression of our love.

I felt a twinge of sadness. My thrilling musical career at the Conservatoire had ended before it began. If Mama had lived, everything would have been possible, I told myself.

"I love you Mama," I whispered as my mother's body was carried out of the room.

I learned later that in Vyborg Mama had stood outside the flat where my father lived, unable to knock on the door. She struggled into the street and collapsed a few yards away. For two days she lay unconscious. The doctor who returned her to the Pioneer Camp explained that a blood vessel burst inside her head as a result of intense psychological pressure, resulting in paralysis. The emotional trauma of the last few years had taken its toll.

Mama's funeral in Leningrad was attended by over three hundred people, and she was remembered with great love and affection.

2

NOWHERE TO RUN

Uncle Ura and Aunt Tamara and their families occupied a cramped three-room apartment on the fifth floor in Nevsky Prospekt, Leningrad. Although they shared a toilet and kitchen with no hot water, somehow they managed to accommodate another person.

Life at the Pioneer Camp with Mama had been magical and wonderful. Although she had struggled all her life, she had been my guardian and protector. Every patch of earth had a memory. Now I felt hopelessly alone, and at times inconsolably despondent.

When Mama died, I no longer felt a child. I was only eleven, but I resolved to grow up and be a man. Mama would have expected it of me, I reasoned.

When the camp season ended, Ura came to collect me. I loved our Pioneer Camp and it was hard saying farewell to my friends and the teachers.

For the last time I walked out of the main gates, with all my clothes and toys piled into two cardboard boxes, tied with string, which Ura carried with ease. I carried a smaller box containing Mama's shawl, the album of photographs, and the hand-painted Russian doll. I handled it like a treasure.

Aunt Tamara and her husband, Benjamin, had a son named Slavik who was my age. Benjamin had worked as an editor for a military publication, and then in a solicitor's office. One day I was told that Uncle Benjamin had been "bad" and was going away to be punished. He would be going far away and be gone a long time. At that age, it was all the explanation I needed.

Aunt Tamara and Slavik moved to a new flat near Voladsky Bridge. Later, she moved again to another flat in the Vyborg district and became a member of the Leningrad Baptist Church, joining the church choir.

Ura's wife, Vera, was an attractive woman whose eyes seemed to hint at some hidden fear. Their three-year-old daughter Valentina, or Valya for short, had a mischievous smile and we immediately became good friends.

After a few days in my new accommodation, I realised that there were serious difficulties. Ura had a kind heart, but had a reputation for drinking heavily. Ura's habit would cost him good jobs and consequently Vera's meagre salary kept the family in bread and potatoes.

One night, Ura began cursing the potentates in the Kremlin for all our difficulties. He composed an abusive letter to Khrushchev and read it out to us. Vera had learnt never to contest him in his moods, but I was horrified and questioned him.

To Vera's surprise, Ura was amused and laughed off my challenge. "When you grow up, then you'll understand."

"What do you mean?" I asked. "Explain yourself."

"No, you'll see for yourself," he answered mysteriously.

What was worse, on Saturday nights Ura would stagger through the door around midnight, cursing at the top of his voice. I would pull the thin blanket around my ears in a vain effort to block out the noise, while our neighbour thumped on the wall calling for quiet.

Once I heard Ura slap Vera hard on the cheek. When I looked up, she was on the floor at Ura's feet while he tried again to punch her. Valya was up now and ran to her mother.

"Uncle Ura, stop it!" I shouted, climbing out of bed. He was outraged that I had interfered and tried repeatedly to punch me, but I evaded his blows.

Lunging at me again, Ura badly mistimed his step and

smashed into a shelf. Four glasses crashed to the floor showering splinters in every direction.

"Come back here and I'll kill you!" he swore.

"You'll have to catch me first," I shouted back.

Storming into the kitchen, Ura returned brandishing a meat axe. As I dashed for the front door I heard Vera scream, "Run, Valeri, run!". Valya shrieked in terror. I thrust myself into the hallway and jumped down the stairs, landing on my bottom. I could hear Ura swearing in the hall but I didn't wait to debate the issue.

I spent the night walking the streets in my thin vest and shorts, looking for a warm place to hide. By early morning the cold was too much to bear and I decided to sneak back to the flat. Vera had left the door ajar for me. Ura had passed out after further drinking and slept until midday.

It was an experience that was to repeat itself.

Vera tried her best to make the home a happy place, but everything hinged on Ura's moods, which in turn were controlled by the bottle in his hand.

As my twelfth birthday approached, Vera planned a party for me. On December 6th, she baked a special chocolate cake and my Aunt Tamara and Slavik came round. We all wore funny hats and had a happy time together. Ura was in a good mood and entertained us with animal noises. Little Valya's peals of laughter filled the room as she saw a different side to her father.

Snow had fallen early that year and the cold seeped through the walls of our flat. I didn't have many warm clothes, so I wore several jumpers. Leningrad's wintry streets were uninviting and I missed my friends at the camp, running free in the fields and the clean fresh air. When I thought of Mama, I felt a deep ache within my soul and longed to return to the places where we roamed together, hand in hand.

Fire crackers marked the New Year celebrations in Leningrad, but Vera, Valya and I ate dinner with uncertainty, waiting for Ura to return home.

Valya became cranky and Vera decided to put her to bed.
Later, Vera sat on the sofa reading a *samizdat* novel written
by some banned author. I was puzzled why anyone put up
with reading a carbon copy passed secretly from hand to
hand. Why couldn't it be published just like an ordinary book
and be kept on the shelf?

I made up my bed on the floor and kissed Vera goodnight.
Sometime that night I awoke to hear her scream in terror.
Ura was staggering round the room hitting her all over like
a punchbag. The buttons of her housecoat were ripped and
with one hand she clutched it to herself to cover her body.
Unable to maintain her balance, Vera collapsed backwards
and Ura fell on top of her.

Valya had also woken up and began to wail. "Stop that
yelling," Ura shouted at his daughter. Frightened and
confused by his temper, Valya was unable to stop. As she
ran towards her mother in short jerky steps, Ura knocked
her sideways across the room. At this, Vera tried to grapple
with Ura.

Valya's terrified screams served to taunt Ura, snapping
the last reserve he may have felt. As he moved towards Valya
with his fist outstretched, I crouched low and slipped past
him, plucking Valya off the floor. She clung to me as I put
my arm round her and sped towards the door.

Vera realised that I planned to rescue her daughter and
moved swiftly to open the door, slamming it shut after us,
locking herself and Ura inside. Clutching Valya tight I
rushed down the stairs. Behind us, Ura's booming voice
drowned out Vera's cries.

As we reached the fourth floor, the door opened on the
floor above. "Come here, you little bastard," Ura swore.
I wasn't sure whether he was following us, but if he caught
me now I knew he could kill Valya or myself.

The back door of the building was bolted from the
outside. Behind us the noise from the stairs became louder.
My heart was beating like a bass drum, and we were both
trembling.

I tried to open a window, but it wouldn't budge. I stood on the window ledge with my back against the dirty frame and summoned all my strength. A loud crash startled me! The window pane had smashed and I was covered with glass.

Down the hall I heard footsteps and the sound of heavy breathing, but I didn't wait to find out who it was. I reached down to lift Valya across the ledge to safety. Scrambling through the window, we raced into the night.

There had been a light snowfall and Valya was shivering, so I pulled off my tatty blue sweater and slipped it over her. What a sight we must have been as we trudged down the street! A twelve-year-old boy in a vest and trousers and a three-year-old girl in an outsized torn sweater.

I found a doorway into another building and we stepped out of the cold. The lift smelt of cigarettes and urine, but at least it was warm. I pressed a green button on the control panel and as the doors shut, Valya and I slumped down in a corner.

I looked down at Valya as I cuddled her in my arms. She looked beautiful in her innocence and I stroked her hair. Possibly it was one great adventure for her. Within minutes, I too was asleep.

I awoke to hear a shrill voice yelling at us and a dark-haired lady peering over us and wagging her finger. "Haven't you got a home to go to?" she scolded.

The words stung me as I picked up Valya, and like tramps we stumbled back on to the streets in search of shelter. Valya was hungry, and tried to snuggle up to me as we slipped on the icy road. There was no one else to turn to. We had to go home.

With our hearts beating wildly, we stepped into the building and crept nervously up the stairs. As before, Vera had left the door ajar, meaning it was safe to return. Ura had gone out after us but had not returned.

Chairs had been smashed and a table leg was broken. Glasses and cutlery were lying everywhere. Vera's bruises showed that she had taken a severe beating. Her eyes hid her shame. She cuddled Valya and then made us some sandwiches.

Vera told me that she was going to leave Ura and would take Valya with her. She planned to stay with her brother who lived a few miles outside Leningrad. It was clear that there would be no room for me and I would have to remain behind.

Valya didn't understand what was happening, but the prospect of a train ride filled her with excitement. Vera had already packed a few clothes and within an hour she and Valya were ready to leave.

"Take care of yourself Valeri," Vera said giving me a hug. "I hope you'll be OK."

Valya tugged impatiently on her mother's arm but decided she could wait an extra moment as we kissed goodbye.

Without Valya the flat seemed empty and within a few minutes I was filled with a great loneliness. By mid-afternoon Ura had still not returned. I ate the bread and vegetables that Vera had left for me. There was nothing to do alone in the flat, so I pulled on a coat and went for a walk. It was certain to snow very soon and the cold drove me back home.

Two days later, Ura returned home. He was tearfully sorry. But this time it was too late.

Soon Ura began drinking again and he would blame me angrily because there was no food in the house. Life was intolerable and I would find excuses to leave the house before he got violent. The cold made it difficult to stay on the streets for long.

Then I had an idea one evening. I knew some people nearby who owned a TV set. TV had only recently been introduced in Russia, and few people could afford it. I turned up at their door and boldly asked if I could watch TV.

"Of course," the woman replied. The couple had teenage children who were out most of the time, and they enjoyed having young people around.

I showed great interest in everything that was screened

in order to stay safe and warm. In reality, Ura was never far from my mind.

When it became late, the woman asked me if I should return home. Wouldn't someone be worried that I was out this late? "No, no," I assured them. "No one will worry. They're used to me staying out late. I'm nearly thirteen, you know, almost a teenager."

As I stepped into the flat, my eyes turned to the shelf by the window where Mama's precious Russian doll was kept.

The shelf was empty.

Once again, the flat was in turmoil with chairs overturned, books scattered everywhere, food on the floor. Suddenly my eyes fell on coloured slices of wood among the rubble. The doll had been smashed, it could never be restored. Like yesterday, it was gone for ever, a memory that could be visited only in the heart.

Filled with a silent rage, I cradled the broken doll in the palm of my hand as I sat in the ruins of Ura's life.

A week later, Ura informed me that he intended to place me in one of the local "internats", a home for abandoned children, vagrants, and children from one-parent families. I pleaded with him to be allowed to return to the orphanage at the Pioneer Camp, but to no avail.

With only two weeks to go before I left, I thought that little could go wrong. But the weekend before I was to leave, Ura returned home with a prostitute.

She was a tall woman with short hair, dyed red. Perhaps she had once been attractive, but now she looked haggard and old.

As an observant thirteen-year-old, I had begun to notice that girls were shaped differently from boys, but the next few minutes degenerated into a sordid, embarrassing perversion. Ura behaved without shame and the prostitute was tough and callous. I was forbidden to leave the room as Ura mauled her in front of me.

I crawled into Valya's tiny bed and pulled the sheet over

my head. Closing my eyes, I held my hands over my ears to block out the sounds in the room, and tried to sleep.

I had nowhere left to run.

By the time I arrived at Internat No. 10, the sense of isolation and abandonment that I had experienced after my mother's death in June was beginning to give way to a feeling of independence. Alone but no longer lonely, I enjoyed my new found freedom.

In a curious way I missed Leningrad and Ura. I felt more pity than anger when I thought of him. Although his behaviour was deplorable, I knew that he cared for me. Ura insisted that I return for holidays and some weekends. I had no option but to agree, hardly relishing the prospect.

The internat was situated about two hours from Leningrad. Several old, grey buildings housed about a hundred children between the ages of six and sixteen. There were a lot of activities designed for energetic teenagers.

My first serious challenge faced me on the night I arrived. Some older boys had removed the blanket from my bunk and were threatening to report me to the kindly old matron. As the confrontation developed, the twelve or so boys who shared the cabin gathered round.

I might have been skinny, but I didn't lack courage as I stood up to the ring leaders of the plot. Realising I was not to be tangled with, they retrieved the blanket from a cupboard. I received a cut on the chin, but my bruised knuckles bore witness that I was not the only one bearing a scar.

I had passed the test with flying colours. After that, I hung out with the older boys, whistling at the girls and making up jokes that could only be told behind the toilets.

Within a few short weeks, I had become one of the gang leaders and was probably viewed as a troublemaker by the staff of the internat. But the girls liked us!

We found a way on to the roof and made a hideout where we would go at midnight with our girls. The cigarette ends which we dropped alerted the staff, and one night we were caught and severely penalised. But this only confirmed our resolve to be outlaws.

Kurakina Dacha Park, a large wooded area, was nearby. When the River Neva which flowed through it burst its banks, we would undertake midnight expeditions to inspect the chaos.

The park was notorious for muggings, and even murders. Most folk were afraid to go there at night. But not our gang!

The girls from the internat clung to our arms and shrieked at anything that moved. Although our hearts also fluttered at every shadow, we behaved like brave and carefree adventurers.

However, the danger was real and on several nights we were chased. One boy slipped and fell on the ice and was pounced on by thieves. They knifed him in the side, but fortunately he was able to get away.

I was always in trouble and got expelled many times from the internat. The punishment only fuelled my rebelliousness, and as an orphan they were forced to take me back.

"This place can't hold me," I warned the gang. "I'm going to escape, find a boat and sail far away. I'll find an island and live off the land and never have to work."

As I repeated the notion, it took hold of me. The idea caught on, and I carefully selected five boys who pleaded to come with me. This was going to succeed with military precision. I could only take those who were trustworthy.

First of all, we found the ideal meeting place to plot our strategy. Late one night George, who was wiry and skinny, put his hand through a hole in the timber beams in the elevated base of the main building. "Hey, this seems a little shaky," he called out, manoeuvring a beam and squeezing inside. For a few moments we heard him scrambling around inside the structure, and then trying to get out again. Even in the dim light we could tell as we pulled him out that he was covered with dirt, dust and cobwebs.

But his mission had been an overwhelming success. Deep

in the very bowels of the edifice, George had located a space large enough for all of us to meet.

The pirates managed to smuggle a kerosene lamp and other necessary tools down the hole. In a ceremony of conspiracy, we each cut the tip of an index finger and spilled three drops of blood in a circle of earth in the centre of the room. Stealth and secrecy were the passwords. Sasha kept notes of all our meetings and in closing, we drank a toast to freedom with whatever refreshment we could sneak out of the canteen.

One morning, we heard a great commotion. "Fire! Fire!" Screams of panic came from all sides as the alarm went off. Puffs of smoke could be seen rising above the main building. The entire internat ground to a halt as staff and students filled the grounds.

"Right, where's the fire?" the chief fireman called as his colleagues jumped from their red wagon.

"That's just it," replied one of the staff, looking confused. "We can't seem to find it."

Smirking at the joke, we gathered round the fire engine. Smoke was billowing everywhere as I whispered to George, "I just hope our room doesn't burn down."

Suddenly some activity round the other side of the building caught our attention. Firemen ran to point the hose. Suddenly it was getting serious! I stared in disbelief as a fireman began chopping at the hole leading to our hiding place. "Yes, it's in here," I heard him exclaim, to everyone's relief but our own.

I was dumbfounded. Our room had been discovered. It was all George's fault for leaving the kerosene lamp burning. He would be disciplined, I decided. Worse, he would be fired from the team. He had wrecked his chances of escaping with us.

Suddenly, the reality of it hit me. I tried not to draw attention to myself as I moved away from the front of the crowd. Discreetly, I signalled that we should disperse.

At dinner that night none of us felt hungry. I was

determined to escape and this crisis would not hinder our plans. "What are we going to do?" George said, somewhat alarmed. I glared at him. "You mean what are you going to do?" I replied ominously. "We'll meet tonight. Is that agreed?" There were nods all round. I decided to wait until the meeting to inform George of his future with the group.

As we were finishing dinner, I was startled to hear our names called out. We were commanded to report immediately to the chief of the internat. Frowning in puzzlement, I said calmly "It's nothing. Don't be taken in by their bluff. They can't prove anything."

The chief of the internat was a large balding man named Mr Titov who stood behind his desk as we marched in. Looking extremely serious, he went on and on complaining with boring monotony about our scandalous activity.

Did we realize that our irresponsible behaviour could have burned down the internat? As he droned on, it became clear that he knew a great deal about our plot to escape. When he asked us to confess, each of us stubbornly refused. My coaching had worked.

As Mr Titov became enraged, more details of our plan emerged. This tricky piece of negotiation had to be handled by the leader: I couldn't expect it of the rank and file. "It's all guess work," I began, deciding to brazen it out. "Anyone could have gone in there. We deny everything. You have no proof." I was totally convinced that there was no way he could catch us red-handed.

With a flourish, Mr Titov opened a drawer in his desk and cast his bounty on to the table. It was the diary, plotting our escape. Our names, dates, what we planned to do, everything! Complete proof! Sasha must have carelessly left it behind. Gasping in shock, we hung our heads at such damning evidence.

How could I have been so stupid! I breathed a sigh of relief to think I was not going to lead these idiots in search of our own secret island after all.

The following morning, I was summoned to a meeting with the senior staff of the internat. It was agreed that I had been a disruptive and bad influence and I was issued with one final warning. If I didn't change, I would be expelled.

"I don't have a home to go to," I argued. "Get out of here!" Mr Titov yelled. "I don't want to see you!"

One night, blinded by panic and the fear of abandonment, I strung my belt around a beam in the hallway, tying a noose in the soft brown leather. Believing that no one cared about me and with nothing to live for, I climbed on to a stool, strapping the noose around my neck. "Jump," someone in a mask was shouting inside my head.

I jumped.

A million light bulbs flashed. Car brakes squealed. Mud from the road splashed everywhere. A glass smashed against the wall. Mama's face floated across the roof of the sky.

The belt snapped and I fell in a heap on the floor, bruising my leg badly. Suicide could be a painful experience, I reasoned as I was carried to the medical centre.

Little had changed however. Wild and uncontrollable, I was expelled from the internat within a few months.

Ura received me warmly, glad of some company, I think. But the state of the house indicated that Ura had sunk even deeper in his debauchery. There was no food in the larder, clothes were everywhere, the settee was ripped apart and the bed had not been made since Vera left.

Ura had taken a job in the local park, where he earned about fifty roubles which he would spend on alcohol and prostitutes.

Returning home one night, I found Ura with a young girl. He insisted that I stay, but I slipped away again to ride the Leningrad subway. I covered every corner of the city. Where was there left to explore?

Back at the flat I found the prostitute asleep naked on the bed. Ura lay curled up on the floor in his own urine.

Seeing Ura's shame, I crept into the communal bathroom for a shower and felt the spray of water run down my body.

I wanted to wash the events of the night away from me and change my clothes. Then I walked back on to the streets of Leningrad.

Somehow the day passed but I dreaded returning to the flat and rode the subway, tram cars and trolley buses again. I had learnt how to slip unnoticed through the ticket barrier without paying, and took the tram to the last stop on the line. I headed for Labour Square and then into Theatre Square. Slinking along the backstreets I watched the shining neon lights beckon, as smartly dressed foreigners visited the theatre and ballet, walking arm in arm with ladies in bright-coloured dresses.

My feet led me down to the waterfront of the Neva River. Everyone had a home to go to, but I walked the streets with nowhere to turn.

Old men with walking sticks sat admiring the scene. I could see the coloured lights of some ships docked further along the river and crossed the bridge turning left along the bank.

I found myself hurrying along the pavement and soaking in the refreshing, exhilarating atmosphere. The military ships caught my eye with their flags and cannons. I climbed up on to the harbour wall above the blue-grey water to get a better view of the sailors, who looked so dashing in their uniforms. I couldn't think of anything more exciting than to serve our country in the navy.

I returned night after night to the waterfront, totally fascinated. One evening, I could hear music and laughter coming from the pier. A group of young people had gathered round three sailors playing the accordion and singing traditional songs. After a few choruses I felt as if I belonged to the group, who were impressed by my enthusiasm and my high ranging vocals.

They asked if I knew any songs. "Sure," I replied and serenaded them with a bawdy song I had picked up at the internat. The sailors laughed hilariously while the girls blushed and giggled.

I was an immediate hit. The sailors smuggled me on board and I slept in an empty cabin, waking the next morning full of excitement. I was given a guided tour of the ship and then ate a hearty breakfast. I also got my first taste of coffee. The ship had been docked opposite a submarine, fuelling my mind with romantic escapades of the sea.

One group of sailors who served on the smaller pilot boats based in the harbour became my special friends. I told them I was an orphan, and could I spend my school holidays with them? The captain consented, providing me with the holiday of my dreams.

I began to panic when I learned that Ura had alerted the police to my absence. It wasn't long before my "holiday" came to an end.

Ura was insistent that I return to the internat. I landed in trouble on my first day. It was only a matter of time before I was expelled again, without regrets on either side. Ura's annoyance was obvious but his own life was careering out of control, so what hope did he have of taking charge over this fourteen-year-old punk?

And so I went from orphanage to Ura to internat and then back to Ura again. I felt like an unclaimed parcel in search of an owner.

I found Ura collapsed on the floor with a whore going through his wallet. It was empty. She insisted that she was only taking what she was owed for services rendered. Shoving her out of the flat, I tried to move Ura to his bed, which was difficult because of his size. Taking one last look at the flat, I called out, "Goodbye Uncle Ura." His snoring confirmed that he couldn't hear me and I left.

This time I had a plan! I knew that some ships hired youngsters for short-term periods and I was determined to become a sailor. A rugged sailor named Duke negotiated a position for me aboard his ship.

The idea of a ship's boy had captured the sailors' imagination and they took up a collection for me to purchase the uniform I needed, but I was unable to find naval boots in my size. They consoled me by saying I was a modern sailor with civilian shoes.

I was even given an identity card with my photograph, bearing the ship's official seal. My assignment lasted from May to September and I was treated like a regular sailor.

On my first parade I saluted with my head held high. The captain received me with a twinkle in his eye. I could see the others grinning, but I took it seriously.

Soon I knew every corner of the ship. I loved to feel the rough salty sea water spray my clothes as I polished the brass bells and ornaments.

On one occasion I was ordered to paint the anchor and chain, located in a deep, dark corner of the ship. To make matters worse, it had to be painted black! As I struggled in the dark I slipped and upset the balance of the chain, which disentangled and spun around, rolling over me. As I lay pinned under the heavy chain, I felt the sticky paint on my hands and hair.

For several hours I shouted for help, but it was my absence at the meal table that alerted the crew. As the sailors peered into the darkness, my pathetic cries enlisted laughter rather than pity. This was one occasion when I never shared the joke!

I was given the top bunk in Duke's cabin. He was a tall, powerful man but he loved me and nicknamed me "the kid". One night when Duke was on duty I fell out of my bunk. Sleepily, I crawled back into bed and went back to sleep. Duke was alarmed when he saw me in the morning. "What happened? Have you been in a fight?"

"It's nothing," I replied although I did admit to having a headache. Duke insisted that I should see the doctor. I was not going to be cheated out of my turn to be "the flagman". This was one of my favourite duties, signalling to the ships that sailed past.

"I can't do that, I don't have time this morning," I replied with annoyance. "Besides, haven't I got the right to fall down?"

Duke may have been amused, but he looked really serious. "You'll go straight to the medical room, young man," Duke warned, gripping my arm and thrusting me in front of the mirror. No wonder I had a headache! There was a deep cut on my head and bruises all over my face. Reluctantly, I agreed to visit the doctor, who signed me off sick for two days. Those days were the ones I regretted most of my five month trip.

Some weeks later, our ship passed two uninhabited islands in the Baltic Sea called Moishne and Gogland. From the ship we could see bushes, so the ship's chef sent a team to collect berries for making juice and puddings. It was agreed that I should go too, and as we climbed into the dinghies I was warned that this was a serious responsibility.

At first I worked hard. I decided that I should also sample some to test the quality. If they were not ripe, we would be wasting our time, I reasoned.

But they were delicious! My trips to empty my container became fewer and fewer. Finally, it was time to return and we passed our work load up to a round of applause.

As we climbed aboard, the chef slapped my shoulder. "We know how hard you've been working, don't we!" Everyone on deck laughed, but I resented his insinuation that I hadn't worked hard.

I decided to shower, and as I undressed, I caught a glimpse of my reflection in the mirror. To my horror, my lips were completely black! The crew's laughter rang in my ears as I prepared to face them at dinner. When the berry juice was passed round I winced and said seriously, "I've had enough, thank you," much to everyone's amusement.

The ship would return regularly to Kronstadt pier in the months I served. One day I was given the responsibility of steering the small launch ferrying people to the shore. Another motor-launch followed us on our route, which was marked by tall wooden posts indicating the depth. I made a game out of guiding the boat as close to the posts as possible, which the officer on board found amusing.

The launch following us began to do the same, however, the pilot took his eye off the target for an instant and began to swerve into a post. Realising the danger, one of the officers reacted quickly by grabbing the wheel.

When we finally docked, safe and dry, the officer on board my boat congratulated me on my skill. "I can tell that you were born for the sea!" he remarked. I experienced an overwhelming sense of joy as I saluted him. This was a compliment indeed, as the officers were strict with me and made no allowances for my age.

I felt very proud whenever I went ashore with the sailors. I looked like everyone else, just a little shorter! When friends in Leningrad caught sight of me, most were amazed. The first time I returned to Ura's flat, I saw his eyes widen in surprise.

I was crestfallen when September came around. My last night was marked by a special party on board. Somehow I got through that winter shuttling back and forth between Ura's flat and the internats around Leningrad. I lived for next summer, when I could return to sea.

I got a postcard from Duke who told me to look up a friend of his. Through this contact, I was able to obtain another summer posting and sailed the Russian coast once again from May till September.

At the end of that period, I was forced to make a decision. I was no longer "the kid", and finding ships to sign me up was not easy. Getting into the navy required qualifications and formal training. Finally I was forced to admit that I would have to dry-dock all my seafaring dreams, at least for the moment.

I had learned to operate a film projector during my days at sea, and was hired at the Sputnik Cinema on Nevsky Street. I had tried to study, but found it difficult to concentrate. As a street-wise sixteen-year-old, the cinema seemed more true to life.

The Sputnik Cinema, named after Yuri Gagarin's rocket ship with which we had beaten the Americans into space, screened foreign films dubbed into Russian. Among the favourites were John Wayne and Humphrey Bogart. Musicals such as *Seven Brides for Seven Brothers* and *Oklahoma* were also popular. I particularly liked the up-tempo music of Glenn Miller films like *Sun Valley Serenade*, and learnt to sing "Chattanooga Choo-Choo" but never understood the words. It became a personal mission to meet foreigners just to find out what the songs meant.

Many people made illegal recordings of the films' soundtracks, and the tapes would appear on the black market all over town. One night someone loaned me some pirate tapes recorded from foreign stations such as the BBC or the Voice of America.

Listening to these new rhythms was like receiving an electric shock. I had never heard anything like it before. Elvis Presley, Bill Haley and the Comets became instant legends. Boogie woogie, rhythm and blues, twist. I loved it all.

When the cinema showed a rock and roll documentary it caused a sensation. I sneaked my cousins Slavik and Valya in through the back door. It was an astonishing moment. Few of us could understand the words, but there wasn't a communication problem.

I watched every performance with my eyes riveted to the screen. Soon I found I could sing along with the group on celluloid. See you later, alligator!

One night I saw someone squinting continually at me as the film was rolling. He walked across and I heard a familiar voice say, "Valeri, is that you?"

I stared hard for a few moments, "George?"

It seemed unbelievable. George! On stage Bill Haley was leading his Comets into a frantic version of "Shake, Rattle and Roll", as in his audience a joyful reunion of two pirates who were going to escape from the internat together was set to music.

I had bought an accordion and George played the flute, so we formed a band by adding a trumpet, bass and drums to the line-up. We played songs learned from foreign radio broadcasts and found loyal fans in Slavik and Valya who always hung around.

But we were teenagers and took nothing very seriously. The jam sessions drifted into drinking bouts. Bad company and a weak will made it easy to live on the wild side of life. I was soon an eighteen-year-old rebel who had tasted the bitter-sweet fruit of life and had begun to challenge the established order.

Music held a mirror to my heart, the passage of release. It drew from my soul that which I couldn't reveal to anyone else. Bright, buoyant music set my foot tapping and my thoughts roaming. Melancholic music left me desolate. Why am I so lonely? Why did Mama have to die? What am I living for? The questions seemed too solemn for a teenager like me.

"Why should I live any differently?" I once questioned George. "Who knows where I'll be tomorrow? Today is all I have."

With little reason to change, I had become like a railway carriage detached from an express train. Now devoid of guidance or stability, I was hurtling down the tracks at great speed, wild and free with nothing in sight.

And wham! As if from nowhere everything changed. A letter from the army ordered me to report for duty. From being an aimless drifter, I was now to be drafted into a lifestyle of rigid discipline, forced on to me like a ball and chain.

3

RED ARMY BLUES: 1963–1972

Private Barinov! It seemed like a fantastic dream. At eighteen, I would have given everything for the motherland, but all that was asked of me was two years of my life, so I signed up without hesitation. I treated every night as a farewell party and got blind drunk. I'll change when I'm in the army, I promised myself.

The day before I left, Aunt Tamara invited me for a farewell dinner with Slavik, Valya and George among the guests. Tamara loved me dearly and tried to care for me after Mama's death, but had her own difficulties and I was unable to share my heart with her.

During the meal I kept everyone amused by taking a swig from a bottle of spirits whenever my aunt's back was turned. Tamara knew something was up, wagging her finger at me, half in jest, scolding, "Valeri, you're drunk!"

After the meal we crowded on to the balcony, singing songs, and swapping stories. I picked up my accordion and everyone joined me in the chorus of "Goodbye dear mother, I'm off to war". As we lingered in the cool evening, arm in arm, Tamara said wistfully, "If only your mother could see you now, she would be proud of you, Valeri."

She went on to talk to me about God. Smiling and nodding my head, I maintained my image as a level-headed, serious-minded teenager. The others had all gone indoors to listen to the radio, leaving me as Tamara's captive audience.

"God exists, Valeri," she stated emphatically. "When

you're in the army you will hear lots of talk about God. Don't argue, because you don't know who he is. If you have a problem, pray to God with all your heart, and he will hear you. He is a God of miracles but to some people, he is a mystery. You will know him by his action. You can see God in nature. This world didn't just happen. God exists!"

There were no pauses as she continued in hushed tones and I listened out of respect. Her words mingled with the traffic noise from twelve floors below. Like a farmer sowing his seed in a field, her words were carried into the evening air, sprinkled into the atmosphere.

I had mixed emotions as I walked into the army barracks. I loved my country, and carried my rifle with pride, but I would still have preferred to be in the navy.

With my shaved head and starched uniform, I was posted to Riga under Colonel Sergei Sekunov, a renowned disciplinarian. I was commended for my marching skills and selected for special parades welcoming visiting dignitaries.

However, my behaviour was far from that of a model soldier. In exasperation, Colonel Sekunov said to me one day, "Barinov, I love you as a son, but I hate you as a soldier." I remained at attention and replied, "Yes sir! Thank you sir!"

I trained as an assistant radio operator, and late at night I listened to foreign broadcasts. In this way I first heard the extraordinary music of the Beatles. Recalling our pirate tapes at the Sputnik Cinema, I set about producing tapes of their songs as well as the Rolling Stones and Bob Dylan.

One day I decided to liven up the army camp. Usually a drum roll and bugle call roused us from our slumber. Bringing a modern touch to this 5 a.m. army ritual, I woke the entire camp with Bill Haley's "Rock around the Clock". The volume of this amplified alarm call was only matched by the blasting I received from Colonel Sekunov later that morning.

I loved animals, and made special friends of our tracker

dogs, Rex and Boxer. When our unit was on night patrol around our base they waited for me to get drunk and then ate up all my food rations.

I was selected for the coveted position of projectionist, and a sergeant in my unit became jealous. In a vendetta designed to break me, he subjected me to a continuous series of humiliating tasks. His favourite was forcing me to clean the toilets all night long. He tried to engineer my dismissal, frequently putting me on the punishment list.

I found myself fearing the future, confused and depressed. On night patrols the stillness of the stars in the velvet sky created a backdrop for my restlessness. Then a new thought crept into my mind.

Valeri, you have no future here. This world is enemy territory. End it all. It's the best you can do. The logic of this solution found a foothold in my heart.

However, next weekend wasn't any different, and we ended up at an all-night drinking party. Maxim was a burly youth who always knew where to find another bottle, and I was always around to help him empty it. Perhaps it was the cheap wine, but Maxim was in a talkative mood. Aware of my depression, he said. "Life is what you make of it, Valeri. The world is out to screw you, so don't trust anyone and screw them first! Live fast and live for the day, be sure to have a good time."

"Yes but isn't there any real love in the world?" I asked without looking directly at him.

The word sent Maxim into giggles. "Ha! What is love? And how much does it cost? That's the real question. Ask the whore on Karl Marx Avenue. She'll tell you the price of love." Then with finality, Maxim said, "There's no such thing as love, not real love. It's just a word kids carve on trees, you know what I mean, Valeri loves Anna!"

"But what about God, Maxim? Is there a God?"

"Oh, Valeri, what a joke. That's just a fairy story taught by old ladies. What did our great hero Yuri Gagarin see –

God? Of course not!'' Then speaking slowly to emphasise each word, Maxim said, ''There is no God, Valeri. N-O G-O-D !'' Maxim was not keen to waste any drinking time on serious talk.

In bed that night I lay awake. If anyone knew anything, it was Maxim, but this time I didn't believe him.

A few weeks later I was standing guard over a supply depot with Gregor, who was considered boring company. ''Live a little,'' people told him, ''Don't take it all so seriously. America might bomb us any minute, and it will all be over in a lightning flash.'' We spent the hours talking to keep each other awake.

''Do you believe in God?'' I asked, surprising myself with the question.

''I just don't know, Valeri,'' Gregor replied, taken aback. ''I don't think there is conclusive proof of the existence of God. But when you consider the galaxy and the interplanetary system, and the spectacular beauty of nature,'' he paused again before continuing, ''and then the complexities of the atom, and nuclear energy . . . ''. My question had obviously touched something deep within. ''And the mystery of childbirth . . . '' his words tailed off into the night.

''It does make you think,'' Gregor continued. ''I can't say there is a God, but I think there is something there. Don't ask me what it is because I don't know.'' The question never left my mind.

I had known many women but Viktoria, or Vikki, was my first real love. We met at a dance in town where my army buddies all vied for her, but she only had eyes for me. She worked in a fabrics factory near the base, so it was all too easy to sneak away to see her.

Young and pretty, Vikki wanted us to marry, but I wasn't ready to be tied down. Going AWOL had its penalties, as I soon learned, but it was worth it just to be near her.

The army ranked patrol duty as more important than night manoeuvres with Viktoria, and by the end of my second year, in 1966, I was facing a spell in the military prison.

The army's patience with this wild kid from Leningrad was running out. This time, my foolish erratic behaviour brought me before a court martial which threatened to terminate my career.

One night in the prison cell, in despair, I found myself reviewing my life. What was the point of it all? I lost everything when I lost my mother. I missed her world of love and warmth, and recalled memories of sunny Sunday mornings at the Orthodox Church where we shared communion regularly.

Although still young, my experience of life had left me with no illusions about people. Everyone else seemed as lost and confused as I, filled with lies and deceit. The Communist revolution had resulted in a country without justice or freedom. These basic rights were replaced with mass corruption. It was a one-way street to destruction, with no exit.

If my search for truth and love was to be in vain, perhaps it would be better to kill myself and kiss this world goodbye. I thought I had decided my future, and I grew morose and depressed as I tossed and turned that night.

But two days later when I returned to my cell at sunset after my duties, I noticed a tall grey building through the prison window. At the top stood a cross. As the sun was sinking, the dim light revived a sudden flood of memories of a conversation with my Aunt Tamara.

Against all the odds her words had returned to my mind, "Valeri, if you forget everything else I've said, just remember one thing. God exists!"

GOD EXISTS! GOD EXISTS! GOD EXISTS!

Repeating the words to myself gave the idea life in my heart. Yes, I thought to myself, maybe there really is a God.

I knelt down on the cold concrete floor desperately trying to recall how to enter the secret world of prayer. Long ago I had seen people cross themselves in church and tried to repeat the action, but what was the correct procedure?

Startled by the complexity of this ritual, I suddenly found
myself saying:

> Oh God,
> If you really exist, then you will help me
> because I'm pleading to you with all my heart.
> But if you're not there and if you only exist
> in people's minds, then you can't help me,
> and you will remain silent.

That night I fell into a deep sleep.

The next morning I remained remarkably calm as I waited
outside the judicial enquiry office for my tribunal to begin.
To my surprise and delight, I was cleared of the charges.

I had prayed and the answer had come. God exists! I
accepted this as a promise, the first step along my journey.

At last! Eleven days after my twentieth birthday, on
December 17, 1966, I was officially discharged from the
army. As I loaded my rucksack into the jeep to leave, some
nervous-looking teenagers tumbled out of the army bus. I
smiled to myself and thought of my first days as a recruit.

An official escort put us on the train to Leningrad, but
I got off at the next stop and made my way back to Riga,
straight to Viktoria's arms. Vikki was impetuous just like me.
In an impulsive moment we made plans for the future, but
three weeks later, stirred by an inner restlessness, I kissed her
goodbye and caught the train to Leningrad again.

Valya had grown up fast with long flowing hair and a
winsome manner. I was sorry to learn of Uncle Ura's death,
and Valya clung to me in a tearful embrace. I understood
the tensions she had faced as a young person living in a family
at war.

My first few nights in Leningrad were not spent in wild
drinking sprees at the familiar haunts. George and my other
friends couldn't understand what was going on.

Tamara moved elegantly through the room, dusting the flat. Perhaps sensing that I wanted to talk to her, she called out, "Valeri, do you want some tea?"

We sat in the kitchen sipping strong tea with slices of lemon.

"I can't explain how I'm different, but I know I am because I feel like a new person," I said almost in wonder.

"I know what you mean," Tamara said. "The scriptures tell of such experiences. That's what Jesus meant when he said, 'You must be born again'."

"I want to be born again," the words shot out of my mouth. "That's how I feel. There's a tingling in my heart and senses."

"The way to God is through Jesus. He is the door. Once we know him he will never leave us."

"You mean, it's possible to experience God wherever you are?"

"Yes Valeri, God is a spirit and he can be with us everywhere, in every circumstance. Even in this kitchen, he is with us."

I nodded my head, although somewhat mystified by the theology. I was hungry for information and my mind was racing with questions.

How could I be sure I was born again? Did Christian believers really sacrifice their children live on the altar, or was this propaganda? Did Jesus really exist as a historical person, or was the Bible full of fairy stories? Did Jesus really rise from the dead? And finally, could Jesus really change my life?

Tamara fielded my questions which tumbled out the more she tried to explain. My response was enthusiastic. "I want it! I want it!"

Perhaps mistaking my reply for youthful zeal, she explained mysteriously, "You're young, you have your life ahead of you. You have time to decide."

But God looked at my heart. He could see that I really wanted to be his servant. Leaning across the table, clutching my aunt's hands in mine, I spoke in earnest. "Auntie, tell me what I should do. I believe that God exists. I believe in the holy sacrifice of Jesus. I believe that he died for me. Tell me what I should do now."

"It's very simple," Aunt Tamara replied. "Just give yourself completely, all that you have to Jesus. He knows what you need. He will lead you through life by his Holy Spirit."

I stared imploringly at her. Almost at once I began to pray secretly in my heart, "Lord, let her go from this house leaving me alone here with you."

To my amazement, Tamara pushed back her chair and said, somewhat embarrassed, "Excuse me Valeri, I must go and do some shopping now because we have guests for dinner and I need to prepare some food."

The very instant the door slammed shut, I knelt down and cried out to God, "Oh Lord, from this very second, I want to be completely yours."

I was like a shipwrecked sailor who catches sight of a steamer sending out a rescue boat.

Although the earth did not move and there were no miraculous signs, I did feel peace in my heart as I rose. I recognised this as the same peace that I had experienced as a child when my mother recited the Lord's Prayer. I was aware of a spiritual awakening within myself. I knew things would be different and I felt a mounting sense of excitement.

When I awoke early the next morning I thought my heart was going to burst with joy. "Now I really am a child of God," I told myself. "I was an orphan but now I have a daddy in heaven. Praise God!" I wanted to dance through the streets and cartwheel along the pavements yelling, "People of Leningrad, why do you live without God?"

Crowding into George's front room where the new Beatles album was playing, I tried to join Paul McCartney's voice on the chorus, "Good day sunshine, Good day sunshine, Good day sunshine!" The gang were amused that I talked about God instead of cursing and swearing. It was all a big joke. When they realised I wasn't drunk, they thought I was crazy. I related my experience in the army, "I had a problem and I prayed to God. I escaped punishment even though I deserved it. It was a miracle. I know it's true, God exists!"

I had immediately stopped smoking and drinking, and with the bravado of youth, felt I knew all I needed to know about the spiritual life. I had "arrived". But there were many lessons to be learned.

How could I explain that God lived in my heart, and that I was filled with peace and joy? One night alone in my room, I prayed, "O Lord, give me a mouth so that I can share your holy love with everyone all over this world." It took me several years to understand the significance of this simple prayer.

God cradled me in his loving arms for two months. But I was impatient to prove my own capability and independence. I told him, "Lord, I am ready. I will do anything for you, and go anywhere for you. Look I've already stopped smoking and it's been two months since I've touched a drop of vodka."

And the Lord said, "OK, my son." And still cradling me, he placed me on the ground. Of course I was still a child, and as I reached the ground and tried to stand on my own, I tumbled down. Thinking myself to be sufficient in my own strength, it wasn't long before I fell into temptation.

One night I was talking about the Lord with George and the gang but continued to swig from the bottle each time it came round. Somehow I managed to stagger home but collapsed in the alleyway by my aunt's home.

In the frolic my shirt and trouser buttons had been ripped off, and I had picked up an old bugle on which I blew a bawdy bar song.

I awoke in the flat with a hangover, and the little I could remember about the night before made me squirm. Aunt Tamara found me sitting in the kitchen sipping tea. She didn't speak and I was content to ignore her. However, I couldn't escape her probing eyes.

"They're selling winter coats at the corner. Do you want to come with me and see if there's anything you like?" she remarked. Winter coats in summer or swimming gear in winter weren't a surprise. Soviet production has no marketing strategy. Things suddenly appear in shops, street corners and the backs of cars and you buy them while you can. It was all crazy.

I didn't really want to go, but I didn't want to cause an argument. Besides, I knew that Tamara wanted to speak to me about last night and I couldn't evade that conversation.

Leaving the flat we stepped almost straight into our neighbour, a stout woman named Galina. She was a firm atheist, and nothing I said to her seemed to make any impression.

She plunged straight for the weak spot. "What was that song you were singing last night, Valeri? A new song about Jesus?"

Tamara was silent. I stared at my shoes.

Galina was relentless in her pursuit. "Where is your god now? Is this how Christians behave, keeping us awake at night? What a joke." Her mocking laugh rang in the stairwell as we left.

I hung out with the same crowd that night. Within the next few days I couldn't keep up the pretence of a changed life and soon slid back to my old ways. How I shamed Aunt Tamara.

Two months later, Galina confronted Aunt Tamara about my drunkenness. Tamara was remarkably calm, and told Galina, "God knows everything. Our lives are in his hands. We will all have to answer to God personally. Valeri will, I will, and you, Galina, will also have to answer to God."

I was in the flat with my ear pressed to the front door as my aunt dealt with our nosy neighbour. I knew I was in the wrong, but how could I change my ways?

I apologised to Tamara and told her how wretched I felt. "I think the best thing I can do is to leave Leningrad."

Although Tamara was shocked, she quickly regained her

composure. "Yes, maybe you're right, Valeri. But where would you go?"

I already knew of an expedition leaving shortly for Siberia to complete a topographical survey for a planned new airfield, and the group needed an assistant. After a few calls and a brief interview, I was hired. The group was leaving in two days.

I couldn't handle a farewell party, so I only told George I was leaving. Tamara had mixed emotions about me being away all summer. On my last evening at home, I solemnly packed my few clothes and belongings into my army rucksack. Tamara cooked my favourite fried-chicken dish for me, but although we laughed and joked, somehow the sparkle was missing.

"God bless you, Valeri," Tamara said as we embraced for the last time. I loved her so dearly and was distressed that I had hurt her. I knew I would miss Tamara and everyone else in Leningrad.

I was leaving under a dark cloud. A sense of disgrace and loss dominated my final hours. But I felt I had no choice. I knew that if I stayed longer, I could not survive.

Siberia. The thought sent a chill through me. What did the future hold?

4

TANYA THE REDHEAD

About 2,000 km from Leningrad lies the mining town of Uray in the heart of Siberia. It is near Turmin, an old city to which the enemies of the Tsar were banished. Siberia itself has come to symbolise a land of prisoners in a never-ending winter of exile, of isolated communities of log cabins which never appear on any maps.

Progress and the twentieth century were catching up with Siberia's rich unexploited reserves of oil, gas, coal and iron ore. The expedition on which I was an assistant produced site plans and data for architectural drawings for the airport to be built at the developing centre of Uray.

Although the Saturday-night dance was never mentioned in the newspapers, the unofficial grapevine ensured that everyone in Uray was there. An hour before the doors opened, there were kids hanging around at the entrance.

A dance band with homemade instruments played traditional songs but tried to jazz it up a bit.

After playing for an hour, the band took a break and I introduced myself to Jan, the leader of the group. Before I knew it he had insisted that I join the group on stage.

I sang the Beatles song "All my loving", and immediately several of the girls clapped in time to the music. News of the rock and roll revolution had obviously spread, as the dancers were inspired to further improvised movements. By the end of the song, a crowd had gathered below the stage and everyone in the hall seemed to be clapping and cheering.

Jan gave me thumbs up. "Great. Great," he shouted. "By

the way, do you know any other songs?'' We may not have won any musical awards, but we were having fun and I launched into another Beatles song.

My hair was long, and I wore a Beatle-style jacket. As I was from Leningrad, the group expected me to know the latest pop songs and fashions. No one else in the town had tried anything like this, and we were considered daring. During my time in Uray, we gained a reputation for playing rock and roll.

On completion of the airport plans, it was time for the expedition to move on to Annaderth, a remote settlement nearer Alaska than Moscow. At this point I requested permission to stay in Uray. The leader was a kind man who agreed and said, ''Perhaps music is your life.''

I not only missed Leningrad, but also my girlfriend Viktoria from Riga. I sent her the money for an airline ticket to join me in Uray, but I suspected something was not right from the letters she wrote. In spite of her excuses for delaying the trip, she never came.

One day I was drunk and decided to speak to Vikki immediately, so I staggered to the post office. The sweet red-haired girl behind the counter placed the call, and finally I heard her voice on the telephone.

''Vikki, when are you coming to see me, my love?'' I yelled down the phone, much to the amusement of the other customers. Vikki seemed detached and vague, and the call was over much too soon.

The girl at the counter tapped her desk to attract my attention. I sauntered over and called out, ''I'm in love but my girlfriend is in Riga!''

''Never mind your girlfriend,'' the redhead replied, ''you owe me ten roubles for your phonecall.''

''What's your name?'' I asked the girl.

''Tanya.''

She was attractive, but the people behind me were no longer amused. ''G'bye!'' I called, and staggered out of the post office.

I decided to surprise Vikki by visiting her unexpectedly a few days before my birthday. No one was home, so I had to wait half an hour on a bench outside her block. When I saw her we rushed into each others' arms as if in a romantic movie.

We spent the next few days in a lovers' daze, and celebrated my birthday. When the vodka ran out, Vikki's friend Katya took me to a backstreet "fixer" to buy some alcohol. In the taxi, Katya turned to me and said, "Vikki doesn't deserve you. Did you know she has a lover?"

I couldn't be sure if Katya was a troublemaker or making a play for me, but I dared her to give me proof. Directing the taxi-driver to a high-rise block, Katya took me to a nondescript apartment. We rang the bell and a tall bearded youth answered the door.

"Katya . . . " he stammered. "What are you doing here?" Katya was forthright. "Are you Vikki's boyfriend?"

"Yes," he blurted, not giving the word a second thought, ushering us into an untidy room. His name was Leo, and he freely admitted that although Vikki and he were lovers, they weren't all that serious about each other.

As we looked at photographs of Leo and Vikki caught in a lovers' embrace, the proof burnt my eyes. What really hurt was the way she looked at him.

Leo hung his head sheepishly as Katya and I walked to the door. Back at the flat, Vikki immediately knew something was amiss. "What happened to you?" she asked. "I was worried."

"It's no use, Vikki, he knows," Katya replied. "I just couldn't hide the truth from him anymore."

Vikki crumpled into my arms. "Oh Valeri, I'm sorry. I tried to tell you. I'm so confused."

"It's my birthday party," I said, trying to sound cheerful. "This is a time for laughter not for tears. Don't stop the celebrations."

But among the empty vodka bottles that lined the kitchen floor, I felt dazed and alone. Vikki clung to me as though

I was some sailor on his last night in port. The cassette player seemed to be playing songs just for me, as I tried to hide my heartbreak. Vikki lifted a vodka bottle to her lips to drown her tears.

Somehow we made it through the night.

The next morning when I awoke I couldn't find my suitcase among the sleeping entwined bodies in the flat, so I threw my belongings into a cloth sack. Vikki looked peaceful as she lay on the bed, moving slowly in her sleep. "Goodbye, Vikki," I whispered, and walked from the room.

A wave of loneliness washed over me as I closed the door, and Riga suddenly seemed an unfriendly town.

But I couldn't forget Vikki. Back in Uray I began drinking more heavily than before. I tried to pray, insisting that I would turn from my old ways, but I was powerless to change.

I shared a flat with our bass guitarist Boris, and Pavel our drummer, and we became close friends and drinking partners. One night, Pavel saw a religious tract that my aunt had sent me. "What are you doing with this?" he joked.

"I'm a Christian," I replied.

Pavel began to joke about my lifestyle, not realising I was serious. This annoyed me, so I retorted, "My life will change. I love Jesus. I will stop drinking."

"If someone else told me that, I would believe it. But not you, Valeri!" Pavel laughed even more. "I can't imagine what you'd be like without a drink."

I woke up in a sweat after a vivid dream. Uncle Ura was standing in the middle of the room and I approached him burdened with guilt. He looked at me and said, "Clean your feet!" I then looked down and realised that my feet were muddy and that I had left a trail of dirt behind me as I walked into the room.

Understanding the dream immediately, I didn't hesitate to kneel beside my bed. "Jesus, without your help, I will perish," I whispered, deeply moved by the experience. "Lord Jesus, I surrender to you. Help me!"

I felt a release and a sense of cleansing. Although I had turned away from God, he had not abandoned me. I was lost and searching for a way out, but God knew this moment would come, as he continued to work in my heart.

I carried on praising God as I rose from my knees and walked to the window. I also prayed for a girl to share my life. Outside the street seemed tranquil in the silky moonlight. I understood that I was a solitary pilgrim tramping through this world.

For the next few days, I walked a tightrope between conscience and corruption. Boris and Pavel understood that I was caught in an internal conflict, but they were powerless to help.

On Saturday night, April 27th, we joined Pavel at a wedding reception to which he had been invited. We were used to gatecrashing.

We arrived in time to wave goodbye to the happy couple as they left for a holiday on the Black Sea. Minutes later I bumped into the bride again, who had completely changed her appearance and now served wine and wedding cake to the guests! Astounded by the transformation, I soon realised the answer was much simpler.

The bride and the girl were twins.

There was a flicker of recognition as I thanked her for the wine. In a flash, I remembered an embarrassing episode at the local post office. I knew that she had recognised me as well.

There was a sparkle in our encounter and we were hardly out of each other's sight over the next hour.

For once I declined Boris and Pavel's invitation to join an impromptu band. The group began to play Elvis Presley's "Love me tender" as I manoeuvred Tanya on to the floor for a slow dance together. Holding her tight, I guided her towards the verandah as the song was drawing to an end. Still cuddling and giggling like teenagers on a first date, we walked to the end of the porch hand in hand.

I put my arms around her and gave her a squeeze. She seemed to respond. Seize the moment, I thought. Closing my eyes, I planted a kiss on her lips.

Was it an earth tremor after just one kiss? No! It was Tanya's mother jerking us apart. I guess she didn't want to lose two daughters in one night. "I know your kind," she barked. "My daughter isn't going to be led astray by someone like you."

I knew a potential mother-in-law would not see me as an ideal prospect with my long hair and tight black clothes. Risking her wrath I hung around the party for another hour, joining the jam session.

Surreptitiously I arranged to see the redhead after work at the post office during the week.

I just couldn't get her out of my mind. Tanya! Tanya! Tanya!

Although she had a temper to match the legend of the fiery redhead, I found her shy, unassuming and delightful. I discovered that she wasn't impressed by the number of Beatles songs that I could sing in English. Incredibly, she didn't even like the Beatles.

I found that I could relax with her and over the next few months a serious attachment formed between us.

Tanya's mother worked at the local factory and was strict with her children, rarely allowing them out at night, and extremely particular about the boys they dated. In a small town like Uray, gossip spread quickly.

Tanya wasn't a Christian and found it hard to understand that someone who played rock music, wore jeans and loud clothes could also believe in God.

Tanya's family were involved with occult practices, and she had her mother's gift of foretelling the future. "I see you have Baptist eyes," she said to me one evening. Tanya feared Christians, believing that they sacrificed their children in some weird ritual. I tried to explain the Christian faith to her, but she had been steeped in superstitions from

childhood, making it difficult for me to speak about Jesus.
But I looked for an unlatched window into her soul.

Like everyone else, Tanya loved to listen to the radio and
believed everything she heard. After listening to Radio
Moscow for half an hour, I retuned the set to Radio Monte
Carlo. It was a Bible study on the fifteenth chapter of John's
Gospel. Soon I could sense Tanya's growing impatience.

"I can't believe that people listen to this in the twentieth
century," Tanya finally interrupted in exasperation. But I
didn't budge and replied firmly, "I listen to it."

Somewhat surprised, but not wishing to offend me, Tanya
covered her tracks, "Oh! I just thought no one listened to
this kind of religious broadcast."

Sensing a break in the cover, I moved in. Tanya's eyes
widened as I explained to her how Aunt Tamara's influence
had led me into a personal relationship with God. She didn't
share my convictions, but she listened to me.

Despite our differences of belief, I was convinced that we
were destined to be together. I telephoned my aunt and
shared my feelings. "If you are sure about it Valeri, then
go ahead. Don't put your trust in the counsel of man. Learn
to listen to the heart of God. He will guide you. It may be
a dangerous route, but it will be the best one."

I prayed and asked God for direction. *What should I do,
Lord*? Tanya returned to my consciousness at every possible
moment. She was more than a weekend romance.

Tanya was dreamy and I cradled her in my arms as I asked
her the question of a lifetime. Both of us remained silent
for a few moments with our private thoughts.

Then with a mischievous look, Tanya said, "You mean
you are prepared to marry someone who doesn't even like
rock music?" We collapsed in giggles.

Tanya's parents were understandably reluctant. They found
me unpredictable and were horrified by my religious views.

Tanya's mother tried to talk her out of the wedding.
"Why do you want to marry Valeri?" she persisted.

Tanya replied, "Because he has a tender heart."

We both felt that we should be married immediately. We hit on December 27th, 1968 for the registry office requirements, and the wedding was to follow soon afterwards in the New Year. Tamara agreed to come from Leningrad for the wedding and she wrote a short note of congratulations to Tanya.

One week before the wedding, disaster struck. Tanya developed a large painful boil on her face, and I had lost my red internal passport, a document needed for the registry office. There wasn't enough time for me to apply for a new passport, and Tanya became extremely worried. Her mother hinted that I had hidden the document to get out of the marriage.

Without a word of explanation to Tanya, I bowed my head and prayed, "Lord Jesus, if it's your will that this wedding should take place and that we are meant for each other, please help me to find my passport.

"Please touch Tanya's body and heal this abscess," I continued, "prove to Tanya that you have a wonderful future for both of us."

Tanya didn't know what to do. It was her first experience of prayer. I assured her that God was interested in the details of her life.

This simple and somewhat naïve prayer had an electric effect. Tanya awoke the next morning feeling considerably better and in much less pain. In two days the boil had vanished without even a scar.

The day after we prayed, I was at home learning the guitar with Boris. We had just heard the latest Beatles song "Hey Jude" on the BBC, and I was trying to play it. The doorbell rang, and I was perplexed to find a militiaman standing in the doorway. Reaching into his briefcase, he held out a small red document.

My passport!

At the time, Uray was gripped by "the great freeze". That winter was unusually cold even for Siberia, and life effectively stopped as the town was wrapped in a blanket of snow fifty to sixty degrees below zero.

For several days there were no flights in or out of Uray. It seemed unlikely that Aunt Tamara would be able to make the journey from Leningrad in time for our wedding, and I began to be concerned.

Curiously, Tanya seemed to understand the significance of Tamara's presence at our wedding. I comforted her by saying, "If it's the will of God everything will be OK."

No one knew what would happen. The day before the wedding the air thinned slightly. We heard on the radio that the area was still enveloped by the freeze, but a patch of clear weather was predicted for Uray. Abruptly, the conditions changed, turning from minus sixty degrees to minus six.

We borrowed a car and somehow made it through the snow to the airport. We didn't even know if Tamara had caught the plane from Leningrad. "Just pray," I told Tanya. The airport staff knew nothing in the chaos of cancelled flights.

After two hours, spontaneous applause broke out in the arrivals hall as a flight from Leningrad was announced. Then a few minutes later, Tamara herself walked through the barrier.

Dragging Tanya with me, I raced to hug Tamara. "We didn't know if you'd make it."

Tamara laughed with a twinkle in her eye, "God brought me here."

Ironically, the freeze returned on the day that Tamara left again, on December 29th. It seemed that even nature had conspired to celebrate our union.

Tamara brought the wedding rings, the veil, and Tanya's shoes with her. Although she had never seen Tanya before, incredibly everything fitted and Tanya was pleased with my aunt's choice.

On the wedding day Tanya looked beautiful in a

fashionable white mini-skirt she had sewn herself. I wanted to whisk her away and carry her into the sunset.

It was hard to get flowers because of the cold weather, but we were able to locate a tiny patch of earth that preserved a delicate bunch of wild flowers, timed to perfection. Tanya clasped the flowers, looking angelic as the moment to make our vows drew near.

The registry office clerk smiled. I was twenty-four and a man of the world. But Tanya looked an innocent eighteen-year-old maiden. As I handed over the red passport and gave Tanya's hand a squeeze, the lady behind the counter gave us a cheeky smile. "This is your last chance!" she said with the fatal rubber stamp poised over our marriage certificate.

But Tanya clutched my arm tightly and proudly declared, "I wouldn't change him for anyone else. I love him."

Later that evening according to traditional custom, we were brought bread and salt on a silver platter. We were required to dip the bread into the salt and eat it together as a symbol of our union. Then we drank a toast to our marriage and smashed the glasses against the fireplace to a great roar of approval from our friends and family.

I was spellbound when I opened Aunt Tamara's present to us. Inside the cardboard box was a large heavily-bound Bible. This was the first Bible I had ever seen. I opened the book and gently turned its pages. This is God's book, I thought to myself. From that moment I read it avidly.

I prayed continually that Tanya would come to know God, and asked my aunt to explain the danger of spiritualist practices to her. I felt that Tanya listened to Tamara and that the foundation of our relationship was a good one.

We held a party in one of the rooms at the sports hall, and with Tanya and me seated on the stage, the toasts were proposed. As the wine was sipped, our friends roared "Bitter!"

I took Tanya in my arms and kissed her, prompting another sip from the wedding glass, and another roar from the crowd, "Sweet!"

"One-two-three-four-five-six-seven". The count continued as Tanya and I were locked in a lovers' embrace, oblivious to everything around us.

We spent our honeymoon in a rented dacha, thirty days of togetherness. I never touched Tanya until our honeymoon. It seemed quite natural, even though my friends had been amazed at my restraint.

Zhanna, our daughter, was born the following October, weighing six pounds and twelve ounces. She was a delightful bundle of joy, and I sat for hours cuddling her and whispering into her ear. A special bond developed between us that has remained through the years. Zhanna was a blessing from God on our family.

I had found work as a driver and was taking an advanced course in professional driving. Late one night as I returned from an assignment, I reflected on how I had met very few Christians in Siberia, and there was no church to attend. It was as if the land was covered with a spiritual darkness.

Approaching the lights of Uray I felt strangely distanced from all that I saw. God had answered my prayer for a girl to share my life, and had given us a beautiful daughter. But I still felt as if I didn't belong in this dark world. I started to pray, "All I have in this life is a sinner's world, God and myself".

I found that I was repeating this prayer as I drove. Then through his Holy Spirit, God began to tell me, "Valeri, this is your world." On the unlit road the dark night seemed unfriendly and foreboding. I replied, "No Lord, this isn't my world."

Again I felt the presence of God. "Valeri, this is your world." The message was strong and urgent, and would not leave my mind. I struggled to resist it.

"No Lord," I insisted, "this isn't my home. Not this world."

"Then Valeri, why have I placed you here?"

I had no answer to the challenge.

PART II

ROCK PREACHER

5

LOVE AT THE CROSSROADS

Tanya and I decided to settle in Leningrad, but first I had to return alone to my home town to explore accommodation and job opportunities.

I found myself taking the trolley bus to Labour Square, and drifting towards the Neva River. All I could see were the flashing lights of the harbour, all I could hear was the rustling of the leaves. A dog barking, somewhere in the distance, the sound of an accordion playing a sad refrain.

I strolled along the bank and peered into the swirling river, catching a fleeting glance of my reflection in the water.

A fourteen-year-old waif stared back at me.

Over a decade ago I had sought refuge here from Uncle Ura's anger, curled up under a tree, a homeless runaway, an orphan in the storm.

Reliving a moment from yesterday, I was on the verge of retracing the steps of another poignant journey into the past. Like Mama, I had written to the army resettlement office requesting the current address and whereabouts of a certain Red Army soldier, Alexander Sardonikov.

The contents of a nondescript brown-manilla envelope confirmed that he still lived in Vyborg, near the Finnish border, 270 km from Leningrad. I had written before to Father at this address from Uray, enclosing photographs of his grandchildren, but the letters had been returned, with no explanation given.

Perhaps it wasn't my father. Maybe Alexander Sardonikov of Vyborg had never been a soldier.

I simply had to know the answer.

The house on Kraypostnaya Skaya was an old Finnish-style building and the Sardonikov apartment was on the third floor.

On the brink of abandoning my secret mission, memories of the past made me tremble. Battling against my trepidation I climbed to the third floor.

The name on the door looked imposing: ALEXANDER SARDONIKOV.

But no one was in. Undecided, I shuffled along the hallway and knocked at a neighbour's door. Staring intently at the jittery youth fidgeting in front of her, she appeared to recognise me when I mentioned the name Sardonikov. "Andrew, his son, is here. Ask him."

Fifteen minutes later, a young teenager charged up the stairs. Something in the way he moved, the way his hair fell on his face, the glint in his eye, told me this was Andrew.

I used my cover story. A man named Alexander Sardonikov had been my driving instructor and now I was tracking him down. The student had come in search of his master.

Andrew responded with buoyant enthusiasm and welcomed me into an elegant room with a beautiful fireplace. The rapport with Andrew was immediate and within minutes we had discovered some striking similarities in taste and personality. To the kid's surprise, we even looked alike.

But I had to be sure.

"Do you have any photographs of your father?" He sprang to his feet and passed me a photo album. I felt as though I had been dowsed with a bucket of ice-cold water. Here was an old sepia photograph of a dashing young soldier. Mama had cherished this same photo.

It was Father!

The next photo was of a group of soldiers on a troop train. "Don't tell me which one is your father, let me guess," I said to Andrew, who was captivated by the game.

It didn't take a second.

I asked if there were any duplicate copies of the recent photographs. "Of course," he smiled, and handed one over.

The front doorbell announced another visitor to the Sardonikov home. A family friend from another town had come visiting for a few days.

"Mama will be home soon," Andrew explained. The woman introduced herself, staring curiously at both of us, glancing back and forth. "Which of you is Alexander's son?" she teased.

Andrew found this hilarious. "Guess!" he posed the challenge. "And we have so much in common, it's amazing."

Without warning the front door opened and a straight faced woman, aged about forty, entered the room. Andrew jumped up and exclaimed, "Mama, this is Valeri! He's a student of Papa's, but we're so alike it's unbelievable," Andrew chuckled. The woman's piercing gaze seemed to peel away the veneer from my story.

Andrew's mother embraced the other visitor and both of them sat talking together on the settee. Every few minutes she glared across at me. Every second I stayed in the room seemed to increase the tension, so I rose to my feet and headed for the door.

Andrew argued, insisting that I should stay. "You haven't even seen my train set." "I always wanted a train set," I admitted, "but I really must go."

I didn't want to leave, but I knew I couldn't stay.

At Vyborg railway station, the train to Leningrad was an hour late. When it finally pulled in, I searched out an empty carriage and huddled in the corner, pressing my face against the glass. I watched the landscape float by as the train picked up speed. Like pouring rain in a thunderstorm, a thousand thoughts assailed my mind.

But I had found my Father!

In March 1971, five months after Zhanna's birth, I moved

back to Leningrad. Three months later, Tanya and Zhanna joined me. Tanya was apprehensive about moving to the big city, but I was able to allay her fears. I had found work as a driver and some modest accommodation for our first home together.

I had obtained a room in a ground-floor flat in a six-storey building in Babushkin Street. There were three rooms in the flat, each of them occupied by another couple, with shared toilet and kitchen facilities. Such flats are common in Leningrad and Moscow.

Marina our second daughter was born a year after we moved to Leningrad and once again I experienced that incredible moment when the nurse says, "Congratulations, you've got a girl!" I was a proud dad and paraded our tots around the local park delighting in other people's enthusiasm for our girls.

Our cramped living conditions were not the only problem we encountered. I enjoyed my job driving senior executives around town in a luxury Volga car, but the hours were long and the hundred roubles barely covered our food bill each month. Some nights we went to bed hungry.

There were also the usual difficulties faced by newlyweds of growing accustomed to each others' ways. But the tensions increased between us when I started to attend the Registered Baptist Church on Poklonnaya Street.

I tried to attend every meeting at the church, and soon my knowledge of the Bible increased. I found it easy to speak about how Jesus had turned my life around and was asked to share my testimony with the entire church. I couldn't stop speaking about Jesus. In September 1971 I was baptised and became a member of the church.

To my surprise, I had become a respectable member of society. I cut my hair and dressed in a suit and tie. Sometimes I even wore a hat. I stopped drinking, sold all my Beatles records and for two years hardly listened to any rock music.

I was sincere in my pursuit of Jesus but the religious path was a slippery one. I found it easy to judge others, comparing their response to mine. I had confused an appearance of religion with the freedom Jesus gives.

But Tanya wasn't impressed.

One night after a Bible study, I shared with Brother Boris the conflict that Tanya and I were facing over my interest in the church. I respected Boris because of his knowledge of scripture and his position as an elder in the church.

"Will you come and talk to my wife?" I pleaded. "Maybe you can convince her."

Brother Boris pointed out the scripture exhorting us not to be linked with non-believers.

"But I'm sure that my marriage to Tanya was made in heaven," I insisted.

Brother Boris was not amused. He arranged to visit our home on the following Tuesday at 7.30 p.m. Promptly to the minute, the doorbell rang. It was Brother Boris, dressed in a suit and tie. I greeted him and introduced Tanya, who smiled nervously. The table had been prepared carefully with cakes and pastries made by Tanya during the afternoon.

Strutting into the tiny room, the church leader surveyed our home. His eyes fell on some wine glasses in a cabinet, a wedding present from Pavel who had played in the band with me in Uray.

"What are they?" he questioned, peering at the glasses. Surprised, I didn't know what to say.

Turning slowly, he gazed at the television set in the other corner of the room. "What is that?" he asked again.

"We have a small child. She likes to watch TV," I stuttered.

Brother Boris smiled sarcastically as he continued his inspection. This time, a carpet hanging on the wall caught his attention. This was a wedding gift from Tanya's aunt. It was light brown with an intricate pattern woven into the fabric, like the ones made by skilful Uzbek craftsmen, and bought from gypsy traders.

From his questions I understood that Brother Boris assumed that we were wealthy. I sought to explain to him how God had blessed us, but I knew from his condescending manner that he disapproved. He moved on to deal with the matter in hand in a superior tone that made him sound as though he had just returned from a private audience with God.

Then he looked at his watch and announced that he had business elsewhere and he must leave us. We shook hands solemnly at the door and then he was gone.

I helped Tanya carry the cups and plates to the communal kitchen to be washed up. Neither of us said a word. Finally Tanya broke the silence.

"Never speak to me about Jesus again. I don't want to become like those religious people." She had an edge to her voice and a finality in her words. The meeting had only lasted an hour, but the whole evening was a disaster.

Over the next few weeks my efforts to repair the damage led instead to constant bickering and arguments. Tanya was miserable and I could find no peace.

One night after a bitter quarrel I said, "It's no use, Tanya, we can't go on like this. When fish and crab both swim in opposite directions, the current forces them to swim together."

It was late and as I lay on my bed my mind wandered over Brother Boris' eventful visit and a message I had heard in church once about prayer. I recalled that when Jesus took three of his best men to pray, he went on ahead to pray alone. But how did he pray, I wondered to myself. No one knows.

In my simple way I understood that even a church leader can be a stranger to God, like a tourist in God's country. I knew instantly that it was more important for the heart to move freely, than to be wrapped in a religious disguise.

I fell asleep and in a dream, God urged me to trust him in this situation with Tanya. After that I prayed, "Lord help me." But I sensed God saying, "Do you trust me? If you trusted me, you'd have peace." This was a turning point in my prayer life as God challenged me to have faith.

But full breakthrough was preceded by a barrier.

A few days later I was determined not to allow an argument to flare up. Tanya was annoyed, but struggled to contain her feelings. Suddenly she exploded. Her eyes blazed defiantly as she brushed her red hair back and vowed, "I'll never believe in Jesus."

"You've lost," a little voice whispered as her words stung deep within my soul. "You've lost!" But I resisted replying to Tanya and prayed, "Lord, I need victorious faith now!" I was reminded of a scripture which I had read, "He and all his family were saved."

Calmly I tried to relay this message to Tanya. To my surprise she listened. I knew then that Tanya was on the brink of belief in God.

I had been maintaining the guise of a valiant spiritual warrior. But behind the façade, the enemy had attacked and I was spiritually ill. I knew I could cover my sin but in God's eyes, every secret will be uncovered. And how could I make my wife well, when I was ill? The contradiction disturbed me. I felt that humility was the source of strength. I decided to confess my mistake to Tanya.

"Tanya, I know I have told you that my life has changed. Maybe you think I'm an angel, but I'm not." Tanya's eyes widened. What was this? "Don't be surprised," I continued, "God has shown me that I am nothing at all. When I met you, I was at the bottom and you were at the top. But I changed, and maybe I have made you feel that I am superior. Well, I want you to know that I'm not the angel you think I am."

I didn't know how she would react, but I knew that my redemption lay in humbling myself before my wife. Tanya stared at me, listening intently.

"Even though I have failed, I want you to remember one thing. I love Jesus. Nothing else matters to me. Jesus gives me strength to go on."

The Lord had softened Tanya's heart and instead of ridiculing and taunting me, I sensed a new-found respect in her attitude. The experience helped me to mature and taught me that the power of humility was a fundamental principle in God's kingdom. It was to be the turning point in our relationship.

Slowly, Tanya began to change. She was an unbelieving witness to God's intervention in our lives. A seed had been planted and in an invisible way faith began to grow in Tanya's heart. I decided to avoid confrontational situations whenever they arose.

Two months later, Zhanna became seriously ill with an extremely high temperature. We grew worried as she became weaker. Cradling Zhanna tenderly in my arms I could feel her body warm with fever as she seemed to wrestle feebly with me.

"Lord," I prayed, "we are your children. Heal this little one of her fever. It's easy for you, Lord." I continued to pray for Zhanna while Tanya tried to sleep. Perhaps half an hour passed. I was then conscious that Zhanna was much cooler. She calmed down and quickly fell into a deep sleep. Gently, I laid her in her cot. Tanya stirred. "How is she?" she enquired.

"She's going to be OK," I said grinning. Tanya sat up and felt our daughter's cheek.

"She's cool," Tanya said, somewhat puzzled. "I'm sure her temperature is down. What happened?"

"Tanya, God healed Zhanna. I prayed and God touched her," I said.

Tanya raised her eyebrows. "Are you joking?"

"It's true, Tanya." I confirmed.

The next morning, Zhanna had made a dramatic recovery. Tanya couldn't doubt the evidence before her eyes.

Tanya had witnessed the power of God in our home. When either of the girls fell ill again, it was she who asked me to pray for them. Poised on the precipice of faith, all she needed was a little push to believe.

Tanya's mother was urging her to return home so that she could see Marina for the first time. It was decided that Tanya would take both girls early in August and plans were finalised for their departure. As a concession, Tanya agreed to visit the Baptist Church with me before they left, to ask God's blessing on the trip.

It was a moving experience which encouraged my soul. Zhanna and Marina sat perched in the front row while old ladies passed mandarins and sweets forward to them, forming a human chain of kindness which the girls watched with enthusiasm.

The pastor of the church was a kind man who prayed over our family, laying hands on Zhanna and Marina. I bowed my head and prayed, "Jesus, our lives are in your hands."

At the end of the service Aunt Tamara came over and kissed Tanya. Several friends greeted us and remarked on our beautiful children, making me feel very proud.

At the airport the next day, Zhanna and Marina were excited about the journey and oblivious to everything else. When finally it was time to say goodbye, I hugged Tanya but felt a coldness in her kiss as she brushed my cheek.

"I'll miss you," I said.

"I'll miss you too," she replied.

I felt a solitary figure as she turned to wave, picking up Marina so she could see me, and then was gone.

The next few days dragged. I missed Zhanna and Marina terribly and consoled myself with their photographs. Tanya was always on my mind, and I reflected on the past few years with her. "How can we live together?" Tanya had cried one night. "You love Jesus, but I'm not interested." I knew that Tanya's mother would try to talk her into remaining in Siberia. But despite this fear, I had decided not to prevent them going home.

Returning to a cold and empty room each night was a reminder of how much I loved and missed my family.

At the end of September I got home to find a telegram pushed under the door, postmarked Siberia. Ripping it open

I read, "Arriving September 30th. Children well." It was brief but the news was thrilling. I took time off work to pick them up at the airport. The children seemed to have grown much taller even in two months. Tanya was friendly, but somehow I felt a distance in our relationship.

About three weeks after they returned, Tanya said that she wanted to talk with me. It was 10 o'clock and the children were asleep.

Tanya was sombre. With a clearly rehearsed script she began, "Valeri, I'm not unhappy being married to you and we have had some good times, but we've reached a crossroads in our life. I can't go on like this. You must choose either to live with me and the children or to continue with this Jesus business. You can't have both."

I stared at her, and then asked, "Are you serious?"

Tanya looked across at me and said, "Yes."

Although she looked intently, I felt she was following her mother's advice. I recalled the scripture which says, "If you love anyone more than me, you are not worthy of me." But I also knew that it wasn't God's way to ignore your relatives.

I reminded Tanya of the events which had led me to believe in God. "Do you remember how I wanted to kill myself when I was in the army? But I was rescued by God. He showed me what this world is really like. I believe that God gave you to me and that we were meant for each other."

I took her hand and held it gently. "I really love you Tanya, and I love our children. If two people lose each other in the forest, one will call out and the other will hear the cry. We're like that couple Tanya, we're lost in the forest and we need each other. We've got to stick together.

"You know the old saying, 'God gives and God takes away.' If you want to leave me, it's not possible for me to stop you."

Tanya was close to tears. I felt her body relax against me and we cuddled. In a few days it would be Zhanna's fifth

birthday and we were planning a little party. Tanya said she
would call a truce until after the party and contemplate my
words over that period.

Zhanna's birthday was fun. We played games and wore
silly hats. Tanya had made a cake in the shape of a farmyard
with lots of little animals. I mimicked animal noises and
everyone laughed, including Tanya.

That night, as we tidied up together, I gave Tanya a
cuddle. "Thanks for working so hard and making it such
a lovely day." She smiled and threw her arms around me.
We swayed back and forth for a few moments and then I
moved her back towards the old sofa against the wall. Tanya
was receptive and I kissed her tenderly, passion burning in
our hearts. Playfully the evening passed into night.

Later that night I reflected on the ultimatum Tanya had
hoisted on to the future of our life together. Usually, if
lovers fall out and want to dismantle a relationship, they
are poised like enemies across the great divide. Tanya hardly
looked like an enemy. I knew that the move had not been
of her own design.

A week later I came home early from work to find that
the girls had gone out to play with some friends. As we were
alone I asked, "What have you decided, Tanya? The
deadline has passed."

Tanya seemed troubled. "We'll live together but lead
separate lives."

"You're treating our relationship like a child's toy," I
replied. "Our life together is the most precious thing we
have. Either we live together happily or we separate."

Tanya was serious. She looked really pretty standing in
the kitchen surrounded by dirty pots and pans. I recalled
the first time I had seen her in the post office. Her cheeky
yet shy smile had captivated me.

Tanya looked up and smiled. "OK, we'll live together."

In a rush we threw our arms around each other. Neither
said a word as we held each other tightly. I heard someone
cough. Taken by surprise, Tanya and I leapt back. Jonas,

who lived in another room in the apartment, looked sheepish. "Sorry, sorry, I didn't mean to interrupt anything. Don't worry, it's quite legal what with you being married and everything."

Back in our room we collapsed in a heap of giggles. Like doves cooing on a window ledge, Tanya and I kissed and cuddled recreating the romance of our courtship.

I didn't realise it at the time, but an invisible pattern of faith had begun to grow in Tanya's heart. Like a map of the world, first the outline was drawn, and then as each day passed a little more detail appeared, rivers and streams, valleys and hills.

6

"YOU CHRISTIANS SHOULD BE SHOT"

The car depot where my job was based was on Ispolkomskaya, a short ride on the subway from our apartment. It was attached to an export office controlling shipments to the West. Not everyone warranted the attention and personal transport given to these export officials. The higher up in the Party structure, the greater the luxury.

I was proud of my Volga car and arrived early to clean it, and to check the oil and tyres. I was the youngest driver and got on well with everyone at the depot. "Hey kid," another driver would joke, "come and clean my car after you've done yours!"

I was naïve about my faith. "I'm a Christian," I would announce. "Do you have any questions about the Christian faith?" Most people were amused by my youthful fervour and played along. When I was stumped by a difficult question, I would reply with great confidence, "Oh! If you ask my aunt, she'll be able to answer that one. She knows everything."

Each week I had to transport an accountant to the finance department of one of the company's factories. One of the typists, a chirpy blond named Rita, would give me a cup of tea and tease me about the stern requirements of the religious life.

"I could never be a Christian," Rita told me one day. "I could never keep all the rules!"

"But Christianity isn't a rule book," I argued, "it's a way of life." This made Rita giggle. "You'd be shocked if you knew about my life, Valeri."

I replied, "It doesn't depend on where we've been, but where we're going."

Rita considered this for a moment and then said, "No, Valeri, not for me."

Our discussion was joined by others who both agreed and disagreed, a welcome distraction on a boring day. I was told, "You should talk to Mrs Agrova. She's a convinced atheist."

"I'll face anyone, anywhere, anytime!" I replied to the challenge.

Unknown to me, my presence in the office had been reported to Mrs Agrova. Suddenly the atmosphere in the room changed. Everyone looked attentively at their desks, papers rustled, pages were turned to great effect.

Mrs Agrova was a hefty stern-faced woman, much taller than me. As chief factory accountant and communist official she was an authoritative figure.

"Who is the preacher?" she barked.

"I am," my voice squeaked.

She looked at me with contempt.

"Maybe you have some questions?" I asked meekly.

Hands on hips, Mrs Agrova asked with natural dismissiveness, "If God exists, why is there war?"

I answered seriously, "I believe in God but I also believe in the devil. The devil has blinded us, covering this world with darkness. And in the darkness we confuse good with bad. In the darkness we find brother fighting brother, the bad man stealing from the upright, the wicked cheating the innocent. No one is satisfied with what he has, and we'll fight and kill to get what we want."

Mrs Agrova continued the assault. "Why do so many children die?"

I found the question difficult. "There's only one thing certain in this life and that is we will all die," I explained. "Children have a special place in God's kingdom, so if children die, they will be in paradise, and it's good to be in paradise."

This reply infuriated her. "If God exists, where is he?" she taunted. "Have you seen God? Does he have a long white beard?" There were a few chuckles around the room. "Science proves there is no God and that's a fact!"

I was quick off the mark. "Many scientists believe in God, even our legendary mathematician Mendeleyev, whose work is studied in every school. He knew we weren't just dangling in space."

"He was just a crazy old man," she said dismissively.

I pounced, "That's a very unpatriotic remark about a loyal citizen. I would have expected you, above all others, to be more complimentary."

"But scientists have to deal with facts, the Bible deals with myths and legends."

"That's not true," I replied, "The accuracy of the Bible has never been seriously disproved. But scientists are forced to admit their text-books are obsolete when new discoveries are made."

Mrs Agrova now appeared to be on the defensive. "Oh, you are so slippery. You never answer my questions directly, you're being so evasive."

Her face flushed with anger. It was humiliating for a woman of her authority to back down to a young upstart. "I can't stand around talking to people like you. I have important work to do." She turned to face the room where the staff were hanging on every word. "Back to work everyone! Back to work!"

Mrs Agrova strode purposefully to the door, then scowled at me, "Have you finished your work here?"

Before I could reply, she barked, "Out! You've wasted enough time already!" The door reverberated behind her as she stormed out.

I hesitated. Rita looked up with a twinkle in her eye, "Well! The preacher and the dragon!" Around us there were roars of laughter followed by louder appeals for quiet from those fearing Mrs Agrova's return.

Nonchalantly I strolled over to the door and felt its

handle. Grimacing in feigned anguish, I jerked my hand away as though it was boiling hot. Rita stormed across the room in an exaggerated impersonation of Mrs Agrova and announced, "The end of the world has come, preacher." She opened the door and barked, "Out!"

Tipping my imaginary hat to everyone in the room, I walked through the door. Rita grinned at me, "What a performance. You should be an actor rather than a preacher!"

I danced down the stairs and waved to the people standing at the factory gates, who looked somewhat bemused.

As I prayed in the Volga on the drive back from the factory, I knew I hadn't said anything unusual but it had clearly been an unprecedented event for that finance department. I felt that God had given me great power in my witness.

Everything else had gone from my mind and I raced up the stairs into the central office whistling a cheery tune. Nikolai, the depot chief, sat at his desk and beckoned to me. Another assignment, I figured. He worked with an efficiency that was remarkable and highly unusual for Russia, where no one seemed to care what happened.

I stood before him with my hands behind my back. It was like being in the army.

"We've had a complaint about you," Nikolai said looking directly at me. I was genuinely surprised, and it showed. What could it be? My mouth hung open in shock. Nikolai didn't prolong the suspense, but read out a scribbled note. " 'We asked for a driver, you sent us a preacher.' Do you know who complained?" he asked, raising his eyebrows.

"I can guess," I replied. "Mrs Agrova!"

I decided not to say anything as I was guilty.

Nikolai considered the situation for a moment, but then chuckled. "I know the woman. It must have been quite a confrontation. She can usually take care of herself." Nikolai looked at me sternly, screwed up the paper and tossed it into the bin, dismissing me with a wave of his hand.

I nodded and made a quick exit. As my next assignment was not for another hour, I decided to head outside. I wanted to pray for Mrs Agrova and for the impressionable girls such as Rita who had heard the conversation.

I felt as though I was floating down the street, a little confused, but it felt so wonderful to pray like a child to God. I found that my very soul was lifting itself in praise and the hour seemed to pass in just a few minutes. It was easy and natural that my experience with Jesus should become part of my everyday life.

Some weeks later I was to transport a senior Party official from his luxury apartment in Lenin Square to the export marketing office in the city centre.

Dressed in a smart western suit, Mr Latvin slouched back in the car and chain-smoked. The Volga's windscreen-wipers clattered back and forth to clear a light drizzle, and pedestrians hurried away to avoid the spray of brown slush.

After ten minutes or so, Mr Latvin became irritated by the weather. "Just my luck," he moaned.

Sensing an opening I volunteered, "I don't believe in luck. God has a plan for my life."

"God!" Mr Latvin spat out the word.

I said brightly, "Oh, I see you believe in God."

"Of course not," he said mockingly. "There is no God. That's official."

Perhaps Mr Latvin had never been face to face with a real Christian before, so I responded to his abuse with a barrage of questions which he eventually found impossible to answer.

"I don't want to hear any more of this rubbish," Mr Latvin erupted. "You Christians should be shot! We could have wiped you out. Like that." He snapped his fingers in a threatening gesture behind me and continued, "We have spared you because of our greater cause. We have to spread socialism and communism throughout the world. Nothing must get in the way. But your time will come."

Mr Latvin settled back in the car, grunting and puffing on yet another cigarette. He barely spoke to me after that. At the factory I stepped out to open the car door for him, but he was too quick and brushed me aside.

"God bless you, sir," I said in farewell. He stared at me and cursed furiously. I could imagine Nikolai drumming his fingers on his desk as he noted the latest complaint.

I never saw Mr Latvin again but I prayed for him and the experience did not discourage me at all. Rather, it had the opposite effect. Like a boxer analysing his strategy I asked myself, how could I improve my technique? Should I have been more cautious in my approach? I knew that just having the right words was useless without the blessing of God on my life.

It took a day for Mr Latvin to catch up with me. Nikolai was annoyed. Mr Latvin was a far more serious case than Mrs Agrova.

Two days later I was required to transport a KGB colonel, an energetic young man who sat smartly in the passenger seat. I didn't know what problems talking about Jesus would cause me. But I knew I had no choice.

To my surprise, the KGB officer seemed eager to talk to me about God. He told me that although the Party's line was that God didn't exist, he had been guilty recently of dissident thoughts. He even dared wonder if there could be a God, after all.

Regrettably, we only had a short journey together, and as we arrived I said, "I know one thing. Once I was a sinner but Jesus saved me. My life has been changed." The colonel remained in his seat for a minute outside his destination in Nevsky Prospekt. "Very interesting," he remarked and patted me on the shoulder.

Two weeks later, I sat drinking black tea with the other drivers when Nikolai called out to me. My surprise turned into delight as I learnt that the KGB colonel had again requested me as his driver. "He asked for 'The Preacher',"

Nikolai said. "I assume that means you. I could check if anyone else wants to go."

"No, no," I replied. "That's OK with me."

Once again, we did the same short journey to Nevsky Prospekt which was over in a flash. The colonel continued to question me although we had parked. We remained in the car outside a grey nondescript building with no obvious markings or signs.

A traffic policeman strolled by and peered into the car. Recognising the familiar KGB uniform the militiaman nodded and walked on. Finally, the colonel said, "Fascinating. But I must go. I'm late for a meeting."

Handing him his initialled attaché case as he stepped out, I saluted. "God bless you, sir!" He seemed surprised as he acknowledged my salute.

"You asked God to bless me," he said wistfully. The idea seemed to mystify him. He smiled, turned on his heel and walked into the anonymous building.

I couldn't explain why, but I knew this had been an important meeting. *Praise you, Jesus!*

I had been thinking about it for some time. I knew I could borrow the Volga for a long weekend to make the journey to the Finnish border. Then, in the autumn I had an opportunity.

Setting off before dawn, it took about four hours to reach Vyborg. I knew I was close as all the houses looked different. It was a clear morning and old women with long brooms piled the leaves up by the side of the road.

Outside the house I sat preparing myself. Peering up at the third-floor flat, I could see the curtains were open. Someone was in. I got out of the car and walked up the stairs, pausing at the door. There it was. SARDONIKOV.

I pressed the bell lightly, startled by the harsh loud ring. Abruptly, the door opened and a portly, elderly man stared at me.

"Hello, can I help you?"

"Can I see Alexander Sardonikov please?" I replied.

"It's me," the man replied, "Who are you?"

I repeated my name, but no sound could be heard, the words froze somewhere in my throat. He looked tired and old. I couldn't take my eyes off his face. It seemed as though he might disappear and never return. I couldn't turn away.

"Oh! It's you. Do you still live with Schura? I suppose she told you where I was, and that's how you found me," he said grumpily.

"No, no, Schura didn't tell me," I said, somewhat in a daze. "I found your address through the army's resettlement office."

I heard voices and suddenly Andrew appeared. "Valeri? It's you!" At least he seemed pleased to see me. "Come in! Come in! What a surprise."

Andrew dragged me into the house and said, "Dad, this is my friend, the person I told you about. Do you remember?"

"Yes, yes, I remember," the old man said dismissively. We talked for a few moments but he was clearly uncomfortable in my presence. Making some excuse, he claimed that he was late for an appointment and had to leave the house immediately.

"Perhaps I can help you?" I volunteered, "I could drive you there."

He seemed flustered, "What? Oh no, no, that won't be necessary." As he picked up a coat and walked to the door, I explained to him that I also had to leave. "I was only passing through." Andrew looked disappointed.

I wanted a few minutes alone with my father. We walked down the stairs and into the street. He eyed the Volga and said, "It's a nice car."

"Yes," I smiled. "Are you sure I can't drive you somewhere?"

"No thanks," he replied.

I might never be given another moment. "I know life is complicated," I began. "It doesn't matter about the past, I just wanted to see you myself."

My father brushed his hand across the back of his head and looked down at his shoes.

I explained that I had been close to suicide in the army but God had given me a new life.

Father mumbled a little and then looked at his watch. "OK, I must go."

We shook hands and Father turned and walked slowly down the street. In the rear-view mirror of the car I watched his reflection disappear into the distance.

As I drove back to Leningrad I didn't know what to think. I tried to remember his face and the surprised look he gave me at the door. It had all happened so fast. And then he had turned and walked down the street. We had spoken together and then parted like travellers sharing a railway compartment for a few moments.

Some days later a letter arrived, postmarked Vyborg. With mounting anticipation, I saw that it was from Father.

The handwritten note read:

Valeri,
I really knew your mother but I don't want to talk about that relationship because it belongs to the past. I don't think it's a good idea to write to each other and certainly not good to meet. I don't feel that you are a relation of mine. You seem more like a stranger to me.

There was no hello and no goodbye. Across the bottom of the page he had scrawled his signature. Alexander Sardonikov.

I was broken. I felt like a plastic cup floating about amongst the debris on the Neva River. For a few days I carried the letter everywhere with me. It was a heavy burden to bear.

But as I prayed, God reminded me that I had been reborn into his family and now had brothers and sisters all over the world. When my real father had rejected me, my heavenly Father had loved me.

This was the real miracle.

7

SUPERSTAR

One day in the New Year I was drinking tea with some other drivers when I heard my name on the garage Tannoy system, "Valeri Barinov, report to the transport union office at once."

Something was wrong, but what? I prayed for help, and as I walked up the stairs I felt a calming presence come over me. Remember, I told myself, God's Spirit is your constant companion. He will provide words for you to speak.

I sensed tension in the air. The union chief was joined by the depot's personnel officer, a union activist and the chief of another garage. They all had notebooks ready in front of them and looked deadly serious as I walked into the room and was offered a chair facing them all.

The union chief began. "Valeri, I must warn you that you face some serious charges and very likely a prison sentence. But we wanted to question you ourselves before turning you over to the police."

I didn't know Mr Adas as I wasn't an active union member. He wore thick horn-rimmed glasses and a navy-blue suit. His hair was greased back, neatly combed in place.

"You see Valeri," he went on, "many people have complained about your religious activity. It's one thing if you keep it to yourself, but you are forcing your beliefs on everyone else. Such propaganda is forbidden in our constitution. It's dangerous. What if other people were influenced by your ideas?"

The depot's personnel officer shook his head in agreement

as Mr Adas continued, "You see, we sent someone to question you secretly and have all the evidence we need on tape."

Mr Adas frowned and waited a moment, as though they all expected some kind of confessional outburst. "Yes, we have it all on tape. Why, you told everyone in the garage to visit the Baptist Church." Mr Adas looked deeply hurt and offended that this outrage had been perpetrated under his own roof.

"Praise the Lord that you have it on tape," I enthused.

Mr Adas and the others were completely non-plussed by my response.

"I'll explain everything to you," I said, adopting a confidential tone. "You see, when people ask me a question about my faith in Jesus, I reply. Why, it's the least a decent citizen should do for his comrades, provide an honest reply to their questions."

"All I'm guilty of is answering questions," I asserted, sounding equally mystified that I should be threatened for such innocent behaviour. "Do you know what I think?" I asked, leaning forward in my chair and lowering my voice.

Mr Adas was clearly perturbed, "What do you mean?" he stammered.

"I think you should forbid the others in the garage from asking me about Jesus. That would solve the problem, wouldn't it?" I said harmlessly, as if that provided a neat solution to the conundrum.

"As far as all that talk about visiting church," I gesticulated with my hands, "do you know where it is?"

Mr Adas reached for his pen. "Where is it?" he said quickly and sat poised to write down the address.

"Why, we Christians believe in a personal God with whom we can form a personal relationship and who lives with us. There's really no need to go to a building because if God lives within us, then we ourselves are a church," I declared boldly. "My advice is: don't go to church, come to Jesus!"

The personnel officer held up his hand. "We're not here to listen to your advice. Remember, you're the one facing serious charges."

Mr Adas dared me, "Would you become a member of the Communist Party?"

"Oh yes, certainly," I replied, taking them by surprise once again. "I know communism has a high moral code, and a real communist is someone who lives selflessly for his neighbour."

I leaned forward, getting even more excited. "Don't you see? That's what Jesus was talking about, that's true Christianity. I know that when I tell everyone in the Communist Party about this similarity, they will be pleased. Why, it will be a great privilege to preach the Gospel to the Communist Party. Thank you for inviting me."

Before I'd even finished speaking, Mr Adas jerked forward and interrupted. "No, no," he cried, waving his hands from side to side. "It's not possible. You can't preach at a Party meeting."

Mr Adas addressed me with a new-found respect, realising he couldn't trap me. However, he told me that I could not continue working at the depot, and I left the enquiry feeling exhausted.

Tanya was naturally concerned about how we would survive. "Don't worry," I comforted her, "God will provide. A loving Father cannot abandon his children, can he?"

I took a job as a labourer, then as a cleaner, and later as a driver again. I was given a huge lorry to drive. It had a broken gearbox and unreliable brakes, but was not dissimilar to other vehicles in the depot. It was clear that if I complained, someone else would be given my job.

I continued to speak openly about Jesus at the garage. Soon I was under pressure for "anti-Soviet propaganda", which encompasses anything from pornography to the Bible, so it came as no surprise when the manager called me to his office. Another driver had become annoyed with me and complained that I was spreading sedition.

As I was leaving the manager's office, I saw his secretary look up and beckon to me. "Valeri," she whispered, "I want you to know that I'm a secret believer also."

Rema was about forty years old, tall, attractive and well educated. For a few minutes she counselled me about the risk involved in speaking openly to the other drivers. "You'll only get into trouble," she warned.

I knew that God had called her to be a secret believer, so I decided not to argue with her. Some weeks later Rema caught my eye, and when the coast was clear I slipped into the office. "My son is back from the army," she said. "Would you like to come to our flat tomorrow evening?"

As I stepped through their front door I knew that Igor and I would be friends. He loved rock and wanted to play in a band. All evening we listened to the albums he had brought home with him, one of which was to set me thinking in a dramatic new way.

Although the British musicians Andrew Lloyd Webber and Tim Rice were relatively unknown to us, *Jesus Christ Superstar* was inspiring as it traced the life of Jesus in a rich musical pageant incorporating several different styles. We played the album until the grooves were wearing out.

One night when driving the lorry back to the garage, the musical themes from *Jesus Christ Superstar* kept returning to my mind. I was filled with a deep sadness.

Lord! Even the stones cry out to you! You cause this world to praise you even though it doesn't recognise your authority.

Why did Christians abandon artistic traditions to an ungodly world? Why were the pop charts filled with anti-God songs? Why did Christian musicians settle for church audiences instead of taking their songs to the streets? Where were the Christian bands who would challenge the Beatles and the Rolling Stones?

God had given me musical talent but I hadn't done much

with it. In recent months I had played a few gigs at
communist youth clubs and hung out with musicians.
Everyone knew I could sing rock songs in English and I had
an audience whenever I wanted one. But what songs would
they hear me sing? The question disturbed me.

I prayed and asked the Lord what he wanted me to do.
Follow me, he replied, one step at a time.

Meanwhile the difficulties at work had increased. The
garage manager had a dispute on his hands and I was
pressured to quit.

We heard through one of Tanya's friends that Ambulance
Service No. 7 needed drivers. I was hired and impressed the
manager by looking after the beat-up old vehicle I was given
to drive. Two months later it was replaced with a brand new
ambulance.

We served several hospitals in the area and were called
out both day and night. Sometimes people in the street
would hail us, slip the doctor some money, and we would
make unscheduled house calls. On an emergency call I
knew all the short cuts through the backstreets of
Leningrad.

I carried a transistor radio with me and tuned into Radio
Monte Carlo. Also in the glove compartment I kept a
portion of the Bible — incomplete because I had rescued
it from a fire. The pages were singed and entire books were
missing, but it didn't matter. Sometimes just a few sentences
were enough to convey the presence of God.

I was frequently on night patrol which lasted until nine
or ten the following morning. But I liked the hours because
I could spend time with Zhanna and Marina.

One cold night we were called out to Kalinsky Prospekt
to find a woman waiting with her eleven-year-old son in the
hallway of her tower block. The doctor on duty that night
was himself suffering from a cold. "Don't worry," I assured
him. "You stay in the van and I'll check that we have the
right passengers."

The couple were shaking with cold. Too nervous to stay

in their apartment in case they missed the ambulance, they had waited over half an hour.

"Where are you going?" I asked the woman.

"My son needs an operation," she replied. He was clutching his stomach and leaning against the wall. He seemed to be on the verge of tears.

"Everything will be fine. I'm a Christian, would you like me to pray for you? God will bless you."

The woman's eyes lit up. "Yes," she pleaded. "Yes please!"

"But first let's get you into the ambulance." I carried the boy to the van and we sped off to the hospital. As I lifted the boy into a wheelchair in the reception area, the woman touched my sleeve gently, thinking I was about to depart. "Don't forget," she whispered.

"What's that?" I asked.

"You promised to pray for my boy," the woman replied.

"No, no," I chuckled, "I'm not leaving before I pray." I wheeled him into the corner of the room, put my hands on his head and prayed healing into his body and blessing for his life. When I had finished praying, his mother was in tears. "Thank you, thank you," she cried.

As I turned to move away I could see that the doctor had been watching everything. But the woman tugged my sleeve again. "Wait," she said wiping her eyes, and pulled out an apple from her bag. "It's my last one but I want you to have it. Please take it."

I didn't know what to say. I knew apples were expensive but I didn't want to offend her by not taking it. She reached out and placed the apple in my hand. The decision had been made.

The doctor asked me what was going on, so I explained. Rather than the ridicule I had expected, he was curious.

Over the next few weeks I felt an inner strength about my witness. When I prayed for patients their condition improved remarkably; many were simply encouraged or lifted from bouts of depression. I was gaining a reputation among the drivers and doctors. "I don't know if it's voodoo magic, but Valeri's prayers seem to make a difference."

However, I was an enigma for most people who assumed that religious believers wore sombre suits and never seemed to smile or have fun. When they found out that I loved the Beatles and the Rolling Stones and even played their songs with a band, the contradiction was complete.

Dr Zakharova was an elderly lady who practised as a paediatrician, and so most of our calls were to children's homes. Once when I was waiting for her to return from a house call, some kids who were kicking a ball around in a nearby playground came over to the ambulance. My attention was drawn to a pale-faced boy, aged about eight. He was shy at first, but I asked him if he'd ever driven an ambulance? From the way his eyes lit up, I knew we had made friends.

When I showed him my tattered Bible, he told me that his grandmother used to tell him Bible stories although he had never seen a Bible before. I urged him to put his faith in Jesus. "Try it," I said, "you'll be surprised."

The doctor returned and as we pulled away from the curb, I waved to the boy. "I see you've made friends with Misha," Dr Zakharova remarked. "It's a sad case. He's got leukaemia, poor lad. He's only got a few months to live."

I was moved and realised that God had sent me to him. I knew that God chose the people he brought to me.

Dr Zakharova had been baptised as an orthodox Christian and had some knowledge of the faith. Although she wasn't a practising believer, she recognised that God was in my life. "There is something about you, Valeri," she told me one day. "If I could have your faith, then I think my life would change."

"But faith is a gift from God," I reasoned. "Anyone can have it. It's that simple. Try it. Test it."

"I don't know," she argued. "Let me think about it."

We were called to an internat in Leningrad. A great

sadness filled me as I walked in past boys and girls hanging around aimlessly, unwanted and abandoned. We were directed to the sick bay, where boys with dirty faces and runny noses and girls with long matted hair and torn dresses followed us around.

I think we heard the problem before seeing it. A skinny boy aged about two was writhing on the floor, yelling and crying. Dr Zakharova could find no clues to the child's obvious discomfort.

I asked if I could hold the child and was promptly handed a ragged, noisy parcel of arms and legs. Cradling the wailing baby, I paced the floor and prayed within myself, ignoring the noise. The boy had soon calmed considerably, and after ten minutes actually stopped crying.

The sick bay nurse was amazed. "What did you do to him?" she gasped.

Dr Zakharova explained, "He's my driver. He's a Christian and he prays."

The nurse looked baffled. She kept her eyes trained on the child as if averting her gaze would trigger another bout of yelling.

Dr Zakharova quickly prepared an injection for the child I was holding. The boy cried out in surprise, stung by the prick of the needle. I handed him to the startled nurse who was able to restore calm easily. After checking a few other patients, Dr Zakharova turned to leave and pointed to the boy, now sleeping peacefully in a cot.

"I don't know what you do, Valeri, but your prayers seem to get answered," Dr Zakharova remarked.

"You shouldn't be surprised, there's nothing special about me," I asserted. "You know what I mean, don't you?"

Contemplating what she had seen, Dr Zakharova didn't answer me. There was nothing else I could say to convince her. It was now a matter of prayer.

That summer, Tanya and I took the girls away on holiday. It was good to be together as a family and Zhanna and

Marina enjoyed playing with their crazy dad. Tanya and I found time to be together strolling along country lanes and cuddling in front of the log fire.

Back in Leningrad the holiday was quickly forgotten as the ambulance depot was plunged into a gruelling work schedule. There were staff shortages and I volunteered for overtime, figuring we could use the extra money.

I was assigned to work for Dr Medvedev. He was a highly trained physician, aged thirty, but extremely proud and arrogant. He began to quiz me about Christianity. "I hear you're an expert," he said haughtily.

"Not an expert in theological dogma," I replied. "But I know one thing for certain — Jesus is alive!"

Dr Medvedev found this highly amusing. He then proceeded to ask me several questions. Each time I started to reply, he cut me short and gave his own answer. Soon I decided to remain silent.

"A preacher who has stopped preaching," Dr Medvedev taunted. "What a shame! Maybe you've nothing left to say?"

"But you won't let me finish speaking," I reasoned with him.

"You have nothing to say to a modern man like me," he gloated, leaning back in his seat.

"Dr Medvedev, I lived your life, but you haven't experienced my new life with Jesus," I replied.

This made him laugh, his head rolled back and he slapped his leg. "Poor preacher," he chortled, "what do you know about life?" Still laughing derisively, he opened his case and produced a magazine. "I'll tell you about life. Look Mr Preacher! This is life." The magazine was filled with explicit photographs depicting outrageous sex acts.

"Don't crash the car," the doctor joked, amused by his own humour. As he proceeded to relate a running commentary of each lurid scene, I realised how corrupt his heart was.

At last we drove on in silence but I continued to pray for

Dr Medvedev. Back at the ambulance depot that evening, a few of the drivers stood by the entrance to the building. As we approached them, Dr Medvedev cracked a joke about Christians and looked mockingly at me.

To my surprise Ivan, one of the younger drivers, came to my defence. We didn't know each other all that well, but I saw from his reaction that he wanted to protect me. "Why ridicule him just because he's a Christian? Sometimes you doctors can do nothing, but when Valeri prays, people are healed. How can you explain that?"

"Yes, that's true," some of the other drivers agreed.

The doctor started to argue. I knew it was impossible to reason with him but after a few minutes, I joined the fray, answering his questions but intending to reach the other drivers. Sensing he was outpointed, Dr Medvedev withdrew and walked into the building somewhat disgruntled.

But the discussion was far from over and during the next two days Ivan quizzed me at length about how I came to faith in Jesus. My advice to him was, "Try it out. Test Jesus."

One week later Ivan came to me. I knew instantly that something had happened. And it wasn't my imagination. The other drivers had noticed it.

"I tested God and the experiment worked," Ivan told me. "God exists!" He seemed surprised by his own discovery. In the ambulance depot he was an outspoken witness to the extraordinary change in his life and he became a good friend, visiting our family and attending the church.

I knew it was a matter of time. Eventually the manager of the depot questioned me after work. Someone had complained that I was spreading religious propaganda. I denied the accusation and insisted that I should be judged by my work record. Nothing further was said, but I would have to be careful.

8

MOONWALK

The quaint tram-cars of Leningrad were always popular with
the tourists who queued to visit the museums and galleries,
marvelling that such masterpieces as Picasso and Da Vinci
could have been hidden away in Russia.

Few of them saw the backstreets and alleys where the
hoods and pimps patrolled, or the upstairs apartments where
any blackmarket deal could be struck. Leningrad was full
of desperate people on the run from informers, kids strung
out on drugs, teenage runaways, and child prostitutes.

The Moonwalk Club was situated in a notorious side street
not far from where we lived. With the right connections you
could pick up anything you wanted. But it wasn't the place
to ask questions. The only warning ever given was the glint
of a blade in the shadows.

Events at the club were organised by a stocky, dark-haired
woman named Valentina who had a good heart, but no
ability to maintain any kind of order. She was somewhat
disappointed to find that I was not a potential volunteer,
but soon perked up when I offered to play a gig at the club.
She seemed relieved to learn that we weren't asking to be
paid, and our première performance was immediately
scheduled for the following Saturday night.

I learned that Valentina lived near us, so we took the same
bus home that night. As she locked up and stepped into the
street, her demeanour changed.

"What's the matter?" I asked.

"This is a terrible area. Two nights ago someone was

stabbed just round the corner, and last week one of the girls at the club was raped by three men. Even the police don't know what to do," Valentina explained.

"I've got a secret weapon," I said cheekily.

"What's that?" Valentina enquired.

"Jesus!" I replied.

"I don't believe in God," she said. "Anyway what can he do for us here?" I told her about God's protection on the bus home, and she seemed moved.

The band were excited about the gig and we worked out six or seven songs which we knew would be popular. Valentina enthusiastically arranged the loan of a sound system, which I picked up in the ambulance. George, my friend from the internat took charge of the equipment, assisted by Rema's son, Igor.

Boys in leather jackets hung around at the entrance with girls in tight mini-skirts. The sound check ensured that at least we would be heard.

No one knew what would happen. About sixty kids crowded into the hall to hear us. The four-piece band was ready. Playing rhythm guitar on a homemade instrument, I struck an E-chord, walked up to the microphone, and opened my mouth. "It's been a hard day's night, and I've been working like a dog . . ."

We knew instantly that we were a hit. In half an hour we had plundered our entire repertoire, but still they wouldn't let us stop playing. The band looked to me for guidance as the cheers and whistles grew louder. "Jam session!" I announced.

The kids were calling out songs that they wanted us to play. "Chuck Berry!" someone yelled. "Play Chuck Berry songs!" I launched into "Rock and Roll Music" and somehow the boys behind me did an admirable job of maintaining the driving beat.

An hour or so after our jittery start I announced that we would make "Let it be" our last number. I sang with a minimum of accompaniment, but surprisingly the hall was silent. The applause at the end of the song was deafening. Finally I made a space through the barrage of noise.

"I love the Beatles," I began and with that a ripple of applause spread among the audience. "Shhh!" I cried, "I've got something really important to say."

"I love that song," I repeated, "but I also love the message behind the song. It's a message I want you to consider. When you have a problem and you don't know where to turn to, when you think no one understands you. When you reach the edge of life and there doesn't seem to be anything more to live for . . . " I paused as my voice bounced off the walls of the club.

"Hey!" I shouted. "Anyone out there know what I'm talking about?"

Instantly a wave of cries burst out. I knew I had hit a nerve. "Well if that's how you're feeling tonight then I've got news for you."

Again I paused as the sea of faces peered up at me. "You see I was trapped on that island of despair and thought I would be marooned for ever. But do you know who rescued me and changed my life?"

I paused for a moment, and then shouted the answer, "Jesus!"

A buzz ran through the crowd. Questions and curses were yelled out. "Get off!" a tall girl with a long pony tail at the side of the stage cried. But someone near her shouted her down, "No! No! We want to listen to you."

The attention paid to our music was transferred to my closing comments. I suggested that we call another meeting at the club for those who wanted to hear my story. But no one wanted to wait. They wanted answers now!

We moved away from the stage area so that the sound system could be dismantled and loaded back into the ambulance. The questions were hurled like spears as I stepped into the crowd.

"You don't understand," a petite blonde told me, almost in tears, "I've got nothing to live for."

My throat was dry and someone brought me a glass of water which I gulped down. The music had united our hearts in an unusual way, and the kids listened to me as though I was a minstrel prophet. At 1.30 a.m. about thirty teenagers still hung around, caught up in intense discussion.

Valentina was thrilled by the amazing success of the evening although she could get into trouble because the club's closing time had been exceeded. "Could you play every Saturday night?" she asked.

The Moonwalk Club became the turf we patrolled. The kids looked up to us as heroes. Some were drawn by the magnet of music, others were disturbed and needed help.

Lita was sixteen years old but you would never have guessed. For two years she had been passed like a bag of sweets from hand to hand, living with anyone who would keep her. Her face had been scarred by a drug dealer to whom she had owed money, and to support her habit she had turned hooker.

"I'm going to change, Valeri, I really am," Lita told me one night after a gig. "Will you pray for me?"

No one could believe that Lita would make it, but it was the turning point. She took a job washing dishes in a hotel and struggled to kick the drugs that had ravaged her body. One rainy night at three o'clock I answered our doorbell and was just able to catch Lita as she fell into my arms. The drug dealer had stalked her, beaten her badly, and she was soaked to the skin. She stayed with us for the next few days. Tanya and I were often up all night swabbing her face with a cold sponge.

A month later, Lita told me she had decided to contact her family and would I go with her? It was an emotional reunion as they welcomed her back. "My baby," her mother sobbed. "We thought you'd gone for ever."

When she returned to the club it was to join us in talking to the other street people. One night on the stage, Lita declared, "Jesus rescued me . . ."

It was a powerful statement because everyone knew it was

true. There was no greater testimony to the truth than Lita, standing before the Moonwalk Club, her heart shining like a torch.

Word got around at the garage that I was playing in a band and that the ambulance I drove was being used to transport musicians and instruments. The trade union chief Mr Markarenko questioned me about it. I admitted that we now had a "rock and roll ambulance". Mr Markarenko told me that his daughter had heard us at the "Young Communists' Club" on Lenin Street. "You've got a loyal fan," he joked. "My daughter has good taste, of course!"

One night Igor visited me at the garage to show me a new guitar he had made. A few drivers hung around and we listened to a Voice Of America broadcast. When the programme ended, I twisted the dial and located Radio Monte Carlo.

The programme that night was less than inspiring. Ten minutes after it began, Mr Markarenko walked past. We must have made an unusual sight: young guys with long hair, modern clothes and a brand new guitar, all huddled round a wireless listening intently to some dreary hymn sung by an uninspiring choir.

The next day when I saw Mr Markarenko he asked, "Valeri, I didn't know you had such a good band. But who is the Christian in your group?"

"I am!" I replied with a smile.

"Don't joke, I'm serious," he said. "I need to know."

"I'm not joking," I explained, still smiling.

"You! I'm astounded." Mr Markarenko's surprise became annoyance, "No!" he exclaimed, and walked away from me. Although he had always been cordial, he never spoke to me again. I knew I had made a dangerous enemy.

The Moonwalk Club crowd were really rocking. We could have sung the names of Kremlin Politburo members and they would have applauded us. Then through the clamour someone called, "Sing 'Jesus Christ, Superstar'."

It was a piercing cry that stopped me in my tracks. Somehow we made it through the verse and the entire club joined us in the chorus.

"Jesus Christ, Superstar! Who do you think that you really are? Jesus Christ, Superstar!"

At the end of the song, I unstrapped my guitar, signalling the end of the gig. The catcalls and whistles were urging us to continue playing, so I turned to the guys on stage with me, "I've had it! Play some riffs for them. Sorry guys, I've just got to stop!"

The night air would clear my head, so I walked into the darkness, following my feet. Leningrad was settling down for the night as drunks staggered across my path and car-doors slammed. The subway ride seemed to take for ever, but finally I was home. Everything was quiet, Tanya asleep, the girls snuggled tight. The tranquil end of a long day.

But I couldn't sleep. I retreated into the kitchen and closed the door. Like a soundtrack from a film, the words haunted me. "Jesus Christ, Superstar" replayed itself continually in my head.

Even the stones cry out, but my people are silent!

I paced the floor as though it was on fire, crying out to God. "Jesus, I have nothing to bring you, no offering but myself. I want to praise you Lord. I want to cry out to this city of Leningrad about you. I want to praise your name throughout this land, all over this world. Jesus, show me what you want me to do."

How could we reach people who never came to church? How would they hear about Jesus? What about the kids from Club 47 and the other communist youth clubs where our band played?

Even the stones cry out but my people are silent!

If songs like "Jesus Christ, Superstar" could have such an effect, surely God's people could produce songs of greater power? The idea took hold. All at once I visualised the potential for a musical performance telling the true story of Jesus of Nazareth. It should not be an album of individual songs, but a concept album, with every part contributing to the big picture.

A million ideas sprang to mind. But what should I do? I knew that prayer and fasting was the best preparation, so for three days and three nights I prayed and fasted, experiencing the very real presence of God.

My mind was a clear blue sky across which ideas floated like clouds. As I prayed it seemed clear that my mission should be to tell people that Jesus was coming again.

People get ready . . .

No expense was to be spared in telling the whole world about Jesus.

People get ready, Jesus is coming soon . . .

Step by step I prayed my way along the pathway. I would sound a trumpet every human heart would hear.

People get ready, Jesus is coming soon, very soon . . .

I picked up the guitar that lay beside me and strummed a few chords. "This trumpet must sound!" It felt right. I repeated the phrase over and over, repeating it prophetically, praying for God's anointing. We would be a trumpet voice crying out to a lost world.

Tanya brought me down to earth by reminding me that I hadn't been to work for three days. "What are we going to do?" she cried, "that means even less money this month!"

I couldn't wait to tell the band. We're going to trumpet our message around the world! Fantastic! What message? What music? There was a small detail I had neglected. I hadn't actually written anything down as yet.

I spent the next few months composing the music. Sometimes I created bits of the melody while on ambulance duty, sometimes I'd wake up in the night, tiptoe into the kitchen and slip another piece of the jigsaw into place. Some ideas would remain, others were discarded. Sometimes I felt the presence of God filling our humble kitchen and couldn't do anything but bow my head and bask in his glory.

I absorbed myself in the music which was at times bluesy, dark, melancholic, moody. And then bright, rough, rock and roll.

Later on, I heard Paul McCartney explaining how he wrote a lot of his music. He would begin playing and the music flowed. It was the same for me, I would pick up the guitar and the music flowed. I wanted it to sound very contemporary, and at the time heavy rock dominated the airwaves, so I styled the album around these trends.

By spring 1974 the music had been composed, and I completed the lyrics that summer.

"Cry out you trumpet voice!" it began. I was determined that this trumpet would sound beyond the mountains of Russia and into the West, where ironically it was considered naïve and outdated to talk about Jesus although there was complete freedom to do so.

I knew I would have to create an English version of the musical, but how could this be done?

An affectionate, motherly woman called Galina who led a prayer group at the Baptist Church had once said unexpectedly to me, "Valeri, have you ever studied English?"

Startled, I had replied, "English? Oh no!"

"Learn!" she stated emphatically, raising a finger like a stern schoolteacher.

"Why?" I asked, puzzled by the task she had set me.

Galina had never explained and I forgot her comment. Three months later I saw her at the Baptist Church, and as we walked to the bus stop again she exhorted me, "Did you start learning English?"

I shrugged my shoulders. "No, Galina, I just don't have time to do it."

But Galina was adamant. "Valeri," she insisted, tugging my arm, "Listen to me. Study English. We prayed for you and God showed us a vision: you will go to England, not now, but during the last days."

After that someone gave me a cassette player and the Gospels on tape in English. The tapes were recorded from the King James Version, and when I practised my English with foreigners they were amused. But I knew I would be blessed. Not only was I learning another language, but I was also memorising the word of God!

Remarkably Galina had been right. I would need to know English.

I met an English tourist at the Hermitage Museum and struggled to tell him what I was doing. He explained that "Trumpet Voice", although technically correct, didn't quite convey the idea I had. "Trumpet Call" would be more appropriate. Through his words, God confirmed in my heart that this should be the name of the musical.

I was elated. I felt I was making progress. I had a title!

9

"LORD, DON'T LET OUR DOG DIE!"

The years went by and I didn't know how it would be possible to record our music. Early in 1980, two of the best musicians in the band received their call-up papers for the army. I played with other musicians, but not everyone shared my vision.

Having talked about trumpeting around the world, now I didn't even have a band. I was being ridiculed. Valeri the dreamer! Time had passed, and musical styles had changed.

But I knew that my Daddy never lied.

A friend from Chicago brought me a beautiful leather-bound Bible. I prayed and opened the Scriptures at random. My eyes fell on Matthew, chapter 24, verse 31: "He will send his angels with a loud trumpet call . . ."

The words seemed to leap out of the page. I almost fell off my chair. A loud trumpet call! I had never read this verse before and it was a tremendous encouragement from God which strengthened my resolve.

After church that Sunday, I saw two young girls, clearly foreigners, talking to some of the young people. I introduced myself to them in English that King James himself would have been proud of, "How long willst thou stayeth in Leningrad?"

The girls giggled and said, "Two months."

This was it! "God sent you to me!" I replied.

Again they laughed. These volatile Russians!

"But I prayed, and God sent you here to meet me!" I

invited them home for tea to meet Tanya and to enable me to explain to them exactly what I wanted.

Lorna Waterton and Sally Carter didn't know if they had the time to translate the Russian text of "The Trumpet Call" into English, but agreed to try. Two months later, I was given several pages written in English. None of it made sense to me, but I held it in my hands as though it was a map of treasure island.

The English lyrics of "The Trumpet Call".

I never prayed for things for myself. Secretly, I desired a pair of jeans but they were only obtainable on the black market, and we could never afford it. One night as I was praying, God said,

"Why don't you ask your Daddy for jeans?" I squirmed, "Jeans are my desire, and I would like to have them, but only if you want me to have them. I want to serve you Lord!"

One night before Lorna and Sally left, they brought me a present: a pair of Wrangler jeans! The jeans were old and worn, with wide flares, but I was stunned. When they left our room, I hopped and danced like a little child.

Daddy! Daddy! You love me so much you even gave me jeans. And you commanded these English girls to hand them over!

I wore the jeans every day. Ripped at the knees, I assured Tanya that this was trendy. Frayed at the edges, I was convinced that this was how heavy rockers dressed. When the seat disintegrated, Tanya insisted it was time for action. "You are not going out like that and I don't care who says it's OK."

Reluctantly I agreed, and the jeans were shredded to make kitchen towels. Over the next few months Tanya secretly saved roubles in an empty Nescafé tin. For my birthday that December she presented me with the cash. "To buy jeans," she said.

One of our former band members, Sasha, had a friend who had a reputation around Leningrad for being a brilliant tailor. As a friend of Sasha's he would make my jeans at a "bargain price".

Sergei Timokhin was a tall, gentle giant. We shared the same musical tastes and immediately became friends. He played bass and was keen to join a band. Sergei didn't believe in God, but after meeting a few times to fit my jeans, Sergei bowed and prayed, "Jesus, if you are true, reveal yourself to me." By the time my jeans were ready, Sergei had found faith in Jesus.

Sasha and Sergei were both baptised together in church, a powerful declaration of how God can change the lives of those who surrender to him.

The next few months were painful. Sasha developed cancer and left Leningrad to rest in a country house. But the house was damp and his condition worsened. One evening his mother called at our home with the news that Sasha had died.

Sasha's death was a great sadness for our family, and I couldn't believe I would never see him again. Zhanna and Marina loved him and he had always had a lot of time for them. With tears welling up in their big brown eyes they came to me. "Papa, we're sad. Why did Sasha have to die?"

I sat them on my lap and explained that in the circle of life, there is death. "Maybe he would have suffered badly if he had lived? We wouldn't have wanted Sasha to live in pain, would we?"

Marina wiped a tear from her eye. Zhanna whispered, "No, but we are sad that we won't be able to play with him again."

"I'm also sad because he was my friend. But this should teach us to value the friends we have," I explained. I didn't really feel like handing out lessons-for-life at that moment, but I wanted my daughters to understand the fragility of life and to realise that people are precious.

When Marina was born we knew that our cramped apartment would make life difficult, so we lodged a request with the municipal authorities for a flat. Seven years later, we still waited to be re-located but with several high-rise apartment blocks newly erected around town, we decided to re-apply immediately.

When I called at the Municipal Housing Department I was given a ticket, meaning I would have to queue. There were nine people in front of me. Within an hour, the queue stretched all the way down to the ground floor and into the yard outside. No one knew when the office would open, so we just waited. I didn't want to miss such a good opportunity of sharing the good news of Jesus with so many people, so I listened for my chance.

A tall man aged about forty stood tapping his feet on the step in front. Ahead of him, a middle-aged woman was lamenting America's decision to boycott the Olympic Games being held in Moscow that year. They agreed it was a diabolical act of defiance and spite. Sport, they insisted, must be free of interference and political manipulation. The Americans had behaved shamefully!

"But can you expect anything better from the Americans?" the woman mused, philosophically.

"I suppose not," the man said mournfully.

This was my moment! I emphasised that the heart of man was the same. "Russians, Americans, it doesn't make any difference, we are all sinners!"

Queuing is a national pastime in Russia and I had just submitted a significant contribution. Something to do while we waited.

I knew it was controversial and risky. If someone in the building reported me, I could lose all hope of a new apartment. But everyone seemed to be playing into my hands, insisting that I explain what I meant. I agreed.

The hecklers were silent. Convinced that I spoke the truth, some nodded their heads, listening intently.

Finally, the office opened and slowly the queue snaked forward. I gave my personal details and was told that an apartment would be made available. I could hardly wait to see Tanya's face when I told her the news.

Tanya couldn't believe it was true, and was moved to tears. Zhanna and Marina leapt up and down. Our own flat! In August we moved into a three-roomed ground-floor flat in a large high-rise apartment block in one of the northern city suburbs. It was conveniently close to Aunt Tamara and not far from the Baptist Church.

After living in such cramped quarters, three rooms seemed luxurious. The girls ran from room to room. "Mum, come and see this," we heard Zhanna yell.

"Zhanna, where are you?" Tanya called after her, amused at the luxury of space. Laughing together we moved from room to room thanking God for this provision for our family.

Tanya was delighted to have her own home and took pride in keeping it clean and tidy. Her diligence and adaptability were always a surprise. Even though her purse was usually empty, there were always flowers on the table and when friends visited, her legendary Russian salad was prepared. No matter what time of day or night, Tanya was always there.

Zhanna and Marina had both been pleading for a pet dog, and we promised to review the situation after we moved into our own flat. It wasn't long before the girls reminded us of the promise we had made.

"Pray!" was the only thing I told the girls.

Tanya and I agreed that a dog would make a great companion for the girls and an appropriate confirmation of our home. But how could we afford to buy one? We just didn't have enough money.

Someone had given me an expensive electronic watch that could be sold privately for at least five hundred roubles. This was the only way we could afford a dog. A few days later, I asked the girls if they had been praying.

"Yes!" they exclaimed in unison. "Well your prayers have been answered," I replied.

Leningrad's unofficial market was an open secret. Held every Saturday and Sunday on Kandratevsky Prospekt, the police knew that it was illegal, but nothing was ever done to close it down. In an open field behind one of the city's largest housing estates, you just turned up and displayed whatever it was that you were selling. There were clothes, electrical goods, birds, animals, even cars and motor bikes for sale. Anything not on display could probably be found in one of the flats on the estate. All you had to do was ask.

We found a woman who had several pups in a homemade pen. The girls wanted a male pup, so we agreed a price with the woman, and she reached into the cage and produced a cute black pup.

As I cradled the pup in my arms, he seemed completely at home, eyes twinkling and tail wagging. Within a minute, he started licking my face, indicating his seal of approval on the purchase!

Zhanna and Marina squealed with delight.

As we walked away from the market to the bus stop, I felt a trickle of water running down my arm. My new friend looked innocently up at me. This was a great joke for Zhanna and Marina.

On further investigation, we discovered that the woman had sold us a female pup, not a male one. For a moment the girls registered some disappointment, but the pup had already won our hearts.

Zhanna and Marina conferred for a minute or so and then Zhanna spoke up, "You know, Dad, it's probably best that we keep this little one and not return her. You see, we wanted a boy," she continued solemnly, "but we prayed to God and now we have been given a girl. This must be what God intended for us, don't you agree?"

"Yes, I think you have both made the right decision," I reflected. "Anyway, she seems to have relaxed and made herself quite at home," I added, shaking my wet arm in the breeze to dry it out.

We called her Panthera because she pranced and leapt about like a black panther. At night, we all snuggled into bed together, Zhanna and Marina tucked tightly under the covers with Tanya and me, and Panthera wriggled past each of us.

Five months after we bought Panthera, she became gravely ill and for three days she could neither eat nor walk. A neighbour who saw her in this pitiful condition advised us to put her to sleep. "Your dog is going to die and this is the kindest thing you can do."

Panthera peered up at us almost too tired to move her head. The girls were in tears and Tanya and I were equally upset. Panthera had become part of the family and we loved her dearly.

I decided to talk to the girls. "Do you believe that God is our Daddy?" I asked them. "Yes," they replied. "Do you believe that God can heal?" I enquired again. "Yes, we do," Zhanna and Marina confirmed. "OK," I said, forcing myself to sound cheerful, let's pray and ask Daddy to heal Panthera." I felt a lump in my throat as I spoke.

Zhanna, Marina and I knelt together on the floor beside the blanket where our dear Panthera lay helpless. I placed my hand on the dog. Then Zhanna and Marina laid their tiny hands beside my large hand, resting them on the puppy's back.

I didn't know what would happen, but we were placing our confidence in the healing power of God. I found myself praying, "Jesus, we know you can do anything, and the prayer of our family is that you restore our dear dog Panthera to full health." It was a simple child-like prayer.

Zhanna and Marina had their eyes closed and I felt a slight tremor run through their bodies. In a simple expression of faith which wrenched my heart, they declared, "Yes, Lord, we so love our Panthera. Please don't let her die."

That evening Panthera struggled to her haunches, for the first time in three days. Gently sipping milk from a bowl, she was clearly pleased with the affection placed on her.

The very next day, Panthera was able to walk and regained her appetite. Tanya queued for hours to buy some meat for the ailing puppy. As each day passed, Panthera grew stronger, and our faith as a family increased. I had always told Zhanna and Marina that God cared for us and was interested in the intimate details of our lives. Now they had evidence that this was true and we praised the Lord together.

Sergei Timokhin visited our home shortly after this crisis to discuss the possibility of playing bass with a new band which I was interested in forming.

"Where is your fancy new watch?" Sergei asked me.

I pointed at Panthera who responded with a friendly bark. Zhanna and Marina sat on my lap and showered me with affectionate kisses. They knew that I loved my watch but had sold it as a declaration of my love for my daughters. They have never forgotten it. Such moments have tied our family in a bond of love that no power on earth can separate.

I opened the ambulance logbook and prepared to alter the mileage. It was customary practice to change the number of miles and add something extra, selling the petrol on the side. Everyone did it without a second thought. But over the past few weeks my conscience had convicted me that I was participating in something illegal.

I knew I had to make a stand but I was caught in a dilemma. If I entered the correct mileage then I would be exposing all the other drivers and the entire crew would face an investigation. The drivers were wrong to siphon off the petrol, but further up the line, we all knew that the bosses were on the take.

Troubled by this crisis of confidence, I reasoned that my confession would cause a great upheaval but change nothing. It was the system that was corrupt.

I prayed that night. If I couldn't change the system then I wanted to change jobs. I believed that God was calling me to be an evangelist and that I should extricate myself from the entanglements of corruption.

The mileometer incident was a turning point.

The following March was a cold month. I turned my collar up and tugged my black hat down over my ears. It felt good to be in the open air. It was 8.25 a.m. and Nevsky Bridge, under which the ambulance depot was located, thronged with people hurrying to work.

In front of me a portly man slipped on the ice and went tumbling down. He looked astonished as he sank down on the ground. The black bag he carried fell a few feet away from him and his hat blew off his head.

As I heaved him back on to his feet, an elderly woman passing by scolded him, "Comrade, it's too early for vodka!"

The man looked startled. "I'm not drunk, you silly woman," he panted.

Obviously disorientated by the experience, he grabbed his bag from me as I handed it to him. I thought I was going to be scolded for interfering. He muttered under his breath while the other passers-by chuckled. The woman walked on but turned round wagging her finger. "Russians who drink but can't hold their liquor should be ashamed!" she continued. "Better to pack them off to the West. That'll teach them a lesson!"

The man stomped off in embarrassment, with his hat askew. "God bless you!" I called out. Looking more perplexed than ever he hurried off in the direction of Moscow Station.

This had been an amusing diversion, but my thoughts returned immediately to Vladimir Solovyov, the chief of our station, who had summoned me to his office. I had my suspicions about why he wanted to see me.

I prayed and asked the Lord, "If he is going to fire me, let him tell me directly. I don't want him to degrade and harass me."

Vladimir Solovyov twisted uncomfortably in his chair, took a long drag from his cigarette and said, "Sorry, Valeri, you know I respect your religious views. . ." Again he faltered, "Valeri, you must understand me. Please leave us."

I understood the backroom scheming that had forced him to take this decision. "OK, I agree to leave," I replied. "Can you complete my documents so that I can leave from tomorrow?"

Immediately he replied, "Yes, certainly."

Usually employees must work a one or two month dismissal period, but when Solovyov waived this requirement, the pressure of the manipulation he was under became clear to me. I waited in his office while his secretary scampered around the building collecting the required signatures and collating my dismissal papers.

Within an hour it was over.

"Here you are, Valeri," Solovyov said, handing me a file containing the documents I needed. He looked embarrassed but relieved. I felt he wanted to say something else to me but held himself in check as he shook my hand.

Once again I had to break the news to Tanya. I knew she worried about money for the family. I always reassured her that we were in the hands of God. He knew all our needs and would never allow us to fall, no matter how perilous the trail.

As the depot gate closed behind me I felt a weight off my mind. The noise of the road seemed a strange solace. I recalled the mileometer incident and smiled. Perhaps God had answered my prayer . . .

I headed back towards Nevsky Bridge and the cool air stirred something within. *Thank you Lord.* At least the dismissal was instant. I would tell Tanya of God's provision for our family. I must obey Jesus. Nothing else mattered.

As I crossed the bridge I felt the presence of God, and a conviction that the dream he had placed in my heart would become a reality. We would form a rock band and record the album. I didn't know how, but I was convinced it would happen.

Tanya was startled when I turned up at home and became nervous about the future. "This is the work of God. We must trust him for everything," I comforted her.

Within days I had found shift work at another garage servicing broken-down vehicles. I worked two nights every four days, leaving me four days free.

About this time I met an American, Mike McGibbon, who worked for a Christian organisation in the West called Living Sound. When Mike heard my idea, his response was immediate. "We can help you with recording equipment. I'll arrange for someone to contact you."

True to his word, someone came to visit me to discuss details of the recording, but I quickly understood that this man from out of town had received a command from someone in the West, and didn't really want to record my music.

Was this the moment the trumpet would sound?

10

SECRET RECORDINGS

I had to make my move. It was a question of time before
the KGB picked up my tracks again. At work I had become
suspicious of a young mechanic who had recently joined the
garage. Leonid appeared innocent and naïve, and therefore
inquisitive. I couldn't be sure that he wasn't an informer.

Having talked things over with Tanya and Sergei
Timokhin, who had agreed to play bass on the project, three
weeks before I was due to leave for the recording, I
disappeared.

In fact, I stayed at home finalising the lyrics and music
of "The Trumpet Call" and practising my English vocals.
I was missed almost at once. Strangers arrived at church and
at work asking if anyone had seen me. They received the
same reply: the truth. No, we haven't seen Valeri Barinov.
We don't know where he is. He's vanished.

Two weeks after I had gone underground we got the first
of our callers at home. I was busy rehearsing a line that
required a sense of drama, and paced up and down the
bedroom repeating the words: where evil reigns − love
grows cold.

The doorbell rang and I heard Tanya hurry to answer it.
Silently I moved behind the bedroom door which was ajar.

Muffled voices at the door. Footsteps along the corridor.
Into the kitchen and then out again. A flurry of activity in
the corridor. Panthera's bark sounds dangerously loud.
Tanya's enquiry is dismissed. More conversation and the
front door is slammed.

Tanya paused by the door. A few minutes passed and the house was totally silent. Then Tanya cautiously entered the bedroom, followed by Panthera.

"The gasman!" she said in an exaggerated voice. Tanya was dismayed that we were now treated like criminals. The "gasman" had been more interested in peering into every room in the house than in checking the gas meter.

That evening Tanya replayed the scene for Zhanna and Marina, who laughed hysterically as she mimicked our "gasman" racing through the house. On the fifth or sixth time round, I pounced on Tanya and wrestled her to the ground yelling "I've caught the gasman!" Panthera joined the merriment, licking our faces in the bundle.

Days later Tanya was confronted at the door by someone wanting to check the electricity meter. Once again, the intruder showed more interest in the rest of the house, barely glancing at the meter in the kitchen. Tanya was tempted to ask him, "Do you know our gasman?"

More unexpected visitors arrived in the next few days, but each time I was able to evade them. The joke was over as we realised the sinister implications of these visits by our gasman and his accomplices. Our house was under surveillance and I was on the KGB's wanted list.

The night before I was due to leave Leningrad, George and Igor collected my guitar and suitcase from our home. We arranged to meet at the railway station the following evening in time for the 7 p.m. train. As they left at midnight, we embraced and prayed together, asking for God's protection and power to perform his holy will.

Unknown to me, a car nearby sat waiting with its lights on, and George and Igor were followed as they left. Their ordeal in the backstreets ended at 4 a.m. that morning when they eventually shook off their pursuer by hiding in the shadowy courtyard of some large installation.

I knew I would have difficulty in leaving the building, but I was ready for this moment. After preparations lasting an hour, my disguise was complete. My long hair had been rolled up with Tanya's hairclips under an old hat. Dark brown spectacles and ill-fitting clothes created a staid, formal image. As I emerged from the bedroom, everyone had to look twice and even Panthera eyed me suspiciously.

The disguise worked. I slipped out of the rear entrance and headed for the bus stop. I didn't look round but concentrated on walking along the icy pavement. One slip and I risked more than a tumble.

George and Igor arrived on schedule clutching my suitcase and guitar. I was really excited. At last we were going to record. The impossible was coming true.

Three days later at the secret location, the leader of the underground organisation appeared tense and nervous. "The KGB won't stop until they have hunted you down," he moaned. "If they track you to our hideout then our work will be stopped."

I was stung by his words. What could I say? We shook hands and the meeting was over. I couldn't believe it. Why was I being stopped?

As I settled down on the sofa to spend a troubled night before catching the 7 a.m. train back to Leningrad, a wave of disappointment washed over me. A voice in my head whispered, "You will never record this music. Never! Never! Never! Everyone will laugh at you." Had God brought me this close to have the door slammed in my face?

In Leningrad Tanya shared my dismay. But the KGB were still hunting me and she was pleased to see me back safely.

"That's the end of that wild idea," Tanya stated emphatically.

"No, Tanya, I've gone too far to let go now," I argued.

"Valeri," she replied, "Can't you take 'No' for an answer? It's not your fault. You've tried, but it's just not meant to be."

"Tanya, I don't know how, but I believe that we will record 'The Trumpet Call'," I insisted.

Tanya pointed out the risks that our family and friends

were running just because of me. "You need your head examined," Tanya shouted furiously. "No one from this world would attempt the impossible."

"But I'm not from this world," I replied. I sympathised with her, but God alone had placed the dream in my heart.

Tanya was not amused.

At the garage Leonid expressed disappointment to hear that the secret recording had been aborted. He tried his best to find out which town I had visited and details of the underground organisation.

I went to the chief's office. Valentin was a tall young man with red hair and a full beard.

"Barinov! Where have you been?" he called out as I entered the room.

"I'm sorry," I smiled, "I had to go away."

Valentin grunted and shuffled some papers about. "Many people came here looking for you."

"Not ordinary militia," I replied knowingly.

He nodded.

"KGB," I said.

"Yes," Valentin replied. "Unfortunately." He drummed his fingers on the desk.

I could read the signs. I knew that I was at fault for being absent without leave. Classified as a "parasite" my job options were reduced and I could warrant a prison term. Valentin was not being vindictive but merely following orders. He had no choice but to dismiss me.

That evening we prayed together as a family, "Lord, we need your help. We are your children. We know that you will never abandon us."

I decided to try to find work in a large vegetable store near us. Some years before, over a hundred people had been arrested for operating a black market from the store, so there were always vacancies. A stoker was needed to operate their furnace. It was hard work for little money.

At the interview I told the truth and explained why the

secret police were hounding me. The boss was a tall thin man with a dark drooping moustache which he stroked constantly. Although quite surprised by my story, he said "OK, you told me the truth. I respect you for that and I will honour it. Go and work!"

The next few months passed quietly, and in retrospect I began to see the design. Curiously, perhaps since my last meeting with Leonid at the garage, the KGB had lifted their surveillance on me. I was a spent force, a dreamer with empty words.

Seven years had passed and still the trumpet's call was a well-kept secret. Some laughed at the dream, others forgot the idea. As I listened to Bob Dylan's album *Slow Train Coming*, one line scorched itself into my heart: "God don't make promises He don't keep!" I found that the store had a toilet with excellent acoustics, so I continued to practise my vocals in English and never surrendered the vision God had given me.

I worked night shifts with Anatoly, a slim young man with long brown hair. He also liked rock music and we became good friends.

Anatoly had drifted into drugs and now found there was no exit. He was hooked. I shared my faith with him and one day he took the plunge. Anatoly had opened an attic window allowing God inside his life. He never knew how things could change, but he started to feel different. I told him that when he was hooked on Jesus, drugs would lose their grip.

Anatoly tried an experiment. He cut down the amount of drugs he was using, trusting in Jesus. To his amazement, he found that within a few weeks he had jumped off the "drugs' express".

"I can't believe it," Anatoly told me. "Who would have believed that I could be free from drugs?"

I was not surprised. I knew that there is no force on this planet that can compare with the power of God. My new brother in Christ was to play an important part in our future.

One morning I returned home at 8 a.m. as usual and went to bed. A few hours later, Tanya shook me. "Wake up! A visitor from England is here!" I was about to hear some astonishing news.

The stranger began by reminding me of a conversation I had recently had with four visitors from the Ichthus Fellowship in South London. I had told them about "The Trumpet Call", and they had asked me what was needed. "Musical instruments!" I had replied, "and your prayers."

I nodded sleepily as I recalled the four young men.

The visitor explained that he was running a campaign for the release of seven Siberian Christians who had taken refuge in the American Embassy in Moscow. On behalf of his four friends he had brought us a gift on his journey to Moscow. Did we still need a guitar?

The guitar had been "smuggled" into Leningrad and was back at the hotel. Zhanna, aged twelve, accompanied our new friend back to his hotel and they returned with a brand-new red electric guitar. I picked it up and stroked its glistening frame. My heart was full of praise to God.

I rang the underground group who controlled the recording equipment. They couldn't believe what I was telling them, but hastily agreed that if I had instruments, they could, after all, provide the recording equipment and an engineer. The rest was up to us, and with the emphasis on secrecy we should complete the recording as quickly as possible.

We agreed some dates and I also called some of the musicians who I thought would record with me. Sergei Timokhin confirmed immediately that he would play bass guitar. The others gasped in astonishment. "Really? A new electric guitar? I can't believe it! I'm coming right over to see it." Such a guitar could only have been bought on the black market for an astronomical price. However, reviewing the music, I realised that we needed a synthesiser for special effects. In some copies of the *New Musical Express* which my friend had left me, I saw synthesisers advertised. I ripped the page out and asked an American to send it to the campaign group in England.

"Are you ready to record?" the leader of the underground group asked me. I assured him that I was. "What about the other instruments?" I told him that it was all in the Lord's hands. "Oh no!" he complained. "That means you haven't got everything." I admitted that we still needed a synthesiser. I could see that he thought he was dealing with a madman.

The first meeting was planned for the second weekend in March. Still we had no synthesiser, and the underground group were only grudgingly loaning their equipment. If we were caught, they could lose everything.

Anatoly agreed to help by operating both his furnace and mine, enabling me to slip out of the store undetected.

Everyone involved on the project understood the secrecy of it. In a joyous moment, we celebrated communion together, evidence of the Lord's presence with us and the fulfilment of a prophetic vision.

The portable eight-track studio was to be moved around various secret locations in the city, and we devised a complex code for listing meetings. We planned to catch an out-of-town train sometimes, other times we would travel by tram or trolley bus, taking every care to look inconspicuous. When possible, a borrowed car would provide transport with George as a taxi-driver.

As the schedule of recording sessions got under way, mistakes and misunderstandings crept in, meaning that some forgot appointments or others came at the wrong time or to the wrong place.

First we recorded the drum parts, and then Sergei Timokhin played the bass sequences. This formed the foundation for the rest of the work. Before recording each song, I sat with the musician who was playing and taught him the melody and rhythm line. I sang along while he picked it up and played it again for the final recording.

We were now ready to record the synthesiser and again

the owners of the equipment called on me to express astonishment that I was stupid enough to make risky plans to record an instrument I didn't have! Max, the engineer, had located a country house which was empty and nervously he finalised plans to record on a Friday night in April. One day before we were to leave, Zhanna was at home alone when a slim Englishman arrived with gifts for the family and a mysterious black box. When I arrived home and heard the news, my heart missed a beat. I walked over to the black box and opened it up.

A synthesiser!

With unbelievable timing, God had arranged the miraculous. Forty-eight hours later it would have been too late.

In England they had known nothing about the timing of the recording, but God had coordinated everything. I was so overjoyed that I rang Ivan, the synth-man, who reacted with total disbelief. I had to spend several minutes convincing him that the synthesiser had actually arrived. Within twenty minutes he was round at the flat looking absolutely stunned. Ivan was not yet a fully convinced believer, but God was certainly demonstrating his power to him.

Now it was a little easier for people to believe that the dream was becoming reality.

After the synthesiser was recorded, the lead guitarist was then able to hear the music and play his contribution. The extraordinary nature of "The Trumpet Call" was that we never played together as a group. The songs were too dangerous for that, and consequently each of the instrumental tracks was recorded completely separately. Not all the musicians worked their best and some needed pressure to cooperate. However, when they heard the early mix of the English version everyone said they would have played better had they known what it would sound like.

The Russian vocals were kept for the final days of recording. This was clearly wise, as everyone would have understood the Russian words and it would therefore have been easier for the KGB to track us down.

The Russian version was nearing completion when the leader of the underground group visited me. He complained that rock music was not for Christians and that we had used the equipment for far too long. Their group had a project that needed recording and he told me, "Our work is more important than yours."

I pleaded for extra time to complete the recording, to no avail. He was leaving the following morning and within four hours the banks of recording equipment would disappear with him, never to be seen again.

I had a cold and fever, and was exhausted from the last few months of recording. What could we hope to do in four hours? And where could we find a place to record?

Anatoly told me he knew a house that had just been repainted and was empty for the next few days. In one last burst of energy we hauled the equipment to the quiet suburb Anatoly had indicated. Our engineer checked out the basement of the house. He agreed that it would be suitable as the sound would be submerged in the building.

There was one problem. My throat reacted badly to the odour of paint which still hung in the air. The engineer was apprehensive about my ability to perform, but I knew that we didn't have an option. While the microphones and all the equipment were fitted into place, I prayed. This was the last chance to complete the recording of "The Trumpet Call". I had only one take and it had to be right.

I asked God to heal my throat and clear my voice. The engineer pointed to the microphone I should use and asked me to speak into it, to check the sound level.

"Praise the Lord!" I said into the microphone. "This trumpet will sound!" I lifted my hands to heaven and prayed, "I only want to praise you, my Jesus!"

The engineer signalled, the red light was shining. We're on: live!

I closed my eyes and sang with a passion I had not known

before. I felt a tightness in my chest, but I urged myself onward, convinced that we were fulfilling the will of God.

The first rays of sunlight were peeping through the trees in the backstreets of Leningrad as we drove home. I felt drained of all energy and just wanted to sleep. The recording had finally been completed in one year and in five different towns. I don't know how everything held together. Only God made it possible.

But "The Trumpet Call" was not yet complete! I needed one final choral item to conclude the album. The church choir leader gave me permission to record before the weekly practice. Although I had only five days, I somehow managed to obtain a Japanese tape recorder. Despite technical difficulties and the impatience of some choir members, the last take was magnificent.

I was thrilled. Eagerly I contacted Max and informed him that I had the final item. "I have it on tape." I said excitedly. "And I taped it all myself."

"On tape?" he said, sounding surprised. "What speed was the tape you used?"

I stared at him vacantly but quickly regained my composure. "What speed have you used for the rest of the recording?" I countered.

But the engineer ignored my question and went on to explain, "You do know that tapes have different speeds and it has got to be on the same speed otherwise it'll be worthless?"

I nodded vigorously. "Don't worry, God has directed this entire project. Don't you think he knows about the speeds of tape machines? Of course it's the same speed."

With that I handed over the recording of the choir.

Two days later I visited the engineer. He was preoccupied and under a lot of pressure. "I'll let you know as soon as your project is ready," was all he would say.

I asked if he had any technical problems with my recording.

"No, no," he said impatiently. "All I need is a few more hours in the day."

"What about the speed of the tape I gave you on Friday?" I asked casually.

"The speed of the tape? Yeah? What's wrong with it?"

"Is it the same speed as the rest of the recording," I asked excitedly.

"Yes! Yes! It's the same speed!" he replied grumpily. "How do you think I could edit your recording if it's not the same speed? Look, don't worry so much. Don't hassle me, I'll do it as quickly as I can."

I smiled. I knew the Lord wouldn't let me down. "Just trust me," Max continued as he escorted me to the door.

I couldn't resist a parting shot as we shook hands. "No, no, Max. Trust Jesus!"

11

NIGHT TRAIN TO MOSCOW:
December 1982–March 1983

While we were recording "The Trumpet Call", Zhanna and Marina were growing in faith in Jesus and both of them kept asking me to arrange their baptism.

The State banned young people from being baptized in the Baptist Church, so with the help of friends in the Orthodox Church, a date was set for early January. It didn't matter to me which denomination administered the gift of baptism. The real issue was that Zhanna and Marina were sincere in their search for God.

The girls looked gorgeous as they stood in the cathedral in white taffeta gowns that Tanya had stitched. The ceremony itself had a tremendous effect on Tanya and solidified our unity as a family.

Zhanna and Marina caused a stir when news of their baptism spread throughout the school. The teachers were apprehensive but the girls' friends were curious and eventually many in their class found personal faith also.

Shortly after my thirty-eighth birthday, Sergei Timokhin and I began a fast in order to focus our minds on God. We had experienced God's miraculous intervention recording "The Trumpet Call". Now we had to tell the world!

We wrote and signed an appeal to the Presidium of the Supreme Soviet emphasising the non-political content of the album and requesting permission to perform our music "in the concert halls of our country". To ensure delivery, we registered the letter at our local post office on January 17th, but suspecting confiscation by the local authorities, we decided to deliver it personally to Moscow.

Sergei and I made plans to catch the night train to Moscow. The "Red Arrow Express" covers the 800 km journey once a week. It was always crowded with people taking advantage of its exceptionally well-stocked restaurant carriage, where many delicacies unobtainable in the shops were for sale.

We sipped tea in Leningrad's main railway station. Thirty minutes to go. Even at this late hour, the station was busy. A couple near us were arguing loudly. All around us travellers trundled across the station floor.

I felt a tap on my shoulder. A militiaman stood with his hand outstretched. "Let me see your papers," he said. All at once four policemen surrounded us. Where had they come from? I showed them my identity card.

A plain-clothes officer in a smart fawn-coloured coat and trim dark-brown hat joined the group. KGB. We were escorted to the police station and into a sparsely furnished room, where a long wooden table divided the room in half. Behind the table, another KGB officer waited, his sleek black fur-lined coat slung over a chair.

"Empty your pockets," he snapped.

"You have no right," I countered.

"No right?" the KGB official chuckled. "We have the right to do anything we want."

Out tumbled keys, money, two railway tickets, photos of Tanya, Zhanna and Marina. Our bag was rifled through. Scarves, paperbacks, ten manilla envelopes containing our appeal and three unmarked cassettes of "The Trumpet Call".

The KGB investigator picked up one of the cassettes. "What is this?" he asked.

"It's our Christian rock opera about the second coming of Christ," I replied.

"What?" he appeared shocked and cursed. "Strip!"

Here in the freezing room, Sergei and I could barely stand straight for the cold. Naked under interrogation, we endured the humiliation of a complete body search.

The militiamen picked through our clothes. Throughout the ordeal, the KGB officers swore abusively at us. Two witnesses were called in to sign a report that was in preparation. They were passengers from the station, ordinary people in the wrong place at the wrong time. Everyone knew you didn't refuse a request from the KGB.

The entire interrogation lasted two hours. "OK, get dressed." The KGB officer who had arrested us stared coldly at me as I pulled my trousers on. "You're a marked man, Barinov. The next time we meet, things will be different." Then he added ominously, "Don't leave Leningrad."

We picked up our personal belongings from the table. Tanya's photo had been torn and crumpled. The KGB officer leaned across and grabbed the cassettes and envelopes containing our appeal. "I'll keep these," he said, waving them defiantly. "You won't be needing them for the journey you'll be taking."

Everyone left the room except for one policeman. He said, "You can go now, but don't leave Leningrad. You've been warned."

Sergei and I walked out into the night. It was 2.10 a.m. The snowy street outside the station looked calm and serene. It was unreal and detached from our experience of the last few hours.

I tried not to disturb Tanya as I climbed into bed, but she stirred, tucking herself into the folds of my body. Sleepily she whispered, "Valeri, what happened? I thought you were going to Moscow."

"Don't worry Tanya," I replied, "I'll tell you about it in the morning."

I closed my eyes and tried to sleep. The struggle had begun.

The next day, Sergei and I were summoned to the Council

of Religious Affairs, the government's official body for controlling churches and religious activity.

Mr Kirov shook us cordially by the hand and settled into a comfortable leather chair. A framed photo of Lenin watched benignly over the smartly furnished office. A smaller photo of Leonid Brezhnev hung on the wall to my left.

The elegantly dressed KGB officer who had directed our arrest at the station stood by the window with his arms folded, smiling throughout our encounter. Mr. Kirov's secretary carried in a silver tray with four steaming cups of coffee. "Just what we need on a day like this," the KGB man suggested.

"Valeri, you have recorded an interesting musical programme, this, er, what is it called, 'Bugle Alert'," Mr Kirov faltered.

"No, no," I replied, laughing at his apparent joke. "It's called 'The Trumpet Call'."

"That's right, 'The Trumpet Call', of course," Mr Kirov said, shuffling his feet under the table. "We want to help you."

"Yes, Valeri," the KGB man said with a broad grin. "Your music is very good. I understand that you want to perform in public? We can organise concert halls for you. We can even help you with equipment."

"That would be wonderful," I responded. "Thank you very much."

"Well Valeri," he continued, dragging his words out but still smiling, "you must understand that there is only one condition."

"Yes, what is that?"

"Don't sing about Jesus. Change the words. We will help you with everything. I know some influential people. We can really take you to the top. But not with songs about Jesus."

I smiled back at him. "Well, that poses a problem, because the purpose of the band is to praise Jesus."

Mr Kirov lectured me on the tasks of a good communist. "It's our duty to wipe out these old-fashioned ideas about religion," he declared.

It was clear that the discussion was going nowhere, and Kirov had another meeting to attend. "Don't tell anyone about our little talk," he said confidentially.

"That's difficult," I replied.

"Why?" Kirov asked.

"You know the name of our band?" I said, amused at his growing discomfort. "If we are called 'The Trumpet Call', then we must trumpet!"

The pressure was on. We had secretly circulated "The Trumpet Call" to anyone who wanted a copy. But I had kept one tape in a brown envelope in a drawer in our bedroom. I wanted to deliver this cassette personally.

My heart pounded as I caught the train to Vyborg. I was prepared to be turned away at the door, but Andrew opened it and grinned in recognition. "Come in, come in," he said.

The apartment looked the same, but Andrew had grown tall and was now married with a two-year-old daughter.

"Do you like rock music?" I asked.

"You know that I do," he shot back.

When Andrew played the tape that I handed over, he listened in amazement, swaying to the beat and reflecting on the lyrics.

While I was showing him some photos of Zhanna and Marina, I heard footsteps in the hallway, someone climbing slowly up the stairs. It was Father. Breathing heavily like an asthmatic, he walked slowly into the room. He looked ashen, his hair turned to white.

He recognised me the instant our eyes met, but didn't say a word. Andrew reminded Father that I was one of his students who shared a striking similarity to himself. He nodded in acknowledgment and sauntered into one of the rooms locking the door behind him.

With a growing sense of unease, I explained that it was

time to return home. Andrew accompanied me to the train station. While we waited on the platform, I said to him, "Do you want to know a secret?"

He grinned, "Hey, that's a song by the Beatles." I smiled in response. "But what's the secret?"

"Andrew, did you ever wonder why we're so alike?" I didn't know how to tell him. Nothing would ever be the same again. Pausing for a moment, I said softly, "Did you know that your father had another wife many years ago and that there was a baby from that marriage? I am that child."

Andrew looked cheekily to see if I was joking but he realised I was serious. His smile froze across his face and his eyes narrowed in surprise.

"It's true," I said. "Father was married before and had a child from his first marriage."

Andrew stood transfixed in front of me. "Why, that means we're . . . we're half-brothers," he spluttered.

"That's right, we're half-brothers," I declared.

Neither of us had realised that the train had pulled into the station. It all seemed like a dream, but I had to get on the train and our meeting was ended.

Andrew edged up to the carriage as I climbed in. "Valeri," he faltered, "I don't know what to say."

Sensing his unease, I replied, "There's nothing to say. It happened. That's all."

The engine jostled our carriage as we pulled out. Andrew looked so young, just the way I must have been as a young man. "Come and see me in Leningrad!" I called out.

"Yes, I will come," he replied.

Andrew clung on to me as the train gathered speed. I grinned. It was just the kind of thing I would have done, had our roles been reversed. Andrew jogged alongside the train until we were forced to let go of each other.

"God bless you Andrew!" I yelled into the dark sky as the hurtling train carried me into the night.

I settled down into a seat and reflected on scenes from the past. This visit to Father had been different in some way.

Now, I didn't feel so restless. The sense of loss had been replaced with some measure of peace. I couldn't explain it, but I knew I had crossed a line.

After our meeting with Mr Kirov and his mysterious friend at the Council for Religious Affairs, I was called to the military commission and required to undergo a medical and psychiatric examination prior to being drafted back into the army. Again! No one could make sense of it.

But the signs were becoming easier to spot. The examination would declare me insane, and I'd be held in psychiatric hospital. If I refused the call-up, I would be imprisoned for disobeying orders. Either way, the KGB had set a trap.

How could I fight back? I would rather die than abandon the vision planted in my heart. Prayer was my only weapon.

A psychiatrist who wore wire-rimmed spectacles on the bridge of his nose conducted the interview while a nerve specialist made notes in silence.

I was questioned closely about my religious beliefs. When I indicated my suspicion of KGB pressure, the doctor simply smiled and said, "It seems that you think the KGB are watching you?"

I was relaxed. "I don't know if the KGB watch me or not," I replied. "We all have our work to do. My work is to praise my Jesus. The KGB have different work."

The doctor smiled again and said confidentially, "Let me tell you that the KGB called us and they did say that they have you under surveillance."

I realised the importance of every word. If I agreed with his statement I would confirm that I was paranoid, suspicious and maybe crazy.

The psychiatrist closed the interview with words which were friendly, but an unmistakable warning. "I'm afraid, Valeri, that if you preach about Jesus in the army, you are heading for a psychiatric ward."

The official Soviet Army psychiatric report stated:

Valeri Barinov speaks of his role
in the working of divine providence,
of the power of Christ,
and actively preaches divine wisdom.

Miraculously I was later able to obtain a copy, which was
smuggled to Keston College in England where most of my
information was sent for circulation.

The doctor dismissed me with a referral note for a further
examination at a clinic quite close to my home. I didn't need
to be a prophet to know that the questions would be the
same.

This second meeting lasted an hour and a half.
Undoubtedly the medical team were convinced that they
were dealing with a devious traitor.

Dr Maslova introduced herself and handled the
preliminary discussions. I was then interviewed by a panel
of experts who touched and prodded me, asking ludicrous
questions. When I attempted to reply, each would look at
each other, sometimes rolling their eyes in amusement. I was
a spectacle for their derision.

Nothing I said could make any difference to their
prognosis. I was crazy. Every time the doctors spoke, I heard
the doors of the psychiatric prison swinging open.

The next morning, Tanya suggested that if the medical
staff were given a copy of "The Trumpet Call", they would
understand why the KGB were hounding me. We prayed,
and I had peace in my heart that this was a good idea, despite
the obvious risks. Although Tanya was seen promptly by
Dr Maslova, she was unable to engage her in any
conversation.

One afternoon Zhanna came home from school and
declared, "Dad, we're being watched. Three days running
I've seen the same car parked outside our house. They're
still out there."

I was furious and grabbed my coat. "Quick, let's see what
they look like."

Zhanna and I linked arms against the cold January wind and headed for the road. Zhanna was right. There they were. A black Volga hugging the curb.

"Wait here Zhanna," I said and squeezed her hand. Stepping carefully on to the icy street I made directly for the parked car. Barely a few paces away, I could make out the features of two young men huddled together inside. Somewhat startled, I saw one nudge the other. All at once the ignition key was turned and the car sped off into the distance.

Zhanna came up behind me. "What would you have said to them, Dad?" she asked. I chuckled. I hadn't really thought of anything to say. "God would have given me the words."

All through the following months, each time one of us went out we were tailed. Even Zhanna and Marina were followed to school. When their friends asked if they were afraid, they replied, "Of course not, we've got Jesus. He will protect us."

Jesus gave me boldness, and I approached the black car five times. Each time it sped away.

As a result of Leningrad's extensive underground communication network, the secret recording became very well known, and many young people asked when they could hear us play.

"That depends on the Kremlin and the KGB," I joked.

Realising the opportunity we had to communicate the Gospel to the youth of Leningrad, we planned a meeting in the official Baptist Church on February 6th.

Although the halls weren't being used, the doors remained locked and about thirty young people were turned away. I wrote to the elders clarifying the mission of our rock band:

"The Trumpet Call" may seem a strange form
of preaching to you, but thanks to the medium
of modern music, God's word is made accessible
to everyone and many young people hear the Gospel.

Five days later, Seva Novgorodtsev, a popular DJ on the BBC World Service, played extracts from "The Trumpet Call". He also read out our appeal requesting permission to play openly. Finally, Seva announced our home address.

The response was sensational. Young people, mostly non-believers, contacted us from all across the Soviet Union. It was evident that these kids were waking up from a spiritual slumber induced by atheism. Realising that alcohol, drugs or money could not satisfy the longings of their soul, they wrote in to say, "We need Jesus!"

Early in March a policeman called at the door. "Are you Valeri Barinov?" he asked.

"Yes," I replied. "You know it's me."

"You must report for a compulsory psychiatric investigation tomorrow morning at 10 a.m. I have a police car waiting outside. Either you go by yourself tomorrow or come with us now. It's very important that you are not late."

I convinced the young lieutenant that I could handle my own travel arrangements. The next morning, I left the house at dawn and spent the day visiting friends. If I returned to the psychiatric hospital according to the instructions, it would be as a prisoner, not as a patient.

On April 13th we had another visitor. "Hello, I'm Nurse Yudina from the psychiatric hospital," said an elderly, very experienced nurse.

"Why do I need a nurse?" I said in astonishment.

"Because you are registered as a psychiatric patient," Yudina declared. This was news to me. After some haggling, the nurse reluctantly agreed to continue the discussion inside our apartment.

I offered her coffee, but she declined. Immediately to business. "What medicine do you use?"

"I don't use any because I'm not sick," I commented in surprise.

"But drugs have been prescribed. It is most important that the doctor is informed," she insisted.

I confronted her in a quiet confident tone. "You don't have to keep up this pretence because I know who has ordered you to come here today. I know that the KGB have set a trap for me."

Yudina looked startled. "What trap? Why do the KGB want to trap you?"

"Because of our Christian rock group 'The Trumpet Call'."

At the mention of the group's name Yudina raised her eyebrows slightly. "How many play in your group?"

"Seven," I replied.

Without thinking, Yudina opened her notebook and scribbled down the number seven. Mischievously I pointed to her notebook and asked, "Is this my diagnosis?"

Realising her blunder, Yudina yelled and cursed. She threw her notebook into her case. "You're a traitor," she screeched.

"Your reaction is proof that I am well. No one screams like this at ill people!" Stung by the truth of my words, Yudina stormed out of the apartment.

Tanya had heard almost everything from the bedroom and she rushed out. What more could be said? Swaying gently, we embraced in the tiny hallway, both aware of the hidden danger lurking ahead.

Two days after Nurse Yudina's visit I was summoned again to the Council for Religious Affairs. This time there were no cups of coffee or friendly handshakes.

Mr Kirov frowned at me from behind his desk as I was made to stand before him like an errant schoolboy before the headmaster. I refused to be intimidated and extended my hand. "Hello Mr Kirov, God bless you."

He gave me a limp handshake and went on to talk continually for the next twenty minutes, barely allowing me to reply. He complained about the foreigners I was meeting and warned that I was acting like a traitor.

"Our prisons are full of people like you. Do you understand?" Mr Kirov glared.

"But Mr Kirov," I interrupted, sounding puzzled. "That means innocent people are imprisoned in our country."

He raised his hand to cut me short. "Slandering the Soviet State is a criminal offence. You have been warned. You'll end up in the Ural Mountains with your family!"

The Ural Mountains was a popular euphemism for the labour camps. He pressed a buzzer on the side of his desk and a young man in a crumpled suit escorted me from his office. Mr Kirov didn't wave goodbye.

I went straight to George's apartment, where I informed George and Sergei of Kirov's warning. Before I left, we clasped hands and committed each other to God's will.

I arrived home late to find a note from Tanya who was fast asleep:

Some friends arrived to see you today.
The only English word I could use was "NO",
which wasn't very friendly. They will
return at 7 p.m. tomorrow, so come home early!!!
Goodnight, I love you, Tanya.
PS Zhanna and Marina asked me again whether
we can go on holiday this year. Can we?

The image of foreigners knocking on our door to be greeted by a Russian redhead who says, "NO!" amused me. What would they think? Not the best advertisement for detente! I was also reminded of Kirov's warning against "agents of western imperialism".

Promptly at 7 p.m. the doorbell rang and two young Americans stood clutching a piece of paper with my name on it. I liked to entertain friends from the West and made myself available to take them wherever they wanted to go. This couple agreed to carry out some messages for me.

A few days later Nurse Yudina returned. I decided to surprise her to see what her reaction would be. "I know all your tricks and soon you and your bosses will be exposed."

"What do you mean?" She sounded outraged.

I pulled a copy of Tolstoy's *Resurrection* off the bookshelf and lifted out a piece of paper tucked inside its pages. "This is a record of the pressure used to force me into psychiatric hospital," I declared. "It will be broadcast over the BBC shortly. Would you like me to read it to you?"

Yudina's rage could be contained no longer. "You traitor!" she screamed. "Have you no shame?"

The comic scene was re-enacted as the nurse shouted at her patient and slammed the door.

The house was silent as Seva read the statement over the airwaves. What a breakthrough! I could hardly believe it. Suddenly light had come, and the darkness could not hide it. I didn't know how the KGB would respond, but was determined to carry on as normal.

One week later, on May 6th, we celebrated Tanya's birthday. The glow from the coloured candles on the cake which Zhanna and Marina had baked created warmth and cosiness.

Tanya blew out the candles, and for a second or two the room was in darkness until someone switched on the light. "Make a wish, Mama," Zhanna said. "Make a wish for the coming year."

Tanya paused for a moment. "I wish for a peaceful life, that's all I want." And then added, "But our lives are in God's hands."

Sometimes one doesn't realise that seemingly unrelated events are actually linked like tracks on a railway line.

On May 13th, I was told by the boss at the store that he could no longer hire me. I was not fired, but no longer employable. I had entered the danger zone whereby I could be classified as a "parasite" of the state.

The boss wasn't a bad man. He just wanted to get through the day. He didn't really want to discuss my situation with me but I pressed him. Was I a bad worker?

"Well no, that's not the reason," he explained. "It's just

that we can't have someone working here who is registered as a psychiatric patient.''

The design became clear. He was just obeying orders. Whispers from the KGB didn't need an amplification system.

On June 22nd I was visited by a psychiatrist who conducted an ad hoc interview. Three days later I returned home to learn that a police inspector had called.

"He wanted to know why you weren't working and how long you had been unemployed," Zhanna informed me. "I explained that you had been fired because you had been illegally registered as a psychiatric patient."

I gave Zhanna a hug, and she looked at me with a cheeky grin. Zhanna had inherited my humour.

The next assault came from an unexpected quarter and ripped deep into me.

I was told that the leaders of the Baptist Church wanted to see me on June 28th. I knew that they were under increasing pressure from the KGB to keep me "under control". The meeting was formal and the attitude of the elders was cautious. I explained that, although some people might not like our music, our aim was to share the Gospel. I showed them the letters we had received from young people in response to the BBC broadcasts of "The Trumpet Call". But the elders wouldn't look at the letters.

The following evening a church meeting was held. I was prepared for what was to happen and decided not to attend. Nevertheless, it hurt me deeply. My friends who were there told me of the decision to expel me from the Baptist Church.

The leaders had been intimidated by the KGB. But what a tragedy that they had compromised their responsibility as Christ's ambassadors. We were, after all, brothers and sisters of the same family. I determined in my heart that I would not judge them, but forgive them. Those who submit to a lie bear a greater burden than those who live by the truth.

The following reasons were given for my expulsion:

Firstly, my appearance. I looked like a hippie, I wore jeans, tee-shirts and a cross around my neck.

Secondly, my children had been baptised in the Orthodox Church.

Thirdly, I had not always clearly identified with the Baptist denomination.

Fourthly, we played rock music.

I decided to attend church and act as though nothing had happened. I had been judged by man, and was more concerned with the judgement of God. If God was on my side then I had nothing to fear.

For me, the issue was not where Zhanna and Marina were baptised, but whether they believed in Jesus. The leaders had neglected to mention that it is illegal to baptise anyone under eighteen in the Baptist Church. I had always considered myself a Christian rather than a Baptist, and felt at home in all denominations. As for rock music, it was hard for them to understand that our aim was to share the Gospel.

Aunt Tamara was caught in the tensions within the church and it was a difficult time for all of us.

That same day, I decided to fast and pray for a week. Sergei Timokhin joined me. I wanted to keep myself pure before God. We also received many more letters from young people who were curious about the faith so we organised another meeting.

Despite requests to use the church hall on July 10th, once again the doors remained closed. I was disappointed that we had missed another opportunity to share the Gospel with people who would normally never turn up at church.

But July was also a month of great triumph for us. Vindication was to come from a far country. Seva announced on the BBC that a British pop-singer had sent us a message of encouragement. And then Cliff Richard's message was played.

Zhanna and Marina hugged me. Tanya was beaming. Sergei clapped and cheered. I wanted to scream! What a moment of joy. God had used this moment to endorse and support our struggle when we needed it most.

The news spread like wildfire. Cliff Richard, the famous singer, had actually-heard our music! The great thing was that he understood that we were trying to share the Gospel through rock music.

Late one night Tanya asked me if I had remembered being asked whether we could go away on holiday?

"Yes, vaguely," I said.

"I think a holiday would do us all good," Tanya said.

I agreed. The girls had also been under pressure. Tanya made preparations and we spent a few weeks in Odessa. It was a relaxing time. But I was not to know that this would be the last family holiday for several years. While lying on the beach, I remembered an earlier prophecy from God regarding seven trumpets. I had already recorded the first one and had no doubt that I would complete the others. But how? Only God knows.

When we returned to Leningrad, I found work in a local park where construction had begun on a skating rink. I was given the mindless task of hosing water on to a concrete block. But it gave me flexible working hours and urgently needed roubles.

Tanya and I, Zhanna and Marina were being drawn together in a new experience of togetherness. The Lord had strengthened our resilience and our resolve. God was uniting our hearts for the struggle ahead.

12

PSYCHIATRIC TERROR

I glanced at the calendar: October 11th, 1983.

I stood in the hallway pulling on my denim jacket when Tanya called out to me from the kitchen. I couldn't hear what she said. Again she called. What did she want?

"Tanya," I called out. "I need some cash. Is there any money in the house?"

I couldn't find any money in our usual hiding places and went in search of Tanya. She was standing by the stove peeling potatoes.

"Tanya, have you got any money?" I asked her. Tanya looked up at me. "Couldn't you hear me calling you?" she said crisply.

"Yes, but I'm in a hurry," I explained. "I'm meeting George and I'm already late."

"I don't care who you're meeting," Tanya insisted, "I need to know when you'll be home, because I want us to eat together with Zhanna and Marina tonight."

"Sorry, Tanya," I apologised. "You need a medal for living with me."

"Go on," she said, handing me a few coins. "The sooner you leave, the sooner you'll return."

I was going to be late, but George would wait, I reflected as I jogged through the October rain to the bus stop. He had asked me to bring the letters I had received following the BBC radio broadcast. "I've got an idea," he said enigmatically.

Udelnaya subway station wasn't very busy. I heard

someone call my name and turned to find two policemen standing behind me. Now I've really got an excuse for being late, I thought as I showed my identity card.

"Come with us," one of them said, sounding bored. This was surely a misunderstanding that would be soon cleared up. In my bag, bundled together were letters from young people all over the country. If their names and addresses fell into the wrong hands . . . Somehow I had to get a message to Tanya.

A young officer pulled up in a police car. "OK, I've come for Valeri Barinov." He produced a pair of handcuffs.

"Don't worry about me, I'm not going to run away," I told him.

The officer seemed to be in a good mood. "Give me one good reason why I should believe you won't try to escape?" he grinned.

"I believe in Jesus. Nothing happens to me out of coincidence, even this arrest is part of his plan. Why should I escape?"

When the officer realised I wasn't joking, I knew I had moved into a commanding position. He paused for a moment, chuckling, then slapped me on the shoulder. "Come on Barinov! But I'm warning you, if you try to get away you'll really be in trouble."

The officer hummed to himself as we drove through the midday traffic. I said to him, "Do you know why you're arresting me?"

"Because you've broken the law," he said, "obviously."

"But do you know what crime I have committed?" I continued.

"No," he replied. "I was just asked to pick you up."

"I am a Christian rock musician. That's the reason I've been arrested," I explained.

"Rock music and Christianity. That's a dangerous combination," he smiled. "I didn't know there were any Christian rock musicians," he continued, obviously intrigued.

"But there are many Christian musicians. In the West, of course. Cliff Richard, Bob Dylan, Donna Summer."

We talked casually during the rest of the journey. The hunter and the hunted. Strange companions.

Clutching the bag of letters I was marched into a room occupied by three policemen, one of whom hurriedly finished a telephone conversation. His name was Uvarov. The officer I had arrived with talked with him for a few minutes and then walked across to me. "What kind of music does your band play?" he asked.

"Don't speak with him! Don't speak with him!" Uvarov called out angrily.

The driver was taken aback, and moved away holding up his hands. He strode to the door and was gone.

An hour and a half had passed when I heard the screeching of brakes outside. Car doors slammed.

A young medical orderly dressed in a white coat and carrying a case entered and shook hands with Uvarov. "So this is the Christian preacher," he grinned.

Uvarov produced some forms and the orderly signed them. "He's very quiet now," the orderly sneered. "But this is the man who wants to preach the Gospel with a loud trumpet call." He emphasised the last two words.

I remained silent as he told the policeman about our Christian rock group. It was clear that he knew everything about me. "His wish is to play Christian music," the orderly continued, "but I wish him a painful cross to bear." Uvarov and the other policemen joined in the laughter.

"Do you realise that you are completely under our control?" Uvarov derided me, goaded on by the medical worker. "No one can save you." Uvarov walked across and prodded his finger into my chest. "What do you think of that?" he boasted.

"I know only one thing," I answered both Uvarov and the KGB medical worker. "And I want to thank you . . ."

My retort was met with astonishment. "For what?" they said almost in unison.

"Because God makes an advertisement of me through your action," I declared.

Both were enraged. "You swine," the orderly swore. He was about to strike me, but drew back. The interrogation ended. I was hustled into an ambulance waiting outside and driven to the Leningrad Psychiatric Hospital No. 3.

The hospital was surrounded by a brick wall, its front gates guarded by two militiamen. I was asked to wait in the reception. The bag with the letters lay at my feet.

On the bench beside me, a woman dressed in a smart blue coat fiddled nervously with a medical card. I smiled at her and she acknowledged my greeting. She stared in disbelief as I explained briefly why I was detained.

"Oh! you are here because of your religious activity." She added, almost to herself, "That means I'm here because of my guilt."

"What guilt?" I asked.

"I uncovered a plot at the pharmaceutical factory where I work. The bosses were going to steal narcotics and sell them on the black market. I informed our Party boss, and a few days later was asked to attend a medical examination. I came here totally convinced that there had been a mistake, but listening to your story, I wonder if it's because of the report I wrote."

I sympathised with the woman. "The Party boss must have reported you to the KGB," I reasoned.

"But I'm a loyal Party member," the woman confided.

"But this isn't the real Communist Party. These people are more like the Mafia!"

"I do believe that you're right." Turning to me she said cautiously, "Will you pray for me?"

"Yes," I replied, fearing for her at the mercy of such evil people.

I approached a friendly looking woman and asked her, "Could you phone this number and let my wife know I'm in this hospital?'' I prayed that the note would not be confiscated.

I also beckoned to an old lady. "I need your help. Could you get rid of this for me?'' She eyed the package of letters suspiciously, but agreed. "Just throw it away when you leave here,'' I reassured her casually. Soon she had passed through the hospital entrance and was out of sight.

The registrar called my name and took me to Department 20 on the first floor.

"Doctor, why have I been brought to this hospital by force?'' I protested.

He looked startled. "What do you mean?'' The doctor refused to discuss the matter and left the room locking the door behind him. A few minutes later a nurse arrived and led me to another part of the hospital where I exchanged my clothes for white robes. From there a nursing sister escorted me to an unmarked ward where the door was locked behind me.

The ward was large, gloomy, and silent. Like some children's game, all the inmates froze to their allocated site. I felt their eyes inspecting me. The room smelt of sweat and urine.

A tall man with a scraggy beard sauntered over, speaking nonsense. He carried a stick with a handkerchief tied to it like a flag. "You don't have permission to breathe unless the commander says so,'' he informed me.

"All right,'' I told him.

Everyone began to speak simultaneously, shrieking and shouting, pointing at me. One young man pranced around on his haunches making animal noises and deliberately knocking into others in his way.

My hand reached out for the door but it was locked. I sat on the bed nearest the door and was immediately swooped on by an inmate who crossed the room on all fours mimicking the noise of a car. He was extremely upset so I apologised for sitting on his bed and moved closer to the window.

The bars on the window and the thick pane of glass, stained with dried food and vomit, contributed to the claustrophobic atmosphere.

Some of the inmates pointed accusingly at me and giggled. "So you are sending signals through the airwaves?" the man with the flag shrieked, although not aware of my crime.

"What do you mean?" I asked.

"Silence. Permission to speak must be granted before you can obey," he yelled, shoving me away from the window. He pointed to the far corner of the room and I passed through the rows of inmates uttering obscenities and gibberish.

As I prayed, concentrating on the person of Jesus, I intuitively felt constrained to check the window. Risking the wrath of the "Commander" by moving quietly to the nearest window. Somehow my action passed unnoticed.

I looked through the window which faced the front of the building and to my astonishment I saw Tanya peering up. Several hours had passed since my arrival. Obviously my secret note had been delivered. *Thank you my Jesus,* I whispered.

I waved, praying that she would see me before my movements inside the room were uncovered. Tanya stared. Then she waved. I could see her begin to cry. I felt my chest tightening and my throat dry up. A wave of helplessness washed over me, but only for a few seconds. I blew her a kiss.

I had to signal quickly. Telephone, I gesticulated to her. I knew that the prayers of friends and pressure from the West were formidable weapons. Nothing else would influence the KGB.

One of the guards at the gate hustled Tanya away, but her haunting image lingered with me, returning at times of great despair.

This was a particularly violent hospital where many innocent people were broken. There was sadism in the wards and I pitied the genuinely ill patients. Permission was required to use the toilet, which was filthy and overflowing.

Periodically inmates were removed from the ward and returned in a daze. Finally, it was my turn.

"Do you believe in God?" the lady doctor asked, surrounded by books and charts.

"How long do you plan to keep me in this prison?" I replied.

Unruffled, she continued in a calming voice, "Oh Valeri, it's difficult to say. Maybe one month, maybe three years, maybe twelve years. Maybe for ever." She smiled sweetly.

Before I could reply, the professor of psychology entered the room. The lady doctor excused herself and the professor, who I believed was a Jew, continued.

"What God do you believe in?" he asked.

"The God of Israel!" I replied.

"Oh that's interesting," he replied. "Speak to me, speak to me." God had found a way for me to talk with him.

After about half an hour of explaining Israel's significance in world history, the professor realised I was normal. "Oh my, what shall we do with you?" I felt the question was addressed to himself. Despite the influence of the KGB he wanted to help me.

I was to be injected with aminazin, a drug used in schizophrenia. "Minimum dose for this patient," the professor instructed.

Back in the ward I couldn't stand still. I moved from my bed to the floor to the toilet and back again. I realised that the aminazin was taking effect. I tried to pray but found my mind wandering.

Three years. Tanya would have left you. Twelve years. You'll never see Zhanna and Marina again.

I leapt out of bed. Got to get out of here. I hammered on the door unaware that I was screaming.

One of the inmates crept up behind me. I heard him giggle. "You'll never get away from here," he said rolling his eyes. "You're one of us now."

Restlessness kept me from eating and sleeping. Each evening

I was injected with aminazin. It was hard not losing control. I found myself repeating one word over and over. "Jesus! Jesus! Jesus!"

I met one man who had been a loyal communist. We were able to talk reasonably except when we had been drugged. "Why are you here?" he asked.

"Because of my Christian activity," I replied.

"You will be here a long time," he remarked sadly.

He had reported corruption within his factory and was detained on the order of his boss. The doctors had asked him, "Have you been busy at work?"

"Yes," the man had replied.

"Ah, then you must be tired. Are you tired?" the doctor enquired.

Unsure about the question, the man acknowledged that, if he had been busy, then logically, yes, he must be tired.

The doctor then told him, "Since you're tired, by your own admission, I advise you to have a rest here in the hospital."

Unknown to me, the BBC had broadcast news of my arrest. Tanya also protested but was told, "Your husband's views on religion differ so much from those of ordinary citizens that he needs psychiatric treatment."

After six harrowing days the injections were stopped. The next day I was interviewed for an hour by the hospital's Senior Medical Officer in the presence of the Jewish professor, who said nothing. After realising I was quite sane, the questions began to deal with political issues.

"Valeri, Ronald Reagan is a Christian. Yes? Then why does he increase American nuclear weapons?"

"But we have increased our own nuclear arsenal; it's not just the Americans," I responded.

The Jewish professor escorted me back to the ward in silence. On the way we walked through a short corridor. All the doors were closed. We were alone. In a hushed voice he whispered, "Don't speak about politics." His finger was

left
Valeri's mother, Margarette Barinov, in 1955.

below
Aunt Tamara in 1967.

below left
Orphanage days, Valeri in front aged 11.

left
Tanya aged 17.

below left
The wedding day, December 1968.

below
A new Christian and just discharged from the army.

ght
anya with daughters Zhanna
nd Marina in 1973.

elow
home in Leningrad with
anthera, 1982.

ottom panel
983: final moments together
efore Valeri's arrest.

left and below left
Reunion:
shortly after
Valeri's release
in 1986.

left
"Let me preach the Gospel through my music or let me go."

below
January 1987: outside the KGB headquarters in Leningrad where Valeri was held prisoner.

above
Triumphant
arrival at
Heathrow,
November 22nd
1987.

above right
Press
conference on
arrival, with
Danny Smith
and David
Alton, M.P.

right
December
1987: The
Barinovs
celebrate wi
Sheila Wals
and Cliff
Richard at
Cobham
Christian
Fellowship.

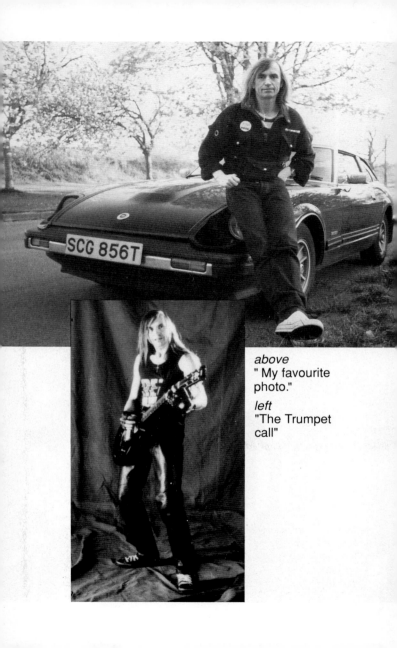

above
" My favourite photo."

left
"The Trumpet call"

raised up to his mouth and he re-assumed the role of custodian.

I understood by his gesture that he wanted to help me, and I thanked God that even in this terrible place he could make people perform his will.

The next day I was summoned to continue the interview. Once again, the professor took notes in silence.

"Ah yes, Valeri, tell us whether you think Russia or America is the military bully?"

"Each side thinks an increase in weapons is justified," I replied. "But you know, I am not interested in the arguments of politicians. I have no interest in politics because I am a Christian. This is my life. The Bible teaches that we can only find peace with God through Jesus Christ. That's the message I want to share throughout this world."

A few more questions followed, and this time a nurse escorted me back to the ward. That day passed peacefully with no more injections or interrogations. I remained in prayer and stayed quietly on my bed. Whenever one of the inmates came to taunt me, God enabled me to endure it.

The following day I awoke early but remained in bed. Today was October 20th. Zhanna's birthday! She would be fourteen years old. How I longed to hug her. My teenage daughter was almost a lady. I felt that my heart would break.

I prayed that Jesus would demonstrate his power. *You can do anything, Lord. Let me be united with my daughter today.*

The day passed slowly. Every hour seemed a torment.

"Barinov!"

I jerked up to see one of the nurses beckoning me. "Come with me and bring your belongings."

I replied calmly even though my heart had begun to race. I wanted to charge out of hospital in my medical gown and run all the way home.

There were forms and signatures but everything was a blur. *Thank you my Jesus!* My heart was singing.

I was out!

I found I couldn't walk slowly. I was jogging down the street. I could think of only one thing. To hug Tanya and Marina and my birthday girl, Zhanna.

And then the moment finally came. When they saw me everyone was amazed. Tanya dropped the plate she was holding and it smashed on the floor but no one seemed to notice. My cousin Valya was at home helping the family, and she shrieked with joy, "Valeri!"

"I love each of you with all my heart," I said as we all hugged in a tearful embrace. *"Thank you Jesus for returning me to my family."*

13

MIDNIGHT RIDER:
October 1983—March 1984

The KGB weren't about to give up. Neither was I. If I compromised, my future would be peaceful, and the trials of the past ten days would be forgotten. I didn't choose to struggle with the KGB. I chose to follow Jesus. If the path of Jesus meant sacrifice, I was ready for death.

The same day I was released, Sergei Timokhin was warned that he would face criminal prosecution. The KGB were everywhere and we walked a tightrope.

Sergei told me that the Baptist Church had prayed for me while I was in the psychiatric hospital, and he himself had written a letter in my support. This was a great encouragement. When one part of the body suffers, the whole body suffers. I was greeted warmly at the church, even though the leadership didn't support me. Everyone knew they had witnessed a miracle.

"When are you going to play?" people asked continually. On November 11th we attempted another meeting at the Baptist Church. I couldn't believe it! Two hundred street people turned up, but the gates remained locked. I knew there was a clubroom on the building site where I now worked as a night watchman, so about eighty teenagers trailed after me and crammed into the hall.

Here in this illegal gathering the lost youth of Leningrad wanted to know Jesus, challenging the State's theft of God from people's hearts. Half an hour later, police and plain-clothes officers broke up the meeting and herded everyone into lorries which took us to the local police station where we were held for three hours.

Zhanna, aged fourteen, was among the group arrested, and along with Sergei Timokhin and myself, she was accused of being one of the ring leaders. I couldn't believe they would arrest someone so young. But she was a Barinov, and no exceptions would be made.

It took a week for the KGB to reach me. I was summoned to yet another psychiatric examination where I was aware that the doctors considered me "not completely well", but allowed me to leave after an hour's questioning.

When Zhanna's school teachers heard that she had been guilty of "disturbing the public order", I was asked to call and see them. I explained everything, including how Zhanna and Marina had been followed to school by the KGB. I don't know what the school authorities thought of me, but they were good people who were genuinely concerned for Zhanna's well-being. As I rose to leave, one teacher clasped my hand and said, "Have pity on your children".

I was moved when I heard these words but kept silent. My pity was for the teachers who didn't realise the Communist Party's greatest crime: the theft of God. Zhanna and Marina had chosen for themselves and found the truth.

During December a new rumour was circulating: that I was a drug trafficker. It was easy to recognise the fingerprints of the KGB. I knew many addicts and had shared the Gospel with them, but had never taken drugs myself. No one who knew me thought I had. Only the KGB's imagination could have stretched that far.

I didn't think there were any accusations to answer so I ignored the rumour. If the KGB wanted to arrest me, I knew the charges didn't matter. Instead, I concentrated on our mission to share the Gospel with Leningrad's drop outs. Our message was simple. Jesus has changed our lives, he can change yours!

Sergei and I spent the week up to Christmas praying and fasting for opportunities to play for young people. Many of our friends asked us when we would record a follow up to "The Trumpet Call". I already had ideas for other songs and albums and I longed for the day when I could work in freedom for Jesus' glory.

On January 30th, we received an ominous sign. A summons from the Leningrad Procuracy warned me that I must stop "spreading slanderous fabrications defaming the Soviet social and state system".

I could hear the footsteps of the KGB getting nearer.

I kissed Tanya for the last time. Zhanna and Marina stood beside us and I embraced them. "Never forget that I love you with all my heart", I whispered.

I had explained to my family that I was going "underground" in order to complete my next recording. The KGB had mapped out my future in Leningrad. I didn't need to be a prophet to read the signs.

I decided not to reveal everything to my family. We were crossing the danger line. If something should go wrong, my family would not be spared the demon of interrogation. If they knew nothing, they could reveal nothing.

Sergei and I had assembled our supplies in January and February: food, warm clothes, homemade skis, compasses and Finnish/English/Russian phrase books. We looked more like pirates than rock musicians.

I arrived early for the 6 p.m. rendezvous. We intended to take a train to Volkastra and change for the next section of our journey.

But Sergei was late.

I was on the verge of calling it off, when Sergei arrived, two hours later. Sensing danger, I asked Sergei, "Why are you so late? Were you followed?"

"No, I wasn't followed," Sergei assured me as we raced to catch a train. Sergei acted nervously and on the train we spotted suspicious characters in black leather jackets, standard uniform of the secret police.

From the map I had seen in Leningrad, Sofporog led to

the border and was inside the frontier zone. But I didn't know that the town leading to the frontier zone, Kestenga, was a closed town. Only those with special passes were allowed in.

When the local authorities realised that we didn't have the passes, we were denied access to the town. Some local people eyed us suspiciously. I was in no doubt that they would inform the police about our movements.

We prayed for guidance. I told Sergei, "I believe we should abandon our plans and return to Leningrad."

Sergei nodded, "I feel the same way. I think we should turn back."

We learnt that the next train was heading north to the border towards Murmansk and not back to Leningrad. We had eighty roubles allocated for our return tickets and we counted that out carefully.

The train was due in ten minutes and an immediate decision had to be taken. We would board the train and change for Leningrad at a station further up the line. We hit on Kynazhaya, a small town en route to Murmansk.

The Murmansk train rolled into Kynazhaya at 9 p.m. that night and we headed immediately for the ticket office. The clerk informed us that the next train to Leningrad would leave at 5 a.m. "There's a waiting room you can use if you wish," he offered.

It had been a tiring journey, and we were exhausted. The waiting room was empty as we settled down for the night. We had brought bread, biscuits and a flask of milk. This had been the first chance that we had to eat anything. We maintained a discreet silence in case we were overheard. Now we only wanted one thing: to get back to Leningrad as soon as possible.

The railway benches were rough, and despite our ski jackets and woollen sweaters, I still felt the cold.

I must have dozed off. The next thing I recall was being woken by voices. I sat upright and was confronted by three militiamen towering over me. Sergei rubbed the sleep from his eyes.

"Papers!" one of the policemen said curtly. We complied.

"Where are you going?"

"Leningrad," I replied.

Our passports were handed back. As they turned to leave I overheard the remark, "It's not them."

Sergei and I exchanged glances. Had we been betrayed from the beginning?

A few minutes later, the militiamen returned. I sensed something was wrong. Once again they asked for our documents. This time there would be no mistake.

A police van was parked outside with its engine running. Sergei and I were hustled into the back and driven to the local police station at Zelenoborsk.

About two hours later, Yevgeny Katchkin, a KGB officer from Leningrad, arrived at the station. Katchkin was the KGB's main investigator into religious affairs.

I was puzzled. How could the KGB man arrive from Leningrad in such a short time? Were we followed from the time we left Leningrad? Had he been waiting somewhere down the line?

The next day, Sergei and I were moved to a special detention centre in Kandalska, the nearest big town to Kynazhaya, where we had been arrested.

My interrogation began almost as soon as I entered the jail. I was introduced to Mr Shelimov, a mild-mannered avuncular figure. He offered me tea and seemed sympathetic to my plight.

"Tell me the truth," he said, "and I will do everything I can to help you. Trust me."

"I will tell you the truth," I replied, deciding to take him at his word. "I wanted to travel to Finland to record some new songs and then return to our country with the tapes."

"And what would you have done with the tapes?" Mr Shelimov asked soothingly.

"I was going to give copies of my songs to the authorities to prove that I am not a political activist and that my songs are not anti-Soviet or political," I continued.

"Why do you write songs?" he asked. "What is your motivation?"

"I write songs to praise my Jesus," I replied. "The KGB have stopped me from continuing my work in Leningrad. I was driven out of the country. I didn't want to leave. After all, my family and friends are in Leningrad," I added. "I wasn't going to leave for ever. If the KGB gave me permission to sing about Jesus, I would never have tried to leave."

"But the police claim you were caught trying to escape," he mused.

"That's a lie," I stated emphatically. "We had planned to cross the border but changed our minds. We were arrested while waiting for a train to Leningrad and can prove it."

Mr Shelimov acted like a kind relative trying to resolve a family quarrel. He told me that twenty people had been caught at this border in the last few weeks trying to escape. "Write down all the details," he told me confidently and handed me some writing paper and a pen. "Would you like some more tea?"

"Yes, please, " I replied.

Mr Shelimov left the room and I settled down to record the events of the last few days. I was tired but tried to concentrate. I knew that exact dates and times were important, but what should I say?

When Mr Shelimov returned with the refreshing tea, I asked him, "Should I record the fact that I changed my mind about trying to get to Finland?"

Mr Shelimov smiled, "I don't think that's relevant. Anyway, you couldn't really prove that in a court of law." Then he added, "No, I think it's best to leave it out."

Without thinking, I agreed.

Mr Shelimov was skilful and I was weary and

disorientated. The document written and signed by my own hand was just the kind of evidence that the KGB were banking on. I had fallen for the oldest trick in the book . . . trusting my interrogator.

14

KGB HEADQUARTERS

The KGB were playing straight into my hands. At last I was going to have a rest! I needed time to recover from the breakneck speed of the last few years. Now I was being provided with free accommodation in Murmansk prison. Food was also on offer. Stale bread, rotting vegetables, thin watery soup.

The jailors were vicious and the cells were dank and filthy. Sergei and I were held in separate cells and not permitted to communicate. Most of the prisoners were arrested on criminal charges.

One month after our arrest, Sergei and I were transferred back to Leningrad. The train had been designed specially to carry dangerous criminals in separate units. I heard movement behind me as I was hustled out of the carriage in Leningrad. It was Sergei. "Hello!" I said. I was nudged in the back with a gun indicating that I should remain quiet.

I could hear the sounds of other passengers on the platform as I marched straight ahead with my arms behind my back. Nine or ten armed guards lined the path leading to a police van. Crouching down on my haunches I held on to the side of the van as it pulled away sharply, siren wailing.

The vehicle's sudden halt signalled our arrival, hurling me across the floor of the van like a cushion tossed on to a sofa. The door opened and I took note of my surroundings. I was in the courtyard of an ochre-coloured building surrounded by a high wall. Six-storeys high, there were many rooms to choose from.

So this was it! The KGB's legendary headquarters on Voinov Street near the Neva River.

I was led into a room at the entrance and told to undress as my documents and clothes were checked and then returned. While under investigation we didn't wear prison uniform.

"I want to contact my wife," I told the guard, but this request was refused. Every time I saw a jailor, I asked them, "Please tell my family I'm in prison."

Wherever I looked, I could see corridors and cells on either side. A red carpet ran along the corridor and no one could hear our footsteps. I could hear voices from some cells, but others were strangely quiet.

We stopped outside cell number 274 on the sixth floor. The jailor unlocked the door and it opened wide, slamming shut behind me.

The KGB headquarters was to be my home for the next eight months. Compared to the other prisons, conditions here were like paradise. Only the most dangerous criminals were held in Voinov Street for investigation, and it was rarely full or crowded. I was moved frequently and kept for intermittent periods on each floor of the jail.

I was alone in cell 192 for several days. Prison legend has it that Lenin was also imprisoned in this room, an interesting twist in my history. How good it was to be alone with Jesus, I thought.

Each cell had two beds, sometimes with mattresses, a wash basin and a toilet. The window seemed designed to prevent light from entering the cell. A naked light bulb dangling from the middle of the ceiling was lit twenty-four hours a day, leaving me with a nagging ache in my eyes. I found that the light damaged my eyesight permanently.

About one month after the arrest, I had a vivid dream. Katchkin, my investigator, tussled with a red dog. I always interpreted dogs as friends, and surmised that the dog represented Tanya. I deduced that both of them had established contact. Months later, I learned that my dream had been correct.

The first evidence Tanya had of our arrest was on April 3rd when the KGB raided Sergei's home and mine. They stayed for eight hours, confiscating all Christian literature, and also personal letters and photographs. Katchkin told Tanya that the search was part of an investigation linked to our criminal case.

"What criminal case?" Tanya asked, shocked.

My wife was then informed that we were to be charged with illegally crossing the border at Murmansk. Over the next week, Tanya and her mother were called for questioning, as were Sergei's wife, Nina, and some of his in-laws.

I was called for the first of several interviews with Captain Katchkin. He was expecting me and I observed that my file was already open on his desk.

"Barinov," he said, looking up at me. I couldn't tell what he was thinking. His expression wasn't giving anything away.

"When will I be allowed to see my wife?" I asked.

"I'm the one asking the questions," he said matter-of-factly. He examined some papers in my file and asked me if I wanted to confess.

I looked at him in surprise. "Confess? But what shall I confess? I'm an innocent man. What am I guilty of?"

"You were caught trying to escape," he replied.

"But I was arrested on my way back home to Leningrad. Where could I have escaped to?" I answered. "Anyway, Leningrad is closer to the border than Kynazhaya, where I was arrested."

"I'm not here to debate the issue with you. It's been decided that you will be charged with trying to escape and I'll find the evidence to convict you. Bet on it! We'll put you in prison and throw away the key!" Katchkin paused waiting for a response.

"I want to contact my wife," I replied calmly.

Katchkin stared at me. "Don't you understand what I'm saying to you? You will be forced to serve many years in prison."

I smiled. "The only person I serve is Jesus!"

The encounter lasted fifteen minutes or so. He pressed a buzzer on his desk and a guard escorted me back to the cells. I was frequently warned that I would be imprisoned for many years and that my children would be married women when I was released.

It was unusual for prisoners to be beaten in the KGB headquarters. They usually relied on skilful psychological tactics to break you.

I was taken to a different cell and held with a company manager who had been caught smuggling things out of the country. Mr Vanou was in his fifties and had obviously enjoyed the good life. His suit was finely tailored and his nails were well manicured.

"I just wanted to make a lemon!" he said with a chuckle. "Lemon" rhymed with million and was a colloquial expression. He didn't consider himself guilty, his only regret was getting caught. Although he was a communist, he hated the government. "You can't do anything without bribing people all along the line," he would say. "It's a government without law. If they steal and cheat, why shouldn't I?"

On reflection, I could trace the hand of God in this placement. Through his experience I was able to gain insight into how to get along in prison. During the three days I shared his cell he told me, "Don't trust the investigators. They'll tell you anything to get you to sign a confession."

On April 18th, I started a fast and wrote an appeal to Captain Starkov, the chief of the prison, requesting permission to see Tanya, pointing out that I was falsely arrested. When the breakfast bowl arrived that morning, I refused it and asked for my message to be handed to the KGB chief.

Around 10 a.m. that morning, I was marched down to Starkov's office. He was a short stout man who took his work seriously. His eyes twinkled as he fiddled with the appeal I had written. "Why are you starting this hunger strike?" he asked.

He looked directly at me to ensure that I understood what he was about to say. "I must warn you that it is prison policy to force-feed you on the third day of your hunger strike. Now do you understand why this is a stupid course of action?"

I nodded and was immediately on my way back to the cells, this time in isolation on the third floor. The KGB chief thought I was on hunger strike, but I was fasting to God, building up my prayer muscles for the battle ahead.

I knew the risks in challenging the power of the dreaded KGB. But I bowed to a greater authority.

Three days passed, and then a fourth. On the fifth day there was a rattle of keys in the lock. Finally the moment arrived.

I was force-fed once a day by two KGB men and a doctor. The violence of the operation was the real torment. The doctor never checked my blood pressure or any after-effects of the force-feeding. Sometimes I could imagine him saying, "It's routine work, nothing special. Someone has to do it."

Within a few days I was suffering badly. As the doctor prepared to leave, I collapsed on the bed, breathing heavily. "Stop this hunger strike or you'll die," he snarled, devoid of concern.

Somehow I managed to continue for twenty-three days. Although the force-feeding was unbearable, God blessed me during that time. I was kept in isolation as part of the tactics to break me down, but this worked in my favour. I was never alone; I was with Jesus! This renewal gave me the strength I needed each day to face the torturers. I never resisted them, but told myself that Jesus' suffering was much greater.

Day by day I could feel my heart becoming weaker, and I was frequently out of breath. Even the KGB officers were a little nervous and the doctor was ordered to examine me. He prescribed glucose as nourishment.

I felt a pain in my heart. What would happen if I died from a heart attack? I feared that Tanya would never know the truth. She would be told that I had suffered a heart attack and died.

The next day when Katchkin asked to see me, I informed him that I was ready to end my fast. He reacted with surprise and relief. It would create an uproar if anyone died in prison. No, they would rather return you home to die.

Starkov stared at me long and hard. Finally he spoke. "Have you been in contact with Sergei Timokhin?"

"No," I replied. It was the truth.

"Then why does he begin a hunger strike on the same day that you are ending yours?" he enquired, his irritation tinged with curiosity. To the KGB chief this turn of events took on the appearance of an orchestrated conspiracy, and yet we had not been in contact. I was amused at God's unique timing.

Later I learned that Sergei had held out for five days, but when the snake tube was inserted into his nose, he decided to end the hunger strike.

After three weeks without food, I found that I could not eat a vast amount. We were fed three times a day, usually soup and bread, sometimes potatoes, occasionally fish and chicken, and on rare occasions, butter. The KGB headquarters knew how to look after its inmates.

The soup was cold and the bread stale, but I knew that God would use even these crumbs to nourish my body.

The KGB routine permitted one hour of exercise in the courtyard each day. A huge concrete grid occupied the inner courtyard, separated into twenty or so units. The cage was locked, and for an hour I stretched and jogged and jumped, covering every inch of the eight square metres.

I loved it when it rained. The mesh that sealed the roof allowed the water to pour into the cage. I stood with my hands raised to heaven thanking God for the raindrops, a reminder that some things never change.

I could hear the sound of trolley buses, the squeal of car brakes. Outside these walls life went on.

Once again I was moved to a different cell, and this time I had a cellmate. He introduced himself as Karl Ivashin from Riga. We shook hands formally as though we were meeting at some society function.

Karl was my height, aged about twenty-eight. He paced the cell, smoking nervously. He had been a documentary film maker and had made several trips abroad shooting footage for broadcast inside the Soviet Union.

"What kind of documentaries did you make?" I asked, interested to gain insight into the secretive world of Soviet television which was not known for its investigative research.

"We filmed negative things in the West like strikes and demonstrations," Karl informed me. "Things which endorsed the government's propaganda programme."

"If people knew what the West was really like there would be a revolution," he chuckled, "so we just feed the lie."

Karl had been caught smuggling pornographic videos back into Riga. "Someone squealed," he said sadly. "Do you know how much you could make with an American porno film?"

"I haven't researched that subject very much," I admitted.

Karl leaned back and a low whistle accompanied his hand as it shot up to the ceiling indicating an astronomically high price.

At that moment the hatch opened and we were offered a copy of *Pravda*. Every few days newspapers were on loan. Karl flicked through and read a news item about the forthcoming American elections. Angela Davis, a black American radical and member of the Black Panther group, was running for President.

Pravda emphasised her left-wing socialist views and suggested that Ms Davis' election was a certainty. All she would have to do was turn up on the night.

Karl believed it. "So America will have a woman President," he observed. "With Angela Davis as President, maybe the United States will finally stop threatening us with the atom bomb.''

"There are several months before the election, Karl," I reminded him.

Karl looked surprised that I should question *Pravda's* opinion. "But *Pravda* has stated that she will be president!"

"Look Karl, in America people can choose, and they will not choose a socialist for President," I asserted. "Anyway, if Angela Davis knew what socialism was really like, then she herself would reject socialism."

With time on our hands, we discussed many things. "Tell me about yourself." Karl listened intently as I told him about the hunger strike.

"What will you do now?" he asked.

"I will fight them," I replied. Karl looked up with a start. "Prayer is my weapon," I declared with a grin.

"I think the best thing you can do is go on television and confess your guilt, even if you don't mean it."

I felt myself tense, but didn't let my suspicion show. I looked across at Karl. He was puffing on his cigarette, apparently giving the matter grave consideration. I decided to call his bluff.

"That's interesting," I said with mock seriousness. "Tell me why you think that would be good."

"Well, if you are in prison for a long time, think about the hardships for your family. Your daughters will be married, your wife would have left you, you wouldn't have any friends. You'll be an old man."

All his reasons were the same as those given by the KGB. I suspected that the KGB had put us together in order to convince me to confess. From that moment on I had to be on my guard when talking to Karl.

A curious incident confirmed my suspicions. It started with a dream I had about selling a bass guitar. When I awoke, I understood that Sergei Timokhin had been broken by his interrogators.

Shortly after this dream, Karl returned from an

interrogation looking agitated. "Sergei is finished," he declared. "He has signed a confession."

Then Karl began to laugh, "I think he has made the right decision. It's the best thing you can do." Karl wore his disguise well, but now I knew he was a conspirator.

Perhaps Sergei had succumbed at a low point to someone like Karl? This spurred me to pray for him.

In the next few days I was summoned by a new interrogator. He seemed friendly. Sifting through the papers on his table, he picked out a single sheet. Almost mournfully, he began, "Sergei has confessed his guilt, perhaps you know?"

I looked him straight in the eye. "What is the weather like now on the Black Sea? Good for a holiday?"

Taken by surprise, he answered, "Good, good, I'm sure."

"Have there been many mushrooms in the forest this year?" I questioned him. He stared blankly at me. I continued, "I haven't been in the forest this year. Neither have I been fishing. I did want to go, but I had to change my plans at the last moment."

The KGB man got the message. He leaned forward and said, "So Valeri, I think Sergei has taken a step in the right direction. It would be best for you to do the same. If you don't, you'll be in prison until your hair falls out. I'm serious!"

"Is that all? Call the guard, I'm ready to return." I spoke politely, but stared at the wall behind him.

Back in the cell, Karl paced up and down. "What happened?" he snapped.

"Nothing happened," I replied, casually.

It was evident that Karl was disturbed, and he began to berate me scornfully. "Jesus can't save you, you fool. Why, he couldn't even save himself. Your only hope is to confess on TV. If not, you'll never see freedom again." Then he cursed blasphemously.

"I'm in freedom now because Jesus changed my life," I replied.

Karl began to giggle, and assuming the posture of a preacher, began to wave his arms about. "Repent, repent," he cried. "Jesus is dead, you fool, don't you know?"

I lost control. The events of the last few hours had left me at breaking point. "If you say one more word, I'll kill you." The words had shot out of my mouth before I knew it. But Karl was laughing, "Jesus, save me! Save me!" Then he saw the glint in my eye and realised that he had crossed the line of acceptability.

I slammed my fists against the steel door, rattling the bolts and yelling for the guard. "Take one of us away! I don't know what I'll do to him!"

The guard opened the door and evaluated the scene. Realising that I was deadly serious, he signalled that I should prepare to move. Karl appeared disappointed rather than angry. Hoping to have gained some special favour through his influence over me, my refusal to confess had left him helpless.

Sleepless nights followed. If I did confess, I would see Zhanna and Marina, if I did confess, I would hold Tanya in my arms, if I did confess, I could walk the street of Leningrad again . . .

15

SHOOTING OUT THE STARS

"Thursday!" the guard announced, rattling the cell door. That meant showers. They were always too hot or freezing cold, but as I stood under the spray, I prayed that the doubts that nagged me about a confession would be washed away. I knew that the benefits of "confessing" were a bitter-sweet illusion created by the KGB.

"God bless you!" I said to the guard as he escorted me to yet another new cell. The greeting was received with a stare, devoid of emotion.

I have a cellmate, and we shake hands. Vasily, or "Vassa" has an open face and a tender heart, and we become friends. Vassa had worked on the railway, and had been caught smuggling jeans into the country through the Czecho-slovakian border. "Everyone does it, so why should I be singled out for punishment?" he complained bitterly. He believed that since only his load had been discovered, an informer had betrayed him.

When Vassa learned that I was a Christian, he admitted that he believed in a "power", speculating whether fortune-tellers or astrologers really could read the future.

Vassa and I spent the afternoon discussing the energy forces that could have brought the universe together. While we talked, I prayed for him, realising that we had been put together for a reason.

Vasily's openness made it easy to turn the conversation towards the existence of God.

Vasily paced the cell. "How can I believe in God?" he asked.

"Do you want to feel God's energy?" I urged him on to the threshold of faith.

"Yes," he said, startled by the question.

Vasily and I stood in the middle of the cell facing each other. The bulb overhead created dancing shadows across the contours of our faces.

"Give me your hand. Open your palm." Vassa obeyed the command, standing before me with his hands outstretched and his palms lifted towards heaven. "Now close your eyes."

I moved my fingertips lightly across his hand, stroking the air, but not touching his flesh. Then, as the tips of our fingers touched lightly, I experienced a wave of power, like a tiny jolt of electricity. "Do you feel that?" I asked him softly.

"Yes," Vassa replied, his eyes flickering almost in disbelief. "I feel it."

"That's the power of God," I explained. "Believe in him and he will change your life."

"When I pray," I continued, "you will feel this same energy."

Vassa was curious. "What is it?"

"It's God's Spirit inside me," I explained. "Prayer is not a repetition of words or actions but enables us to communicate with God."

With his hands still outstretched, Vassa opened his eyes. "Valeri, I want God's Spirit in me." His words sounded childlike, but sincere. Tears welled up in his eyes, evidence that God's Spirit was already at work in his heart. Trembling, he whispered, "Will you pray for me?"

"Lord, reveal yourself to Vassa," I prayed.

He began to rock back and forth. "Valeri, what shall I do? I feel something in my heart but I don't know what it is."

"That's Jesus!" I cried, almost laughing with joy. We knelt together on the cold floor and Vassa prayed a faltering, humble prayer to God.

The prison cell gained the atmosphere of a sanctuary as God's Spirit visited the altar of our hearts with a physical presence so real that I thought I could reach out and touch the hand of God.

Vassa and I were cellmates and brothers in Christ. We shared cells together several times, and each time it was a renewal of celebration. Our physical circumstances could not hinder or diminish our inner joy.

One night after this, I was woken by Vassa. "Valeri, I just had a strange experience," he said. "I was lying in bed but couldn't sleep. You know, the light kept me awake. I found I was dreaming, but I wasn't asleep. It was a vision in which I saw you clearly."

"It was winter, very cold, snow on the ground, and I saw an aircraft on an airport runway. You walked to the plane and you waved to a crowd of people who had gathered. And then the plane was streaking through the sky, flying through the clouds."

Without waiting for my comments, Vassa said, "It's so strange, but I know within myself that you will definitely leave us and go to the West. I know this for a fact," Vassa asserted.

"Thank you Vassa," I replied. "That's a message from God for me."

"I've never known anything like it," Vassa said, and still a little confused, lay down and fell asleep.

I was now the one who couldn't sleep as I tried to unravel the thread. Could this mean that I would be whisked to the West from my own prison cell? I believed this with total conviction. But when would it happen? The minutes turned to hours, and before long I was aware of the dawn's early light desperately trying to break through the barricaded window.

Instead of the journey I was prepared for, I was summoned to a psychiatric hospital. From the grapevine I knew that conditions in hospital were considerably better than prison, and inmates were always conspiring to be sent there.

Under the supervision of armed guards, I jogged into the courtyard with my arms behind my back. Judging by the time gap before the van set off, I was not the only inmate being moved to the hospital.

Twisting and turning through Leningrad streets, the vehicle pulled up at Kresty Prison and extra prisoners boarded the van. It was going to be a full load.

When we reached the psychiatric hospital, I recognised Alex, a young fascist I had met briefly in prison.

Although we were carefully guarded and our contact was limited, there was a delay in registering the prisoners at the hospital foyer, providing Alex and me with a stolen moment together.

"Hi Valeri, how are you?" Alex whispered as we waited for the staff to sort out the blunder. Apparently Kresty Prison had sent an extra prisoner, and the guards did not want to wait while the hospital staff decided what to do. If the choice had been put to us we could have cleared things up easily. But no one was asking our opinion.

The psychiatric investigation took a month. Compared to the KGB prison, it was like a holiday camp. I was detained in a ward with ten others, only some of whom really were mentally disturbed.

One night I had a dream in which I saw a fire raging in the distance. When I awoke and considered the implications, I wondered if this meant that Tanya had been able to reach the West with news of my imprisonment.

I prayed and asked for confirmation that I had interpreted the dream correctly. Tell me something today. Give me a sign.

That day the doctor said to me, "Did you get any letters from the West?" He looked at me with a smile, but I could tell that he understood everything.

Katchkin and the other investigators had tried to break me by insisting that no one cared. Now this hint came as an answer to prayer and was confirmation that people knew about me.

Alex was moved into our ward after two weeks. He was eighteen, very intelligent and a keen student of chemistry. As a neo-fascist, Alex was interested in European politics and believed that a new order would purge the country of the communist mafiosi who oppressed and corrupted our land.

We were joined in the ward by a dark-haired youth with round spectacles. Alex and he had shared a cell sometime in the past. Gregory was also a committed fascist who hated his mother because she had married his father, who was a despised communist.

When I spoke about Jesus, they listened intently. Gregory found the idea of forgiveness unacceptable, and although Alex endorsed the concept as a form of release and purification, he could not declare his allegiance to the formality of religion.

"But I'm not a religious person," I argued, which took them both by surprise. "I don't believe in religion, but the freedom that Jesus gives. I'm talking about a way of life, not an institutionalised dogma."

One night, I awoke to hear Alex calling to me from his bed, which lay next to mine. He had been troubled with stomach pains and could not sleep. In obvious discomfort, he croaked, "Pray for me, Valeri."

I agreed, and then he added, "I want to check your energy. To see if God really can do anything for me."

"It's God's energy, not mine. If you want me to pray for you, I will, but there's no magic in my prayers," I said quietly. "But you pray sincerely to God and discover the truth."

Around us, everyone slept as I knelt beside the bed. The next morning Alex found that his pains had vanished. He didn't know how to explain it, and a small flicker of faith burned in his heart.

The daily investigations were all a game, and I played along. It was on a Wednesday that an orderly escorted me to the hospital reception. I wondered if I was going to be taken directly to the airport? Would Tanya be there?

And then I saw the familiar blue of the KGB officers'

uniform, and the van awaiting me. No tearful reunion with Tanya. No holding hands with Zhanna and Marina. No Leningrad airport. No midnight flight to freedom. No sound of the trumpet call. Not this time.

Once again I am hustled up the steps into the reception of the KGB prison on Voinov Street. My records are checked. Yes, I am Valeri Barinov. Yes, we did play rock and roll. Yes, I am a Christian. No, no, it's a mistake, I wasn't trying to escape. Why, Leningrad is nearer the border than the place where I was arrested. Sorry, I wasn't trying to argue, I was just pointing out . . . Yes, I will remain silent and only answer those questions that are asked me . . .

And then, back up the stairway in solemn procession with the guard, the familiar red carpet, the rattle of the door, the cell with dim light and dirty mattress, the smell of the toilet, and the hole in the wall which could so easily have been a window, now barred, sealed, closed.

But I feel no sense of despair or anxiety. A peacefulness beyond explanation falls like a cloak around my shoulders. With a twinge of sadness, I imagine my family huddled together on the sofa in our apartment.

Jesus, you alone are worthy of this sacrifice. What a privilege you give me to sound a trumpet call about your holy name. You know my loneliness and pain. I trust you, my Jesus, and I commit my body into your hands.

I feel a physical presence surround me like a wave and lift my heart in praise to God. The shadows in the cell are transformed into dancing rays of sunlight. I forget myself and prance around the room, praising God.

Over the next few weeks the KGB moved me frequently. My investigation must have been coming to a head because Katchkin summoned me for interrogation almost daily. I learned to judge the moods, realising that his attitude and response were merely tactics in the overall strategy to break me.

Katchkin himself had his orders. Who played in The

Trumpet Call band? How did we record the music? Where was the equipment hidden? Did we have a list of people who had copies of the cassette?

During interrogations I was able to examine the documents as I stood in front of Katchkin's desk. It astounded me to learn that the police had questioned over one hundred people in many different cities and villages all across the Soviet Union. It was a costly and time-consuming exercise. In all, it totalled thousands of pages, and was bound in four separate volumes.

And then I saw it! A secret order issued from the high command of the KGB:

> The Christian rock group The Trumpet Call must be banned. None of this music must be allowed to spread in our country. This group must be destroyed and the operation kept secret.

As I skimmed the page, committing every line to memory, it became clear that I was considered an enemy of the State. Someone who spread dangerous ideas.

Katchkin regularly quizzed me about the recording of "The Trumpet Call". I feigned ignorance, reminding him that it had been a long time ago.

"How could you have forgotten?" Katchkin said disbelievingly. "This is your recording, isn't it?" he demanded, holding up the cassette.

Pretending to call upon hidden memory banks, I peered closely at the tape as though I had never seen it before. In exasperation, Katchkin produced a tape recorder. "Perhaps this will refresh your memory," he growled.

As the opening refrain of "The Trumpet Call" filled the investigation room, my heart was bursting with joy at the unexpected privilege of being given a personal audience here in prison.

But outwardly my face was masked in mystery, occasionally shaking my head in puzzlement. Katchkin glared back at me, confused by my lack of memory. He began to tap the table top in time with the music, but stopped himself.

Katchkin wised up to my scheme. The next time I suggested that playing the music might refresh my memory, he just scowled.

One day towards the end of September, Katchkin sat me down with him at the wooden desk. Unusually, the table in front of him was bare. No notebook and pen, not even my familiar brown file.

"Do you want some tea?" he asked, "or maybe coffee?"

"Coffee, please," I answered. "Thank you." We could have been colleagues at an office, meeting to discuss business.

"Valeri, today no investigation," he said matter-of-factly. "I wanted to talk to you directly, man to man."

I smiled in response. Now he appeared friendly, no longer the intimidating investigator.

"Valeri, I saw your wife recently," he said sympathetically. "She's having a very hard time without you and wants you home. Your daughters are very pretty, aren't they? Very clever girls," he said with a chuckle. "They miss you, you know that, don't you?"

My smile froze on my cheeks. I felt my throat dry up and gripped the arms of my chair tightly. He spoke slowly to drive each point home. His remarks were like darts hitting the bull's-eye. "Your family need you with them."

"But you know my situation," I answered, trying to sound normal. "What can I do?"

Katchkin smiled. "It's very easy. I will help you," he said, speaking calmly. "Confess!" the word sounded soothing and comforting. "Tell us everything you know."

"But I told you everything," I replied.

Katchkin teased, "You know what I mean. Tell me, how did you record "The Trumpet Call"? Who were your accomplices?"

"Why do you ask me about the recording? You arrested me because I was trying to escape. Let's talk about that!"

Recognising that this would not provide a winner, Katchkin concluded, "So, Valeri, consider carefully what we talked about today. If you want to sign a confession, call me at any time. Just ask one of the guards to contact me."

After this interrogation I shared a cell with Vassa once again, to our surprise and delight. Vassa had many questions about the faith. Was the Virgin birth a fairy story? What about Noah's ark? Did Jesus really rise from the dead?

Vassa was also curious about such issues as baptism, and I explained that it symbolised our new life with Jesus. On the third day of our detention together, Vassa asked me to baptise him. I was amused by God's humour. Here, in the very heart of enemy territory, the secret agents of mercy were at work.

We spent the day in prayer and fasting. Not wishing to alert the attention of the guards, we kept the food that was served in one of the prison bowls. The other bowl was held in preparation for the baptism.

Vassa knew the risks. If we were caught both of us would have been punished severely. We knew that no hour was safe, as the guards checked us throughout the day and night. As we prayed I had the conviction that the baptism should be carried out at dawn the next morning.

Before dawn I heard Vassa moving around in our cell. I was awake in an instant, and could sense a genuine excitement in his eyes. He looked fresh and young. Vassa told me that one of the guards had checked about ten minutes earlier. Soon the morning bell would sound and the guards would be rattling the door. This was the time to conduct the baptism.

Vassa sat on his bed with his shirt around his shoulders. I sat opposite and reminded him that I didn't practise any special brand of magic. He was entering the presence of God, and this should remain his strength and fortress. Then we prayed together.

As we were praying, the window of our cell door was unlatched and a face appeared at the hole. Not suspecting anything, the face disappeared and the hatch was slammed shut.

"This is the moment!" I declared.

I picked up the tin bowl full of water and Vassa tossed his shirt on to the bed. We stood in silence and then prayed quickly over the water.

Vassa leaned over the bowl maintaining an attitude of prayer. I looked at Vassa and said, "Vassa, I baptise you because of your faith in God . . . in Jesus' name!" I poured the bowl of water over his head.

I swiftly picked up the towel, and handed it to Vassa. He dried himself in short, rapid movements and sat on the bed again.

Once again we sat facing each other. Bread and water stood on a table beside us.

"Now it's time for communion," I said. In an extraordinary way, it was like a celebration.

"Thank you Valeri," Vassa said, his eyes brimming with tears of emotion.

"Don't thank me," I replied, "thank God!"

The experience had an anointing that was unprecedented. Basking in the joy of God's presence, we were brought back to earth with the familiar sound of the cell window being unlatched.

"Still in there?" the guard asked with a smirk.

"Where can we go?" I answered with a smile. But surprisingly, it didn't feel at all like captivity.

16

"MY CRIME IS I'M A CHRISTIAN"

"Swashbucklers of Rock and Roll" appeared in
Komsomolskaya Pravda on September 16th, 1983. The
author of the article, Y. Filinov, charged the rock medium
with subversive influences and identified Seva
Novgorodtsev, the DJ, as a renegade. Seva was a legend
among young people throughout the country. He had
emigrated from the Soviet Union in 1977, and worked for
the BBC's Russian Service broadcasting jazz and rock back
into the USSR. Mr Filinov also charged that our band was
unpopular and played badly:

> Seva Novgorodtsev, absolutely overcome, is making out
> that this dreadful work ("The Trumpet Call") with its
> wretched text is the greatest achievement in the field of
> music. Well what of it? Pay someone for lying, and he'll
> deliver the goods.

The publication of the article could not harm Seva
Novgorodtsev. He lived in London. It could, however,
influence my trial. It was quite customary for slanderous
articles vilifying political and religious dissidents to appear
in the Soviet press before their court appearances. Filinov's
article was the strongest indication that my trial was
imminent.

I used the time to maintain my physical discipline. I tried
to keep my weary body alert with push-ups, skipping, jogging around my cell imagining I was hurtling across the park.

One day as I walked down to the exercise yard, I caught a glimpse of someone from the labour camps who was held on our floor. He was dressed in black trousers with his name and zone number marked on his jacket. He was a "tenner", that meant ten years of hard labour, and was looked upon as a hero. Dark tales of the indescribable evil of camp life trailed along the prison network.

A sense of dread and foreboding came over me. But what of the vision and the silver bird soaring through the sky? The crowd waving farewell at the airport? Would I be spared the ordeal of labour camp?

My trial was scheduled to begin on November 23rd, 1983. A few days before, I was moved to a cell on the third floor. As I entered the cell, I barely managed to contain my joy. It was Vassa!

Vassa told me that he had been convicted of smuggling and sentenced to eight years. I quizzed him about the transfer from police van to court-room. That night I prayed, wondering if it would be possible to escape.

I wanted to send a message to friends in the West but my eyes were weak, so Vassa willingly detailed the false evidence prepared against me on a scrap of paper three inches by one. The miniature document was magnificent, but I had two immediate problems: smuggling it out of prison and getting it to Tanya or someone else who could publish the news.

Despite the pressure, there was a glint of sunlight. Vassa and I were not split up but remained cellmates until my trial. The night before, we prayed together and once again experienced the presence of God's Spirit. I felt like a gladiator waiting to be called into the arena.

But I was not afraid! I had spiritual weapons that could withstand the assaults of the enemy. Like a fighter in the ring I pranced around the room shadow-boxing. "I'll beat this devil!" I yelled as I lashed the air, striking a mortal blow at an imaginary enemy.

Vassa collapsed in laughter as I swung round and felled

an assailant who crept up behind me with expert karate strokes. "Take that, you communist devil!"

Vassa's eyes signalled behind me. A face peered at us through the hatch in the door. Undeterred, I stepped up the assault against the powers of the air. This duel of death required total concentration, but a glance at the door confirmed that my game had caused great mirth in the corridor. Now a new face appeared as another guard suppressed a chuckle.

November 23rd was a chilly morning. I awoke early and committed myself into the hands of God.

The shoelaces of my Adidas trainers had been confiscated in case they were used as a noose. I had made laces from a narrow strip of cloth, and this had been permitted. I hid the secret note inside the lace cloth and tied a tight knot at the top of the running shoes.

"Valeri, how is it?" Vassa asked me. I gave him the thumbs up.

Without informing the authorities, who would use it as a pretext to delay my trial, I resumed my fast. The struggle was not with flesh and blood, but against principalities and powers.

At 8 a.m. I was summoned to the investigation room and ordered to strip in order to check that I was not smuggling anything out of prison. I threw my jeans casually over my running shoes. The guard appeared easy going, but his examination was thorough. I was asked to rinse my mouth out to ensure that nothing was lodged in my throat.

Then the guard checked my clothes. I remained impassive as he picked up my shoes. He checked the heel carefully, and then the inside.

The shoes landed on the floor with a thud. "Get dressed," he said.

The officer waited for me to dress and then escorted me to a lorry-type vehicle parked near the prison gates. The gates were open, but six armed-guards stood watching me.

Two vicious dogs strained at their leashes. I loved dogs, but didn't wish to tangle with this pair.

Could I escape? There was only one way. Roll under the lorry and dash twenty yards to the gates. Would they really shoot me in the back?

I gave up the plan and climbed into the long narrow compartment. In the cage next to me I heard shuffling. It was Sergei Timokhin. We had a few moments before the guards climbed on board.

"Sergei," I whispered, "why did you sign a confession? It's a trick. They won't let you out." I tried to imagine Sergei's face. He must have faced terrific pressure.

The front doors opened. One more question. "Sergei, did you tell them about the studio and the band?"

"No!" he called back.

"Stop talking!" the guard yelled, slamming the bars with his pistol.

As we drove to the courtroom, siren blaring, I tried to imagine what a small boy, pointing to the police van, might ask his father, and how his father would answer?

Our trial was held in the Central Courthouse of the Leningrad Procuracy, a huge building in a busy street. Hands behind my back, I was hurried at gunpoint into the building. Inside, people were milling everywhere, and I was led like a dog on a leash through swing doors and corridors. Keys unlocked a padded cell and I was ushered in.

A slim man with brown hair sat looking forlorn on a bench by a window. Few introductions were required.

"Murder," he said.

"Christian," I replied. Noticing the impact of my words on him, I enquired further. "Is it over?"

"Yes." At that moment my escort arrived. "God bless you," I said quickly.

I saw his eyes widen. To some it was just a phrase obscured by constant usage, but this doomed man received it like a letter from home. "Thank you," he replied.

Indicating his displeasure, the guard grabbed my shirt and

pushed me into the hallway. Television cables marked our path to the court-room, where our arrival was filmed under bright spotlights.

I heard several people call out my name. I tried to acknowledge the familiar faces with a smile.

And suddenly, there was my Tanya. She looked so frail and weak although her blazing red hair and tender green eyes were just as I remembered her. She looked worried and on the verge of tears, but waved bravely. I longed to leap over the partition and sweep her into my arms like a knight in shining armour. She'd soon realise that everything would be fine.

Sometime later, I learned that Tanya hadn't been told in which court-room my trial was to be held. She had seen the cable of the TV crew and followed it to where the "Barinov trial" was performing.

Here she found the seats filled with KGB agents, preventing her, or any of our friends, from attending. When Tanya threatened to phone the West to complain, she and some of my supporters were allowed in.

As the proceedings began I sat in the dock wondering how I was going to get the secret note to Tanya. I assumed a comfortable position with my leg up on a wooden panel in front of me, and cautiously removed the note and bunched it up in my fist.

When the court was adjourned for lunch, I was ordered to follow the guards out of the court. As I passed the rows of spectators, I casually flicked the pellet across at Tanya in a mischievous gesture.

The reaction was astounding. I heard someone scream, "Over here!" Everyone followed the missile's flight as though a million roubles had been tossed into their midst. KGB agents scrambled across the floor. I saw Tanya looking for it.

"It's here! It's here!" someone called out.

Agents swooped on a middle-aged woman and emptied the contents of her handbag on to the floor. But the note wasn't there.

"Here it is! I have it!" One of the agents held it up, and passed it to the Procurator. He squinted and frowned at the tiny message. Addressing me, he enquired, "What's written on this piece of paper?"

"It's a message for the West so that everyone will know that this trial has been fixed," I declared boldly.

The judge glared at me. "No! No! You're not permitted to send such messages to the West," and with that he confiscated the note and included it with the accompanying documentation in my case.

During the three days of my trial, witnesses were called who had clearly been coached in their evidence by the KGB.

One witness, a cellmate from Murmansk, claimed that I had asked him to draw a map of the border and mark the best escape route. Such evidence could hardly prove my guilt. At the time we were imprisoned in the local jail!

Another witness whom I barely recognised, admitted that he was a psychiatric patient. His evidence was garbled and confused, and most people pitied him.

The next witness was a hardened criminal with whom I had shared a cell. During his obviously rehearsed testimony it emerged that he had signed a KGB statement without reading it. At hearing this, the judge appeared perplexed, and questioned why he had not read it first.

"You see sir," the convict began, "if they want to get you, they will. I was told to sign it and I did. It's just the KGB way." At this, the judge called a halt and he was hustled away.

Katchkin was called upon to give evidence, and as he spoke about our arrest at the border, I challenged him. "How did you get there so quickly? Did you fly?" I asked.

Katchkin glared insolently at me as the judge reprimanded me, "Don't point your finger at the witness."

Finally it was Tanya's turn. "Tell us about your husband, Mrs Barinova," the prosecuting attorney began.

With a trembling voice, Tanya replied, "I know that if

everyone in our country was like my husband, this would be true communism."

With each of Tanya's answers, it became clear that the case against me was slipping through their fingers. Abruptly, she was told to be quiet and dismissed from their proceedings.

My friend Sergei Timokhin sat in court looking haggard and despondent. Under intense psychological pressure he had agreed to appear in a televised confession. It was a sad moment as he faced the cameras disconsolately and admitted his mistakes and misunderstandings of the constitution and religious law. Sergei claimed that the capitalist system had manipulated him.

I could imagine the KGB investigator convincing Sergei that this was the best way, the only way. But it was a trick.

On the final day, Sergei Timokhin and I were commanded to stand as our sentences were announced. Sergei was visibly shaken when the judge sentenced him to serve two years in a labour camp.

For daring to sound a trumpet call declaring that "Jesus is coming!" I was not surprised to be awarded two and a half years in camp.

Tanya was in tears when she heard the severity of the sentence. The judge asked if I had any last words to say to the court? In a short speech I declared the true reason for my arrest and imprisonment, "My crime is I'm a Christian!" It was all that I could say. But I knew I would be given another moment for the final word.

As I walked from the court-house, Tanya and our friends flocked around me. Even as I climbed into the police van to return to the KGB prison I could hear their cries ringing in my ears.

Our case had become a cause célèbre, and eventually it hit the newspapers. On November 27th, 1984, *Leningradskaya Pravda* published an article which stated:

Even in his school years, Barinov was beyond the control of relatives and teachers alike. It was his aunt who, in the hopes of saving his lost soul, advised him to turn to God. To her surprise, he seized upon this idea.

Of course, he didn't really believe. He learnt to use the name of the Almighty as a cover for anything. Barinov remained true to himself, and at the trial he stubbornly maintained the story he had thought up: voluntary abandonment of commission of the crime.

A day earlier, an official Tass bulletin had published a similar report under the title "Leningrad Trial of Renegades".

I decided to end my second fast on 6th December. It was a curious date. It was my fortieth birthday, I had been imprisoned for forty weeks, and I had been on hunger-strike for a total of forty days. Somehow I was able to draw strength and encouragement from this knowledge.

The hatch of the cell was drawn back, and a guard called out, "Get ready, you're going to have a meeting." I was led out, down through an underground labyrinth of corridors that left me disorientated and into an investigation cell.

Satisfied that I wasn't smuggling any contraband, I was led into another room. As the door opened, I could see Tanya sitting behind a glass panel. All I could see was her face and chest. Beside her were Zhanna and Marina, both craning their necks to catch a better glimpse of me.

Tanya was weeping helplessly, and the sobs racked her body. The girls held her tightly, their eyes never leaving my face.

I placed my hands over my lips and transferred a kiss on to the glass partition. Instantly, hands reached out to own the kiss. For a second it seemed that we were actually touching.

"Have any friends in the West been helping you?" I asked Tanya.

"Nothing," she replied sadly.

On looking closer, I noticed that the girls were both dressed in old clothes. My heart sank.

"Show daddy your shoes," Tanya said. The girls leaned back and somehow raised their feet to the level of the window. The soles had been worn through, and the freezing weather had arrived. "Even coming here today has caused them discomfort," Tanya said, wiping away the tears.

"Don't cry, Tanya," I said softly. "God will lead us away from here and we'll be together."

Tanya stared back at me and said, "How do you know?"

"A vision from God has confirmed this," I replied.

"A vision or a fantasy?" Tanya called back.

If she doubted God's abiding affection for us, I wanted to encourage her. I went on to explain that a cellmate who had become a Christian had a dream that I would be released and would leave the country with my family and travel to the West.

"I don't know when this will happen," I concluded, "I only know one thing: trust Jesus. Everything else will fail. Jesus is our only security."

We talked about Zhanna and Marina, and details of family life. "Panthera misses you, Dad," Zhanna said.

At either side of the panel, KGB guards recorded our pitiful conversation in notebooks. When Tanya began to ask questions about my last six months inside "the big house", the guards called out, "Stop talking about prison, it's not allowed."

After about an hour, we were informed that the meeting was over. The guard on my right sat impassively observing the tearful scene. Turning to him, I pleaded, "Can I kiss my children?"

"No," he replied firmly, "It isn't permitted."

"Please!" I implored him.

"No!"

"Tanya, don't weep for me. You know that Jesus is my

judge and I stand here as an innocent man. Why should we fear these earthly powers?''

Still sobbing, Tanya raised her hand in a futile embrace. Zhanna and Marina stood with their arms round their mother. I could tell that despite their sorrow, they were proud that daddy had remained strong and unbowed.

At the door I turned to wave at the faces at the glass. Hands waved back, smiles amidst tears were the final memories that I carried back to the cells with me.

The next hour was hardest. Images hurtled through my mind of the girls clutching Mama's hand on the cold journey home. My heart was aching for Tanya and my girls. The road was hard and darkness seemed to be all around, but there was no turning back.

Jesus, I need your strength to withstand this torture.

Alone in my cell, I celebrated Christmas. I knew that Christians all over the world would be celebrating as families united together to mark the birth of the Prince of Peace. Yet here I was, separated from my beloved wife and children.

As I prayed, I experienced the compassionate presence of God's Spirit encompass me.

My time at the KGB's "big house" was nearing its end and I was allowed one final meeting with Tanya, Zhanna and Marina before leaving Leningrad for the labour camp.

Although we were happy to be together, the meeting was tinged with sadness, as we realised that this was to be our final hour together for at least two years.

I prayed for each one in turn and prayed that God's presence would become a daily reality.

Zhanna and Marina tried to cheer me up by telling amusing stories, and we talked about the day that we brought Panthera home from the market.

It was an unusual meeting and lasted longer than the allotted time. Goodbye seemed such an inadequate word. Lord, I prayed, how I long to hold these loved ones in my arms for one last time.

But the meeting was over. Tanya, Zhanna and Marina rose together and left. At the same time, the guard accompanied me out of the visiting area. Mysteriously, we met together as we waited for the connecting door to be opened.

But the door didn't open. I don't know what caused the delay, but I just looked across at my wife and daughters who stood a few feet away.

Suddenly, Marina left Tanya's side and flung her arms around me and kissed me. Marina had barely reached me when Zhanna followed.

The guard was too stunned to react. The last time that we had met, the KGB guard had forbidden such contact, but we had prayed and God had intervened, giving us one final embrace.

I clutched Zhanna and Marina close to me, kissed them tenderly and whispered a blessing in their ears.

In a few seconds it was over. The door was unlocked, the guard had moved me away, and the girls had returned to Tanya's side, their eyes twinkling with merriment. The memory of that moment would never leave my consciousness.

But Tanya's tears began to flow, bringing us back to the reality of the tension that we lived in. Zhanna and Marina tried to console her as I was led back into the belly of the dragon.

PART III

ANOTHER COUNTRY

17

EASTER SURPRISE: 1985–1986

After a three-day train journey in a prison carriage full of filth and rubbish, I was taken out at a town called Vologdar. Once again, I was given an armed escort, once again my papers were checked carefully in case I was an imposter. Imagine someone desperately wanting to break into the prison network of the Soviet State. The height of black comedy, I mused.

I was held for a month in the local jail which had been built to house twenty prisoners, but was occupied by nearer fifty. The KGB prison seemed like paradise compared to this hole. The fleas leapt visibly between the two bunk beds which were supposed to accommodate four or five people.

In early March we were shunted like cattle in the freezing cold to the labour camp itself. A sign at the main gates stated:

We hope your stay here will be beneficial as we work together to build communism on earth.

We had arrived on another planet. Even the air smelt different, a dry, stale, rancid stench that was all around us. The camp was situated on a murky, infectious swamp in the Komi region, one of the Soviet Union's autonomous republics well-known for its labour camps and slave-labour gangs.

Two thousand inmates occupied the cramped facilities

designed for eight hundred prisoners. A wall topped with barbed wire encircled the settlement, punctuated by searchlights and watchtowers thirty metres high.

Our first three days were spent in the quarantine area. There were five new prisoners with me from Vologdar prison, and about forty-five more joined us. Some were deserters from Afghanistan, young boys who didn't want to fight.

Keys rattled and the huge frame of a guard filled the room. He introduced himself with a mocking grin, hands on hips. "I'm Captain Zhora, you're not going to forget me!" he barked. With that, he lashed out at a man to his left. Taken by surprise, the man fell backward, blood pouring from his mouth. Gasps could be heard around the room.

Zhora appeared amused. Everyone shrank back from him as he strutted across the room, launching into an obscene tirade of orders and commands designed to terrify the new recruits. "Are you listening to me?" he yelled in the face of one nervous-looking man. "What did I say?"

Before the man could reply, Zhora's clenched fist crashed down on his head. Zhora was infuriated that the man crumpled at his feet. His boots dug into the fallen man's body as he lay helpless on the floor.

No one knew what to say. Our words had been frozen. "Now maybe you'll pay attention to me." The front line ducked out of the way as he swung his fists. A wicked gleam appeared in Zhora's eyes. "I want you all to get on to the top bunk bed!" he commanded, picking up a wooden broom stick that leaned against one of the walls.

Now, pinned against the far wall, we wondered how we could fulfil such an impossible and insane demand. Who would be sacrificed to quench this guard's thirst for sadistic pleasure?

It was then that I understood why this camp had been nicknamed "Bloody Special". We would spill our blood here at the hands of torturers and the legend of the camp would live on. Zhora had been our first introduction to life at Labour Camp No. 27. Nothing would change. We were, after all, in another country.

I sensed that the KGB had sent some secret communication about me to the camp administration and to Lobanov, the deputy commandant. "KGB Prison," I heard one official remark to another as my file and credentials were checked.

Zinchenko, the camp commandant, was sympathetic towards me, but he didn't want to tangle with the KGB. "Musician," he said, checking some of my papers. "Rock band The Trumpet Call," he smiled.

"Now you will trumpet here."

There were twelve groups in the camp and the leaders were represented at this meeting to assign newcomers to their section. "Who will take him?" Zinchenko asked. No one wanted to assume responsibility for me. Even in this pit, fear of the KGB sent them scrambling for cover.

Finally I was assigned to "Group Twelve" in one of the two wooden barracks situated to the west of the camp and ordered to remove my clothes. The replacements were tatty, torn, and ill-fitting.

A vicious caste-system operated in camp, governed by cruelty and violence. Group Twelve was made up of the highest, most brutal category. As tough, ruthless criminals, the "Stealers" were mostly serving life-sentences for murder and their commands were enforced.

For the "Traitors", or informers, betrayal was a way of survival bringing meagre rewards, favours or food. The "Workers" carried out most of the menial chores and duties. The lowest, most despised caste were the "Homosexuals" who were merely there to be abused. It was common camp policy to punish inmates by moving them from one class to another.

"I'm Barinov, from Leningrad," I called out. Someone looked up, but no one acknowledged my greeting. At the end of the hall I spotted an empty bed with a ripped, filthy mattress, wrecked with fleas and other insects. I threw a tatty blanket over it and staked my claim.

The camp was about one hundred metres wide, by two hundred metres long, stretching from our barracks on the west over to the brick dining hall on the east. Beyond that the punishment cells were sited in an enclosure sealed with barbed wire. Adjacent to the arrival zone, a two-storey administrative building led to the private quarters of the camp staff.

The first day passed uneventfully, although I knew I was being watched. At around dusk, we queued five in a row to eat a dismal meal of cabbage soup, eating in shifts in order to accommodate everyone.

The cabbage smelt rotten, and I struggled to swallow it. "Shall I help you?" asked my neighbour. I nodded, and in a flash he had emptied the contents of my bowl into his.

"First day?" he enquired.

"Yes," I replied. "How did you know?"

He grinned knowingly.

The "pahan" in our group noted that I had returned to the barrack and watched me closely. Pahans or "fathers" ran the work groups and each one was a long-term prisoner on a criminal charge.

I determined that from the outset I would serve only one authority. Jesus!

I introduced myself to the pahan as an innocent man imprisoned for my Christian activity. He seemed uninterested and instructed me that my duties in the barracks would consist of sweeping the room and cleaning the toilet. Behind him, the leaders of Group Twelve watched this exchange.

"I won't do that sort of work," I said politely but firmly.

It was clear that the trial of strength had begun. I couldn't back down. All I could do was pray . . .

One of the gang stood up and pushed me backwards,

almost toppling me off my feet. "Who do you think you are?" he said venomously.

"I don't really fit into any of these classifications. I'm not a worker. I believe in Jesus, I'm a preacher."

Everyone listened to me as though I had told them I had landed on a space ship from Mars.

Someone cursed, and I felt a sharp pain on the side of my head. I never saw the blows come as my side and back were hit, with boots as well as hands. I curled up on the floor and put my hands over my head.

The side of my head felt wet with something trickling down my face. It tasted salty. I grunted as the blows ripped into my body.

I prayed for strength to endure this trial.

Someone gripped my shoulders and hauled me on to my feet. There was a tearing sound and cold air tickled my left side. I heard one of the gang issue another warning. All the words seemed to be tangled.

"Thank you Jesus," I heard myself gasp in reply.

The contest had lasted about an hour and I faced the beating with a smile, answered every abusive salvo with a blessing. What could be done with this man of mystery? My body carried the marks, and my face had swollen up, scarred by the battering it had received.

The next evening, as we queued to enter the dining room Captain Verona, an officer in charge of personnel, eyed my bruises. He snapped his fingers and ordered me into one of the interrogation rooms. Assuming that I was seeking revenge and was therefore a prime candidate for the role of informer, he asked me, "Who did this to you?"

"No one did it. It was an accident," I replied.

The officer was infuriated and warned me that I would risk another beating if I didn't identify the culprit. He swung his baton perilously close to my head.

"I stumbled and fell," I insisted.

I had made a dangerous enemy, and I reached the service area to learn that the food for our rota had gone.

Back at the barracks, one of the workers carried a message. "Micky wants to see you." Another contest? I hauled my aching body over to the middle of the room, where everyone on the "inside" gathered. If you didn't belong, it was not the place to linger.

"You wanted to see me," I said, not knowing who to address.

One of the gang stood up and placed his hand on my shoulder. His grin showed teeth stained with nicotine. "You did well," he said, grateful that I had not informed on them, indicating that I had passed their initiation ritual.

"Are you really a preacher?" someone asked. "Yes," I replied, "it's true. I wouldn't lie to you."

I saw that my reply caused some dismay. "Valeri, if you want revenge, we can easily find you someone to beat up," another blurted out in earnest.

"Don't worry, as a Christian, I don't hold grudges."

I returned to my bunk and tried to sleep. Life was turning, and no one could predict the future. My life hung by a thread and I could be killed at any time. But I was certain of one thing. Only God determined whether I lived or died.

The next morning I was assigned to a work detail that was the envy of every inmate. We were permitted to venture out of the labour camp! Group Twelve regulated the rota of convicts sent by the camp administration to work in local forests.

I just couldn't believe it. Everything seemed so easy. The civilian driver dressed in brown overalls signalled to the guards and the automatic gate slid open.

Our task was to chop trees and saw planks of wood into manageable sizes to load onto the truck. It was hard work, but a welcome respite from camp life.

The next day I rode in the cabin and got chatting to the driver. To my surprise I learned that his brother was a Christian and he indicated that he could assist me in getting information and documents out of the camp.

"What are you whispering about?" Karl, one of the prisoners, asked.

Not wanting to compromise the driver, and aware that I could be betrayed, I replied, "I was asking our driver if he could bring a guitar for me so that I could play and sing for everyone in camp."

The driver didn't need any prompting. "That's right, I think I can get hold of a guitar. I'll let you know the next time I'm on duty."

Karl frowned suspiciously, but did not pursue the point.

Through contact with the friendly driver I was able to secure an amazing coup. His brother passed me a carefully wrapped parcel which I slipped into my parka, and tucked into the crotch of my trousers. It was a delicate balancing act.

Miraculously, I was ushered back into the camp with a cursory search from the guards at the gate. In the barrack I surreptitiously unwrapped the treasure. Five special Easter cakes, and so many Easter eggs! I counted the eggs. Seventeen!

Easter was celebrated in homes throughout our land by exchanging specially baked Easter cakes and hand-painted eggs.

I couldn't sit still. "Hallelujah! Praise Jesus!" I cried out. But the barracks weren't empty. "What's going on?" someone called out. "What's happening?"

"It's just the Christian," someone else replied. "He's a little crazy."

The distraction passed unnoticed. Despite random searches by the guards and persistent pilfering by the prisoners, my booty remained intact.

One day after breakfast, I spotted three of the leaders of Group Twelve smoking by the side of the barracks. Piotr, Boris and Sergei were among the toughest men I had ever met. Undeterred, I strode forward. "Did you know that today is Easter Sunday?" I asked with a grin.

The trio were dumbfounded. None of them expected to be questioned by a lowly convict. "Is this a joke?" Piotr snapped.

I beckoned them to my bunk and unveiled my trophies. The religious symbolism of the Easter eggs and cakes evoked precious memories of childhood in the country, memories of another time, another place, when things were strangely different and innocently simple.

In stunned silence these tough, hardened criminals gazed at the treasure laid out before them.

"But it's impossible," Piotr spluttered. "How . . . how did you get all this?"

"Jesus is risen!" I declared confidently. "Jesus makes the impossible happen."

"I just can't believe it," Piotr repeated, mystified. "I wish my grandmother was alive so I could tell her. She was a believer, you know."

"Take one," I said cheerfully.

"Come over to my bed," Boris invited. It was an honour to be included in this inner sanctum where the leaders met. Boris reached behind his pillow and produced a bottle of homemade alcohol. This clearly called for a celebratory drink.

If God had led me to this group it was for a purpose, I decided, and that was to preach Jesus.

Quickly I told my story. They stared at me listening intently to every word I said. The bottle passed from hand to hand, the cakes and eggs were munched.

"When the KGB began to persecute me," I concluded, "the devil whispered in my ear, 'It's the end for you,' but I was not afraid because God told me, 'He is risen!' Everything is possible because Jesus is risen!"

While we were talking, one of the convicts had crept towards Boris' bed. With a scowl, Boris raised his fist and the convict slunk away. When I suggested that the eggs be shared among the others in our barracks, Boris asserted that they should be shared with the other gang leaders.

Incredibly, these leaders enabled me to gain access to several key figures in the camp underworld. As their ambassador, I was ushered in bearing Easter gifts and repeating my message.

Vlasenko lay on the ground behind the barracks, a torn blanket covering his crumpled form. A number had been attached to his foot and soon he would be dumped unceremoniously in the camp graveyard, essentially a hole in the ground.

A rag had been stuffed into his mouth to stifle the screams, and he had slashes all over his body as well as a gaping wound in his back. Surely someone must have seen or heard the assault? No one was talking. Rumour had it that Vlasenko had been selling information about Armenian brandy that had been smuggled into the camp.

Betrayal was in the very air we breathed. It wasn't safe to turn around. Even asking innocent questions could prove risky.

The technical group was run by a civilian who visited the camp each day. It attracted carpenters, electricians, painters, teachers; not that you had to be skilled in any of these trades. Rather, it enabled you to stay out of the killing zone. Everyone kept to themselves and got on with the work in hand.

It was here that I met Yura Taikov, a kindly old prisoner with a thick beard and a twinkle in his eye. Yura became my mentor and confidant, and was a good man to know. He was extremely shrewd in picking up on camp gossip and usually knew what deal was being struck and consequently whom to avoid.

Yura had been a mountain climber and kept me enthralled with some of his yarns. He told me that climbing was a tremendous way of maintaining concentration, but paradoxically was also good for relaxing. "I'll take you with me one day, Valeri, and teach you to climb," Yura kept telling me.

"Promises! Promises!" I teased. "When are you going to do it?"

Immediately after Easter, I had an exceptionally violent dream. In the final scene, my clothes were ripped and my body was covered with wounds. But I had been victorious and the enemy lay slain at my feet.

Intuitively I knew that the warfare was spiritual and concerned an attempt by Tanya to visit me. From the dream, I understood that in spite of this "attack" we would meet.

That morning I received a message ordering me to report to the administration block. A blond young man with shining eyes sat behind a desk piled high with papers. From his clothes, I saw that he was a prisoner too.

"I've got a surprise for you," he smiled sympathetically. "It's your wife," he explained. "She's come to visit you."

"When can I see her?" I enquired, a smile spreading across my face.

"Right now," he replied. "I need to write out a pass for you. Can you wait a few minutes?"

I nodded vigorously. Yes, I had time, lots of time.

The man's name was Vadim. I prayed silently for him as I waited. He told me that Tanya had been in camp for two days, appealing for permission to see me. Although she had initially been refused, the officials had finally taken pity on her. The dream's interpretation had been correct.

Vadim handed me a document authorising a twenty-four-hour visit with my wife. "Take this to the duty officer at the gate," he explained. I accepted the paper gratefully as if it was a cheque for a million roubles.

Near the front gates there were rooms set aside for prisoners to meet their families, but visits were handled like rewards and punishments. Sometimes inmates would be told that their wives and children had arrived at the camp but they wouldn't be permitted to see them. This mental anguish could break your heart.

During my imprisonment, Tanya made the two thousand

km journey six times, but I only saw her twice. The other times she returned home desolate and depressed without even a glimpse of her beloved.

I took Vadim's paper to the gate, where I was given my civilian clothes so that the fleas, bugs and lice would not be exported to civilisation. A body search completed the preparations, and I was escorted by an armed-guard to the reception area.

Her red hair looked wild and uncombed, her clothes were crumpled and slept in, most unusual for Tanya. Head bowed, she sat nervously on the edge of her chair.

When she saw me, she sprang to her feet and rushed into my arms. Tears burst out and trickled down her cheeks. Gently, I led her across the wooden floor and down the hallway. We had room number two.

She clung to me like someone lost in a dense fog, as though she would be lost for ever if I disappeared. I understood that her distress was as great as any physical pain I had to endure. Her eyes were red, and she was clearly near exhaustion.

The room was spartan, but we weren't looking for luxuries. A cooking stove, sink, table, two chairs and a bed were somehow crammed inside.

"Why are you crying?" As the words slipped out of my mouth, they seemed absurd.

"You look so pale," Tanya replied, equally shocked. Then she caught sight of some bruises, the result of a beating. "What happened to you?" she asked.

I was in a quandary. "It's nothing," I muttered, "we don't get any vitamins in our food here."

"But can't you talk to the chiefs of the camp and ask for a different diet?" Tanya asked, with a puzzled look.

I nodded and agreed that I would do what I could. Tanya looked uncertain, but did not press the point.

There were a thousand things I wanted to ask about Zhanna and Marina and our Leningrad home. Tanya did her best to handle all the queries and then took charge.

She had brought me a parcel, but some things had been confiscated: two cartons of cigarettes, which were always good for cutting a deal. She hadn't resisted, but would gladly have turned over the entire contents of the parcel in exchange for a few minutes with me.

Tanya's small brown case was a veritable magician's trunk, and my eyes began to bulge. I had forgotten what eggs looked like, and I could have eaten the roll of sausages straight from the paper. Brown powder which filled the room with an intoxicating aroma. Coffee! I stared at the jar as though it contained precious jewels. There seemed no end to Tanya's box of delights: macaroni, an assortment of meats and chocolates.

Tanya is an exceptionally skilled cook, and soon she produced traditional Russian cabbage soup for the first course of our meal. I held the bowl and warmed my hands.

But I couldn't eat. After the camp diet my stomach had shrivelled and hardly matched my appetite. I don't know if Tanya completely understood, but she didn't interrogate me unduly.

Our hearts were overflowing with joy and appreciation for these precious few moments together, and as we thanked God for our food we didn't need many words to convey our feelings.

Tanya handed me a package. I carefully unwrapped the blue linen cloth, and there in my hands lay a copy of the New Testament. How had she managed to smuggle it into prison camp? Once again, God had done the impossible. As I clasped the book tenderly I felt a sense of power fill me. With this book, no force on earth could defeat me.

"Thank you Tanya, thank you," was all I could say. One of the drivers in the town could slip the Scriptures to me, as I would be searched thoroughly once I returned.

Tanya had taken two jobs, and the pressure was on. Sometimes the family went to bed with only tea to drink. Another disappointment was that some close friends in

Leningrad had received help on our behalf from concerned people in the West but this hadn't been passed on to our family. I was surprised. Why don't people pray and help? Aren't we one family? Weren't we all God's children?

"Don't put your faith in people, trust only in God," I counselled Tanya. I reached for the holy book, and flicking through its pages, I found the Psalm I wanted to share with Tanya. Clasping her hand, I began to read:

> I will lift up my eyes to the hills
> From whence shall my help come?
> My help comes from the Lord
> Who made heaven and earth . . .

In the stillness of the moment God's Spirit moved in our hearts. Outside our window we could hear the guards on night patrol calling to each other as their heavy boots tramped the ground. But their words seemed distant and strangely foreign.

We clung to each other that night discovering our love almost anew. I pulled the sheet over our bodies and our room breathed the peace of a sanctuary.

The sounds of camp life roused us from sleep. The pass ended at 2 p.m. and every moment of our time together seemed precious.

Tanya prepared breakfast in bed, with eggs and coffee.

"Don't expect the same back in Leningrad," she joked as she poured me another cup of coffee and we settled down to savour the hours that remained.

Tanya told me that she'd had some visitors from the West, including David Alton, a British Member of Parliament from Liverpool. I was glad to hear that we hadn't been forgotten.

But as Tanya paused to remember other details of the campaign for us in the West, the door to our room swung open. Not quite room service, I thought to myself.

"You've got two minutes to clear out," the young guard called, snapping his fingers.

Tanya spun round and looked at me in despair. "No, there must be some mistake," I said quietly. "My wife's permit ends at 2 p.m. this afternoon. It's only 9 o'clock now. We have five hours together."

He stared impassively at me. "I don't know anything about that."

"But it's true," Tanya pleaded.

But the guard was deaf to her cries. "Two minutes," he snapped. "If you're not out, I'll throw you out. Get it?"

I tried one last time. "But we have permission, it's legal."

"That was yesterday," he said curtly. "New rules today and I have my orders. Out!"

And so it was over. Tanya hurriedly packed her case and was shuffled unceremoniously down the corridor. A hand on my arm ensured that I didn't follow her. Craning our necks to be sure we didn't miss a single moment, our eyes alone were permitted one final embrace.

The torn and sweat-stained prison uniform was exchanged for my own clothes and immediately I began to itch. I was glad for this bizarre rule about changing clothes. Tanya had been spared this pathetic sight.

The snow seeped through holes in my prison boots, and the cold reached deep within, as though my bones rattled with each step I took. In this raging hour of madness I turned my face to the biting wind and followed the armed escort back to camp. In the grey sky, I saw Tanya's face, a haunting image frozen in time. Her face at the door in the closing moments of our encounter.

I tried to envisage the scene. How's Papa? How's Papa? my daughters cry. How does Tanya reply?

I can see her face. Weary from the long journey, she moves her lips. But her words are frozen . . .

I pray for Tanya, Zhanna and Marina. "I will lift up my eyes to the hills . . ." I whisper under my breath.

A rifle butt nudges me in the back and a grunt from the guard orders me to keep silence. The KGB doesn't even play by its own rules. They cheated us of five whole hours together, a move intended to devastate my morale. The enemy had encircled our encampment, but just being with Tanya was a victory in the battle.

The next morning, I awoke strangely elated, recalling the emotional power I had experienced when I held the holy scriptures in my hand. The New Testament was a dangerous book. With help from people outside eventually the scriptures were smuggled inside the camp.

In this pit of despair where every heart seemed to have lost hope, the word of God raised a match in the darkness. Life in the labour camp was intense spiritual warfare. Sometimes I was like a monk, praying every second, every moment, with every breath I took.

I wrote a letter to the Presidium of the Supreme Soviet appealing for an amnesty based on the fabrication of evidence and the false testimony of several witnesses. In addition, I managed secretly to obtain some of my trial documents as proof, and wrote a short message about conditions in the camp for Tanya to send to the West. I was running a risk.

I couldn't be certain, but I think it was Arkady, who played both sides of the street. I had been warned about him being a traitor, but when he asked me to read the "Shepherd Psalm" we struck up a friendship.

I heard someone call my name and looked up at the watchtower. The sentry told me to report immediately to the administration block.

Boris lurked by the door. He scratched his chin, and with his fist clenched, his thumb went down. "Someone's ratted on you," Boris rasped slyly, his lips hardly moving and his eyes looking in the opposite direction.

Was it Arkady? It hardly mattered, who could you trust?

Punishment cell! The words spelt dread and terror, but

they also had a sense of unreality about them. How much worse could it really get?

I followed the armed escort into yet another bizarre nightmare world of desperate men.

18

BLACK SNOW

There were no rules, and no one could be trusted. You could be betrayed by a cellmate for a crust of bread. A wrong turn, a word out of place, even a misunderstanding, and I would be dead. Jailors and guards would turn the other way as the jagged edge of a broken bottle lashed out. The walls were streaked with blood and the ground absorbed the tears. No one would know anything. The administration would inform my wife, "Prisoner Barinov is dead." That would be all.

In the ten-foot-square cell, five men eyed me suspiciously. "Hello," I grinned, attempting a wave.

My greeting was met with ominous silence. The cell was dark and dingy. The wooden floor felt damp, and water had collected in the corner by the window. The thick walls were lumpy, as though the cement had been slapped on at random, and filthy brown stains ran down the whitewashed surface. Every punishment cell bore the stains of its victims.

The stench in the cell came from the open toilet in the corner. Flies buzzed around, and the scratching of rats could be heard in the pipes. The drainage system was less than adequate, and frequently the toilet overflowed, turning the entire cell into a sewer.

The next few moments would seal my fate. It was easy to spot him. Obviously the boss of the cell, the others looked to him to exert his authority over the newcomer. He stared insolently at me, like a huge machine with greasy matted hair.

The machine sauntered over to me and dabbed me in the chest. "Who are you?" he said menacingly.

I knew there could be no compromise. If I was to die, it would be defending his name. "I'm a Christian!" I declared boldly, smiling, and extending my hand towards him.

Someone laughed mockingly, and the uncertainty of the moment left me hesitant. The machine glared at me. He was also unsettled by the amusement my words had caused. Perhaps he figured that he should be the one to decide what was acceptable for derision. Turning round, the machine lashed out with his fists at a convict who gasped for breath and flung himself against the wall imploringly.

Turning back, he towered over me. "Christian, eh?" he said, now a little quieter after his outburst. "Tell me about it. I'm intrigued." The tension in the air had eased and everyone began to relax.

"Thank you, Jesus!" I said aloud.

The machine stared at me. "You talk to Jesus? Are you crazy? Only madmen talk to imaginary people."

I grinned. "Jesus is alive. He's real. He protects me even here in this labour camp."

Calling for silence, the machine addressed the others in the cell. He commanded them to give me their undivided attention. "I've always wanted to meet a Christian," he said. He shunted the others off the bed and settled himself into a comfortable position, offering a space near the end to me. I declined, and he didn't move.

I had a captive audience!

Machine took a liking to me, and this ensured my safety. He was a killer who controlled the criminal network in camp, blind to his folly and not knowing any better. Yet I liked him and I sensed that his heart was tender, someone who God could reach.

We were fed three times a day, but the food looked like left-overs from someone else's plate. Machine would divide the bread and soup into three portions, insisting that he and

I take the first two, leaving the others to pick apart what was left.

I picked the white of the bread, leaving the crust for last. Now it formed a bowl. "I think I'll bake a pie tonight," I mumbled. Rolling my eyes, I pranced over to an imaginary larder plucking invisible vegetables from the shelf. The charade captured everyone's attention and I was goaded on to continue the performance.

"Potatoes!" I exclaimed. "Sausage!" I continued, dragging out the word, sniffing the air, as my audience groaned with appreciation.

"Salami!" The word sliced the air with a torment of things remembered.

"Salami?" I repeated with a mysterious air. "No, not salami again!" Machine slapped his thigh, amused by my game.

"Carrots?" I chewed on a sample with an expression that conveyed the delights of a raw carrot.

I ran through every vegetable that came to mind, gaining a rollicking response from my audience. The game went on too long, but in prison things got distorted and it was hard to think rationally.

My pie was ready to be consumed. "It smells delicious," I confided in the group and proceeded to devour it.

Although everyone in the camp behaved like wolves, when a prisoner was held in the punishment cells, his "family" would secretly send food and supplies to him. Machine had agreed to allow other prisoners to use his network to purchase food.

Everyone knew that one of the older guards, Boris, would do anything for the right price, and soon a deal was struck for cigarettes and a portion of the cognac. The risks of betrayal from the other guards were nevertheless high.

Machine worked on the base of one of the bars in our cell with a tin spoon during the afternoons when it was less likely that we would be disturbed.

To my surprise, once the bar was loosened, it could be

swung forward to reveal a huge hole. Now the big man proceeded to reconstruct the window ledge using beige prison soap to stick together the shavings of cement which had been painstakingly collected in a cloth.

It was an astonishing feat.

Next, Machine made a hiding place in the wall, which was about three feet thick. A nest was hollowed out to about half the thickness of the wall, and a cover formed for it. Once again, soap and water were used to stick larger pieces of cement together.

The cover was delicate, and once it was in place, we crept like ballet dancers to the other side of the room, hardly daring to breathe.

Gingerly tapping the cover after allowing it time to dry, we ascertained that it would not come tumbling down. Our nest was secure.

Two nights later when Old Boris was on duty there was a voice outside the window. "Hey! Number seven! Anyone awake in there?"

Everyone was awake, but no one dared stir, fearing a trap. Finally, Machine crouched by the window and whispered, "Snake, is that you?"

"Course it's me, who were you expecting, Leonid Brezhnev?"

Snake quickly negotiated the clandestine delivery. "Don't worry, you'll get your share," he called out to Machine.

Chocolates! Meat! Tea! Vodka! Armenian brandy! Everyone entered the tantalising conspiracy, and rouble notes were rolled up in a brown handkerchief and thrown out of the window, where a disembodied voice confirmed its safe arrival.

Now we had to wait. Rags were shredded into long strips and tied together to form a rope. A full day had now passed since the money had been tossed out of the window, and the tension was mounting. What if it turned out to be a shakedown?

Without warning, a piece of paper sailed through the

window and landed in a wet patch on the floor. "Tonight at two," it said.

It was possible that the message was designed to trap us. But sure enough that night there was a voice at the window.

"We need ten minutes to get ready," Machine said in a throaty whisper.

"OK, I've got two other deliveries to make. But if you're not ready in fifteen minutes, the deal's off."

Machine and I set to work on the bar, while the others sprang to remove the cover from the hole in the wall. We didn't have long to wait, and soon we heard movement outside. With that, we tossed our homemade rope up at the window. Perhaps it was nerves, but the rope didn't quite make it.

"What's happening in there?" Snake said, not attempting to disguise his annoyance.

Machine aimed more carefully, and this time it sailed through the window. A tug on the rope ensured that we were in business. "OK, haul her up," Snake instructed. A cloth packet appeared awkwardly at the opening and tumbled to the floor. Hands quickly ripped off the cloth. Tea!

With no time to dwell on the intoxicating aroma, it was bundled into the hole, in a sheet of *Pravda*. Snake worked away at the system, and the nest welcomed its clandestine treasure.

"Last one," the voice called. Machine tugged at the rope.

Perhaps it hadn't been securely fastened, or Machine had jerked it awkwardly, but without warning, the parcel span around the room, erupted in mid-air, and crashed to the floor. On this short but momentous journey through space, a torrent of black jets was unleashed.

A blizzard of tea! The entire cell was covered with a trillion flakes of tea! At first it was funny, but the darker side of the drama hit home. How could we explain it to the guards? Black snow?

The bar was repositioned, and the cover to the nest remoulded with soft soap paste, but what could we do about the tea? How much time did we have before the cell was hit, spelling disaster for everyone?

Machine's leadership was jolted by this turn of events. Suddenly he turned to me with a wild desperate look in his eyes. "Valeri, I want you to pray to your God for help!"

I didn't know what to do, but my heart transmitted an urgent telegram to heaven. "We must pick up every flake of tea," I replied.

"But that will take hours," Machine replied, "and the guards search us every few minutes."

Old Boris was due to finish his shift shortly, and the change of guards would mean someone would be here to check us any minute.

"If we truly seek God then he will help us!" I declared boldly.

Everyone followed Machine's lead. I had never seen the big man so contrite. I asked them all to kneel down on the ground with me as I prayed a simple prayer to God requesting his help. I ended by saying, "In Jesus' name!" To my surprise, everyone repeated the phrase and the name of Jesus echoed around the walls of the cell.

Then, armed with a piece of cloth, everyone began to pick up each single flake of tea. The tea was on the walls, even on the ceiling. Black flakes floated in the toilet water. As we worked quickly I prayed aloud, and soon my words were being repeated by Machine and the others. "Jesus, help us. Keep the guards away!"

I told them the Gospel story, acutely aware that my audience were probably hearing it for the first time. "Jesus is alive. He died at Golgotha but he rose again."

All at once we heard the familiar sound of footsteps in the hallway. Voices of guards and boot leather scraping. Everyone looked at me. I didn't need them to fill in a questionnaire to know how they were feeling.

Someone was at the door. The rattle of keys was indisputable. We froze. It was just hopeless. Scouring around the cell, it was clear that we had made an impact, but it wasn't enough. We needed a few more minutes. Machine gave a look of total despair.

"Just pray," I whispered, trying to sound calm.

At that moment the sounds outside the door stopped. Voices called out. The guard was summoned by an officer in the reception area. Machine's jaw dropped, and he looked disbelievingly at me. The others stared spellbound at the door.

"Quickly, let's get to work," I insisted. "We can do it!"

Living on borrowed time, we continued to pick up the tea leaves. My joints ached, and there were bouts of cramp. But we worked with new-found energy.

Finally, it was over. We combed every inch of the cell until we were sure that no tea remained. Exhausted by nervous tension as well as the task, we sank down.

"I've never known anything like it," Machine marvelled. The others agreed. "It's magic!"

"Not magic," I cut in. "But a God of miracles!"

Seconds later, there were keys in the lock and the door swung open. "Cell number seven!" a harsh voice barked, and one of the guards sauntered in.

The search was only a cursory look around, but the few minutes felt like an hour. As he passed the nest, our hearts missed a beat, but he didn't suspect anything. Instead it was merely continuing the prison tradition of harassment, intimidation and torment.

As the guard turned to leave, his gaze fell on Yevgeny, an inmate from Riga. "Why are you wearing two sweaters?" he snarled.

Taken aback by the question, Yevgeny stammered, "I'm . . . cold. It's damp in this cell . . . and I've been sick. I've got a . . . cold."

"Nonsense," the guard answered. "You can't wear two sweaters. Take one off now!"

Keen to avoid any confrontation, Yevgeny obeyed and handed over the dark brown woollen sweater. The guard took it from him and strolled out of the cell as casually as he had arrived.

As the door slammed shut, every one was dumbstruck. Eventually Machine broke the silence, "It's a miracle. I just can't believe it."

His words came from the very centre of his being, conveying heartfelt conviction. At a desperate moment he had turned to God for help, and to his surprise the stone wall of silence had disintegrated and in its place, he had stumbled into a freezone, the uncharted territory of faith.

Over the next few days Machine questioned me repeatedly about Jesus. Then one night he startled me. "Valeri, I'm going to heaven when I die."

"How do you know that?" I said, somewhat taken aback.

With a twinkle in his eye, Machine grunted, "Because I've lived in hell here on earth."

"Showers! Showers!" Old Boris yelled. Cell number seven joined the queue to the changing room at the end of the corridor, and then into the showers. There were three showers, and usually the water was cold, even in deep winter.

We were allowed ten to fifteen minutes to shower and wash our clothes. Then a few extra minutes were permitted for shaving. Razors lay in the sink and everyone shared the same blade. Communal lifestyles were very influential in the planning of the Revolution but this was carrying things a little too far.

You got used to seeing the homosexuals hang around the showers. The system decreed that they were just there to be used.

On the way back from the showers, Yevgeny spotted the guard who had confiscated his sweater. Something about him looked familiar, but he couldn't quite put his finger on what. And then he saw it. A patchwork sweater using yellow, red and two shades of brown. And one of these shades was quite unmistakable.

Yevgeny couldn't help but stare. The guard couldn't help but notice.

As he walked past, the guard lashed Yevgeny across the shoulders with his night stick. Taken by surprise, Yevgeny was knocked off balance and crashed heavily against the wall. Groaning in pain, he tried to rise and then stumbled again.

The guard moved closer, tapping his stick against his side. He was sure to use it again unless Yevgeny moved quickly.

The injustice of the episode and the brutality of the guard sickened me. The camp system wouldn't tolerate any interference, so I remained silent. I prayed that Yevgeny would find strength to rise quickly and that the guard would be restrained from launching another attack.

Just at that moment, Old Boris strolled along, alerted by the commotion. "What's going on?" he asked the guard. "Trouble?"

"Trouble," the guard confirmed. "But I'll handle it. He's being insolent, so I had to teach him a lesson."

No one said anything and Yevgeny shuffled forward, linking up with us as we returned to the cell.

But the incident was not to be buried. The next day the guard confiscated several inoffensive items from Yevgeny's belongings.

Yevgeny stood helplessly at his side. Ten minutes later, Yevgeny was taken for an interrogation, during which he was severely beaten. On the way back to the cells, Captain Zhora saw Yevgeny and asked what had happened. "He fell," the guard replied.

But Zhora wasn't a fool and quickly realised what had happened. Smiling, he said, "You've got to be really careful here. These cells are so slippery."

Back in the cell we tended Yevgeny's wounds. He was due for release in two days' time, having served the usual fifteen day term, but to his dismay he learned the following morning that he had been penalised for the recent "indiscipline".

An additional fifteen days!

Sentences could be extended at anyone's whim and we feared for Yevgeny's safety. Weakened by the prison diet, his spirits sank lower than ever. Yevgeny feared that the guards would kill him.

"Your only hope is getting to the hospital," Machine counselled. "And you know what that means." Yevgeny looked despondent but nodded his head, indicating that he understood the coded message.

That afternoon, Yevgeny told Machine, "I'm ready. Will you help me? Will you break my arm?" he added chillingly.

The brisk efficiency with which Machine went to work made it clear that this was not the first time that he had engineered such an operation. He soaked a towel in water, squeezed it dry, and wrapped it around Yevgeny's left arm. Already a loose floor board had been removed and lay on the bed.

One of the other prisoners stood on the end of the bed and peered through the window above the door. He gave Machine the thumbs up sign. Yevgeny was given a rag which he inserted in his mouth, and sat next to the bed.

Machine picked up the plank and placed it across Yevgeny's arm on the bed. Then he poised himself.

"Stop!" It was Yevgeny who broke the silence. Turning to me, he cried, "Valeri, if I don't get into hospital I am going to be killed. Will you pray that my arm is broken?"

It was a heart-rending appeal. I had seen the sadistic way the guard tortured our cellmate. I had to respond to the plea for help. I nodded my head and lifted my arms, inviting God to take charge of these desperate moments.

Crack! A light snapping sound. It reverberated through my body, rocketing around my brain.

Tears streamed down Yevgeny's face as his teeth pierced the rag in his mouth. A trickle of blood appeared where he must have bitten his lip. His whole body wriggled in anguish, thrashing from side to side.

The arm hung limply at his side. Sneaking a glance, Yevgeny whimpered in torment, "Ah! That's good! That's good!"

Swiftly the props were all replaced, and then Machine hammered on the prison door, yelling for the guards. Eventually someone arrived and the door was unlocked. Yevgeny lay crumpled on the floor, his broken hand twisted across his fallen frame.

"What happened?" the guard asked. "Anyone see what happened?"

"No one saw anything, unfortunately," Machine volunteered a reply for us all.

The guard bent down beside Yevgeny who squinted in pain. "What happened?"

Yevgeny groaned and chose his words carefully. "I fell," he said, adding, "These cells are so slippery."

Two days later the doctor arrived at our cell and confirmed the diagnosis. At last Yevgeny heard the word he longed for. "Hospital."

"Valeri, thank you for praying for me," Yevgeny said when the doctor had left. One hour later a prison orderly arrived to escort Yevgeny to the hospital. Yevgeny grinned at us. We had saved his life.

19

ZHORA THE TERRIBLE

I lay awake, unable to sleep. I kept thinking about Tanya and prayed for her. My thoughts drifted to my daughters Zhanna and Marina. I knew that in spite of the outlaw image that the government had imposed on me, my girls were proud of their dad.

The night played tricks with my mind. I closed my eyes and in the darkness vivid images danced in the prairie moonlight. Tall grasses blew gently in the breeze, the stars twinkled like diamonds on soft dark-blue velvet. She glided towards me, her smile as hypnotic as ever. Behind her were the sounds of children playing. The sound of a brook gently flowing into the stream.

I could hear her speak, but the words were vague and distant. I felt a weight pressing down on me as I lay on the ground.

Is it her?

I awoke with a start. For an instant I thought I could hear Tanya moving around in the other room. No. The punishment cell, the stench from the toilet. But I was aware of another noise, moving in short jerks across my body.

A rat!

Racing across my stomach and hurtling over my chest, aiming for the contours of my face, its squeal rang loudly in my ears.

With a start, my arm jerked forward, blocking the advance of the rat and knocking it off me. I leapt to my feet, and to my astonishment, two rats fell off me hitting the ground with a thud, yelping.

My hand fell to my side. The rats had gnawed their way through my pocket, nibbling on the bread I had saved from dinner. I removed the bread from my pocket and placed it on the window sill. I still heard the sound of rats scratching in the prison wall and had little confidence that they wouldn't mount another offensive before daybreak.

Moments later I was fast asleep and unaware of any intruders.

My fifteen days in the punishment cell was drawing to an end. Two days to go. The dank conditions and appalling food had drained my strength and left me debilitated.

The next day the cell door opened and the guard led a youth into the cell. Looking weary and exhausted, he had the appearance of someone with a major illness.

The prison rituals to which he would normally have been subjected were waived. Sergei was about eighteen years old, but prison had aged him. His skin was bruised, with eczema and bites, and like over half the prisoners in camp, he was suffering from tuberculosis.

Sergei should have been in hospital receiving treatment, but instead he was forced to maintain a rigorous work schedule. Unable to work, he fell behind the daily quota and found himself in the punishment zone. Machine undertook to help Sergei so that his food and safety were guaranteed.

In a curious way the degradation of the punishment cell had bound us together in an unspoken pact. I could never forget my cellmates or the excruciating moments we had shared.

Intuitively I knew that I would not escape further spells in the punishment cell. I would not seek this way through labour camp, but I could not ignore the inevitable.

In a few moments the guard would arrive to escort me out of here. From one hell to another. There was nothing to say. Machine looked at me and nodded. I smiled. Sergei was propped up against the wall staring into deep space. The others in the cell were silent, each meditating on their own thoughts.

Back in the camp nothing had changed. Nothing, except that during my stay in the punishment block four people had died and been dumped in holes in the ground marked with a numbered stick. One had hanged himself, another had been stabbed, someone else had died of malnutrition. The very air we breathed seemed to have been polluted with a sense of doom. It felt as though everyone had been alerted to some collective piece of bad news.

As always the first task of the day was to pick the fleas, lice and bugs off our clothes. All you really had to do was to stand up and jump around, and the trespassers fell in a heap on the ground. Ninety per cent of prisoners had lesions on their bodies from flea bites. Some of these had turned into septic open wounds, and blood trickled through the dirty rags used as makeshift bandages.

One cold rainy night we huddled close listening to the rain ricochet off the roof and drip into our barracks. As we heard the clatter of the food trolley even the prospect of soupy water seemed to offer us hope by its very warmth.

We should have known better.

"Hot soup on a cold night? Whatever for?"

Taking a decanter full of cold water, Captain Zhora poured its contents into the soup bucket.

"Why did you do that?" the guard pushing the trolley enquired.

"Let them die!" Zhora snarled. "That's all they can hope for in this life."

After leaving the punishment zone and re-entering camp life, I learned that I was no longer allowed to work with Group Twelve. This was a blow. Most of the 150 people belonging to Group Twelve linked up with Group Seven and were allowed to work outside the camp.

But the camp administration had decided to limit my

contact with the outside world and I was transferred to Group Eleven. I realised that I had to exert extreme caution in this new group, as I could be betrayed by traitors and informers in order to win favour with the bosses.

But I also made a friend in Group Eleven. It was Vadim, the young man who did clerical work in the office and had issued me with the pass to see Tanya.

I was assigned work producing nets. Each prisoner's daily production quota was twelve nets, on completion of which the camp administration gave a reward. With this money, one could buy cigarettes, chocolates and selected foodstuffs from a special general store that was open for a few hours each day.

But in the given time and bad work conditions, it was only possible to produce three nets, meaning that every work shift failed to avail itself of the camp administration's generosity. This was a punishable offence.

I refused to work on the nets and declared a hunger strike that lasted about two weeks. During this time I noticed some discarded slices of bamboo on the floor in the technical centre. As I polished them a sheen appeared on the surface and the transformation was remarkable. Using twine, I tied the bamboo slices together to form a cross.

I wore the cross to remind myself that although my body had been trapped behind the red barbed-wire, my heart was free. I was not a captive of the godless Soviet system, but a servant of Jesus.

Captain Zhora's eyes were drawn to the cross like magnets and he stared at me in virtual disbelief. It was as though I had pulled a revolver on him. Striding across to me, he grabbed the cross and tugged it viciously from my neck. Feeling the full force of his strength, the twine snapped and Zhora crushed the cross with a curse.

The officer was in a fury, but I maintained an outward calm, perceiving the violence of the seizure to be an act of confession.

Weakened by the fast, I was sentenced to the punishment

cells for failure to work. When fifteen days were over, I learned that I was to be transferred for a psychiatric examination and that my sentence in the cells was to be extended.

"But if I'm crazy," I argued, "then why am I imprisoned in a labour camp? I should have been sentenced to a psychiatric hospital. It doesn't make any sense."

But the doctor wasn't there to make any sense out of it. His job was to find me guilty!

The hospital itself was located between two labour camps, and there were many prisoners there under treatment. The prisoners looked just like the patients, haggard and ill.

My interrogation lasted nine days. In frustration, the doctors decided to abort their assignment. It was all over in a flash and within an hour, I was in a police lorry.

Back to camp. Back to the cells. Back to normal.

"You're quite a celebrity in the West aren't you, Barinov?" Lobanov the deputy commandant grinned and puffed on his cigarette.

The hair on the back of my neck began to bristle. "I don't know what you mean," I replied nonchalantly.

"Well the BBC seem to be taking an interest in you and we get these cards and letters from people in the West." Lobanov sounded mystified.

Again, I sounded non-committal and shrugged it off, but inwardly I felt a surge of strength rush through me. Lobanov had inadvertently confirmed that my friends in the West had not forgotten me, as the KGB had warned would happen. On the contrary, there seemed to be an active campaign being waged on my behalf.

I was thrilled and wanted to learn more, but Lobanov wouldn't be drawn. Instead he began to scold me for spreading sedition among the prisoners.

Again, I felt a spiritual victory. I wanted to praise the

Lord and dance, but I had to conceal my joy. Lobanov's questions confirmed my suspicions. The camp authorities knew that my New Testament was in circulation and had tried to ban it, but they couldn't track it down.

"It must be your book," Lobanov insisted. "We never had this problem with anyone else.

"Barinov," he continued, "you've got to stop preaching or you'll never get out of here alive. Do you want your wife and children to visit your grave here in the Komi Mountains? Is that what you want?" Lobanov pointed to the door, terminating the interview.

I spent the next two evenings in the camp library composing letters of appeal. Squinting hard, I wrote a letter to Tanya urging her to inform the West of my plight. I also wrote to the Presidium of the Supreme Soviet, believing that if anyone in authority took time to study my case, they would realise that I was innocent.

To remain alive in camp I would have to remain silent about Jesus. I just couldn't do it. The risks were considerable. If the camp underworld came to learn of Lobanov's threats, I wouldn't last a day.

Two days later, as I queued for bread and tea, I stood next to someone from Group Twelve who worked outside the camp. His name was Nikolai but I didn't know much else about him. Like everyone else, he was imprisoned for "economic crimes".

"Do you want my bread?" I asked him.

"Sure," he said. "Aren't you hungry?"

"Yes, I'm hungry but I'm fasting to God today," I replied.

He looked startled, so I explained that I was a Christian and that prayer and fasting tuned my senses towards God's Spirit. Taking him into my confidence, I told him that I needed help in sending a message out of camp. He came into contact with local people. But could I trust him?

He looked around, speaking quietly. "I may be able to help you. But what's in it for me?"

He wanted cigarettes, food, or cash, preferably all three. We hit on a deal and agreed to meet in two days' time allowing me to gather the required items.

Some of the younger guards were quite impressed that I could sing rock songs in English. They were in a relaxed mood, and after half an hour I had collected twenty cigarettes.

The songs were also popular among the prisoners. Others wanted me to read the scriptures. "I'll do that for you anyway," I joked. I also traded food and tea to boost my cigarette stash.

I was still uncertain about my new-found collaborator. What if he took my cigarettes and then turned me in, collecting a reward from the guards as well?

The next morning I asked Nikolai, "Are you sure you can get this message to my wife?"

"Don't worry about a thing," he replied confidently, accepting the cigarettes. "It's best that we don't meet again," he told me, sipping his tea.

"But how will I know what happened to my letter?" I enquired.

"You will know," Nikolai grinned. "You will definitely know." He was right, I would know. Sooner than I thought.

In the dinner queue that evening Captain Zhora caught my eye and signalled to me with his index finger.

"We know your tricks!" he growled. "There's an urgent message for you at the office."

I hesitated, but Zhora thumped me in the chest knocking me backwards and winding me. "Go at once," he ordered, raising his voice.

Within minutes I was confronted with the evidence of my crime. In my appeal I had requested that the Soviet authorities give me permission to leave the country. This was taken as confirmation that, given the chance, I would try to escape.

The camp authorities proposed to solve the problem in the old familiar way: the dreaded punishment cell!

I still had the New Testament on me when I was arrested,

but as I was searched, the guards in the punishment cells were distracted by some innocent scribblings.

"It's the lyrics of a song I'm composing," I explained.

The guard looked at me to see if it was a joke, but I told him I was a rock musician and this provided a strategic distraction as it concluded the search.

The New Testament was in the punishment cell!

The book gave me strength and was fascinating for my cellmates who insisted that I read extracts from the "holy book".

One night at around midnight I was awoken by a disturbance in the cell directly opposite ours. Someone was hammering at the door crying for help. I climbed on to the bed and peered in vain through the window above the door.

There were scuffles and blood-curdling screams, "Help me! Help me! They're trying to kill me!" It was Zardok, who had assisted Snake in selling supplies to Machine.

The guard strutted unhurriedly to the scene. He ignored the dispute, refusing either to negotiate an honourable peace within the cell or offer Zardok any protection.

From the prison grapevine we learned that Zardok had died from the terrible beating he received. The guard could have prevented his death, but had instead abandoned him to his fate.

I could never have imagined anything worse than this labour camp, stranded on an island on the edge of the world, drifting to hell.

I was transferred to a makeshift medical unit for a psychiatric examination and tested for "delusions of grandeur". A man in a grubby white coat questioned me, "You want to be a rock musician so that you can be famous?"

"No, I want to sing not for fame and fortune," I corrected him, "but for Jesus!"

"It's a puzzling case," he remarked. "I think you need further examination and professional help. A lot of help!"

Back in the punishment cells I was warned that such

examinations could have severe repercussions. I learned of other prisoners who had been sentenced to ten years in psychiatric hospitals. "If you're not crazy then they make you crazy."

Over the next few days I was moved constantly. A cold north wind blew in through the windows and I caught a chill. Without warm clothes I found myself getting feverish.

The guards mauled me, and I sensed that it was "open season" on the rock musician from Leningrad.

I must have been an enigma to the guards. Every time they shoved me, I said, "Thank you! God bless you!" It was not easy, but as I took the first step, the next ones followed and my security came from knowing that I was fulfilling God's will.

As fifteen days drew near, the bread ration was halved without warning. We declared a hunger strike against the food that was dished out. The word spread and other prisoners in the block agreed to join us.

When the guard doling out bread and soup was met with a cacophony of tin bowls banged against the doors, Captain Zhora stormed out of his office swearing furiously. "You'll be sorry," he raged, "you'll all be sorry."

For Captain Zhora the protest had turned into a "riot", and he was determined to punish the culprits.

Within an hour he was back, accompanied by a tough prisoner named Black. Zhora's holster was unstrapped and his revolver glinted ominously. In his left hand he held a spray can.

Zhora ranted about the "riot" and named the three criminals he considered culprits. I was among them.

I remained silent. To protest my innocence was to betray the others. And in any case it was a spontaneous protest that could be resolved by giving us food.

I refused to sign Zhora's document confessing the crime of inciting a riot. Black witnessed my refusal and initialled the document. Zhora informed me that it would be placed in my file.

Zhora grinned at me. "Your days are numbered, Barinov!"

Raising his right hand to his neck, he ran his finger slowly across his throat. There was no mistaking his message.

Without warning the officer raised his left hand and sprayed me in the face. Taken by surprise, I couldn't move fast enough and the jet of tear gas caught me full in the face.

I crouched down on my haunches, my arms flaying from side to side. I tried to dust the air, but it was hopeless. My eyes were streaming as I gasped for breath. Both my cellmates were coughing furiously as they turned away. As Zhora sprayed me, Black lashed out with his feet as though I were some irritating insect, a pest that he had to destroy.

Trapped in a time-warp, the tear gas assault seemed to go on for several minutes, yet it must have been over in seconds. The burning sensation lingered for many hours, but Captain Zhora's words lasted longer.

My cellmates were alarmed, assuming me to be a dangerous criminal. "If they mark your card, there's nothing you can do," one said sadly. The next day I was moved yet again, and they both sighed with relief.

"Good luck," they said in unison as I prepared to leave.

"I don't believe in luck," I told them. "Things don't just happen by chance. Just pray to God. Take a step of faith," I said speaking quickly, aware that I could be moved at any second and never see them again. Both seemed gripped by what I had said and asked me to pray for them. As the words tumbled out of my mouth, the door to our cell swung open.

"Barinov . . ."

20

RED STRIPE

"Barinov! I've got something for you," Captain Zhora snarled. Then he tossed me a cord about one and a half metres long. As I grabbed it, I noticed that he had tied a crude noose on one end.

"Do something useful," he chuckled. "Use it!" For several minutes Zhora and another officer laughed at their own joke. I could smell liquor on their breath.

"I'm not afraid to die," I told them. "When I die I know that I'll be in paradise."

They stared at me for a moment. "This man is crazy," Zhora muttered.

My fifteen days in the punishment cell had been extended by a second term, but there was little point in appealing against this injustice. Every time I moved cells, I carried my New Testament with me like a passport, and the other prisoners would listen transfixed as I read from its pages.

When the guards discovered the Holy Book, I argued that I hadn't smuggled it in, just carried it in. "Anyway, I told them confidently, Lobanov has given me permission."

At the mention of the camp's second in command, questions ceased. The guards knew that I was an unusual prisoner and that Lobanov had indeed issued a confidential directorate concerning me. Perhaps he had also allowed me to keep this religious book.

To my surprise, Lobanov himself carried out an impromptu inspection of the punishment zone, and an enthusiastic guard asked him, "Sir, did you give prisoner

Barinov permission to keep a New Testament in the cells with him?''

Lobanov's denial was emphatic, and he demanded furiously that I hand the scriptures over. I had no choice but to hand the well-thumbed book reluctantly to the guards.

God hád given me supernatural power to resist the tactics employed to break me, and I didn't think the pressure on me could be increased. But it was.

I was placed among the hard-regime prisoners, the toughest criminals in camp, and a vicious rumour was spread among them by the authorities. ''Barinov is a KGB agent, an informer, sent to spy on the prisoners.''

It was a plan that could not fail, as the KGB were hated by everyone in the camp. How better to strike back at the system than by taking revenge on the secret police plant? I didn't have a chance.

I was watched closely, and my story of Christian activity must have seemed like a stupid cover story. When the jailors brought me food, I always thanked them, and one day ''Gypsy'', one of the gang leaders, challenged me directly.

''Why are you thanking them?'' he threatened. ''Are they friends of yours?''

''No,'' I said calmly, ''I'm a Christian, and this means I must love even those who hate me.''

''Who do you think you are? The Pope?'' another prisoner named Ivan began.

The confrontation reached its climax on the third day when the beatings started. I was pinned against the wall and hit, slapped, kicked, without respite and without cause. I had taken a stand as a Christian and knew that if I backed down my authority as a preacher would be broken. It would confirm their fear, that I was a KGB plant.

I slumped against the wall, collapsing in a heap on the floor. Now my own blood mingled with the stains on the wall. I had pain in my kidneys, bruises all over my body, and it felt as though I had several broken ribs.

I didn't know how long I could bear the attacks. Fearing

that I was near breaking point, I recalled a scripture, a promise from God: he would not let me suffer more than I could bear.

Gypsy, Ivan and the others were surprised by my resilience and determination. "Admit that you're a KGB spy and we'll stop beating you," they promised, surrounding me.

"I am a Christian," I replied and prepared for their bunched fists to hurtle down into my body.

One night as my battered body kept me awake in pain I prayed, "Lord, perhaps it is better if I lose consciousness and enter your presence. Then this pain will end." Then I added quickly, "But Lord, I just want to perform your will."

The assault to discover my true identity went on for about thirty days. This was the signal for the respite: Gypsy restrained another of the inmates from a punch aimed at my head.

"Enough," Gypsy declared, clutching his cellmate's wrist. It was the word I had waited to hear. I didn't know what had brought this change of heart, but my heart sang praises to God.

"Don't be afraid," Gypsy told me. "Now we believe that you are not a KGB agent, but that God sent you to us." Before I could say anything he put his hand on my shoulder and announced, "I have something important to ask you."

"Valeri, tell me," he began hesitantly, "will your God punish us for what we have done to you?"

There was a hushed silence as everyone waited for my reply. "Of course not." Everyone relaxed visibly. Then half-joking, I added, "God will not punish you if you receive Jesus into your heart, and I can tell you more about him."

The response was immediate. "Of course we want to hear about Jesus." Once again, God had extricated me from the trap that had been set, replacing it with a captive audience. During the next three months those prisoners who had been set up to be my executioners turned out to be my protectors. Special honour was afforded to those convicts who had endured "hard regime" sentences. When I finally emerged from the punishment zone, I found a reception committee waiting to welcome me back to camp.

In the barracks, special food had been laid out for me. To my astonishment, there was tinned fish and meat, chocolates, and an assortment of drinks, berry juice, milk and tea.

I quickly caught up on the camp gossip. Someone told me that I had been one week too late to partake in some unusual food. I recoiled in horror at learning that a dog had strayed into camp and never got out alive. It had been caught one night and stewed by several prisoners, deprived of real food.

Strangely, I lost my appetite.

My hand tapped my leg in an insistent rhythm as I stood behind the locked door. I could hardly wait. Behind the door was Tanya. Haunting images of her blazing red hair and tender green eyes floated across the room. The last time we had been together was tinged with the bittersweet memory of our parting, cruelly separated although we had permission to meet.

How I longed to take her in my arms and cradle her tenderly, wiping away the tears that would flow.

As I was ushered into the adjoining room I bumped awkwardly into my escort, who turned to scold me. Like a schoolboy on his first picnic, my enthusiasm could not be quenched.

But there was to be no private reunion. Dealt another blow by the authorities, I found myself in a large hall with several other prisoners sitting in front of a glass partition.

Then I saw Tanya wave, and rushed over to her, pressing my hand on the glass. Now it was her turn. Tears streamed down her face as she moved her hand to clasp mine. All I felt was the cold pane of glass which separated us.

"I love you," I said, full of admiration for the woman who had stood by me and shared my suffering. Sometimes, even when she hadn't agreed with my plans, her devotion to me had swept her along.

When words are inadequate, the eyes dance and God binds us together in an everlasting embrace.

Tanya held up some photographs of Zhanna and Marina, and I squinted through the thick, grubby glass at the beautiful young girls in the pictures. I couldn't help smiling, but I felt an ache deep within me.

"They miss you," Tanya said amidst the bustle of the visiting room. "And they love you!" At this my spirits lifted.

Tanya confirmed once more that a campaign was being waged in the West on my behalf. Although there were no exact details, I was encouraged, and sensed that prayers were being offered up for me.

There was so much to say, but time was restricted and behind us the guards stood, ensuring that we did not betray "state secrets". It had been rough for Tanya, and slowly her story unfolded.

Tanya had suffered a breakdown due to the pressure of supporting the family, and had been hospitalised. But through it all, she had experienced God's intervention. The KGB had coerced her boss to fire her from her office job when articles about my criminal activity appeared in local newspapers. Although her superior, Vassily, was not a Christian, he was sympathetic to Tanya's situation and had defended her vigorously.

"Why punish the wife for the behaviour of her husband?" Vassily argued. "Why should I dismiss her? Think of the two children, they are the future of our country. We can't treat families like this."

And so this courageous man defended his decision despite sustained harassment, and remained a very real protection to Tanya throughout my imprisonment. Tanya told me that he had become very interested in the Christian faith in recent months.

"He'll be the first person we invite for dinner as soon as

I'm home," I told Tanya, and thanked God for this man of strong principles in such a strategic position.

"I'm counting the days for you to come home," Tanya smiled, wiping away the tears. I nodded in agreement. "Pray. Just pray. God knows everything. My life is in his hands."

During our meeting, Captain Zhora walked past. "These are our re-education instructors," I told Tanya humorously. She didn't manage to find it funny.

It felt as though only ten minutes had passed, and there were so many more things to say. But an arm on my shoulder told me that it was time to go.

"One twenty one!" I shouted out to Tanya. She nodded, recognising the Psalm that had brought encouragement and strength. We pleaded for extra time, but it was useless. I would have given anything for one embrace, one kiss.

The sorrow of parting seemed to overshadow the joy of anticipation that I had felt. Once more, we didn't know when we would meet again.

I was a dangerous high-risk prisoner, and would be shot if caught trying to escape. Public enemy number one!

In case there was any doubt, my photograph was hung at strategic locations throughout the camp. The picture was marked with a diagonal red stripe — a distinction which was seen as an award among the prisoners, and which I shared with the most violent criminals who really were hellbent on breaking out.

Lobanov, a committed atheist and loyal communist who took his job seriously, told me that there were new rules that applied to me because of the threat I posed.

"I'm a Christian," I explained, "I'm not going to escape."

But Lobanov refused to open the subject for debate and informed me, "You will have to report to the duty officer every two hours. If you fail to report on time, then you will be put in the punishment cell."

In an unguarded moment, Lobanov said to me, "We know that you are a troublemaker because Katchkin told me about the problems you caused in the KGB headquarters in Leningrad." There it was, proof of his KGB liaison.

I asked innocently, "Oh! So you know Katchkin?"

Without thinking, Lobanov replied, "I've known Katchkin for years."

From this, I deduced that Katchkin was not unaware of my present difficulties, and Lobanov was probably taking orders from him.

Soon I realised that the red stripe had considerable benefits. The authorities had inadvertantly guaranteed my protection, among some of the prisoners at least.

It also meant that I had total freedom to travel anywhere in the camp, which was separated into several zones with barbed wire. Normally special permission was needed to go from one zone to another. Now I found I could slip through the zones by identifying myself and I used this free access to the full.

"It's Prisoner Barinov," I explained to the guards on point duty. "I'm a red striper."

The guards came to know me and they all assumed that as I was due to report every two hours to the camp office I would be given special tasks to perform. In fact I spent most of my time speaking about Jesus to the other prisoners, among whom I found a deep spiritual hunger.

At night, the guards would check to see that it really was me under the blankets trying to sleep.

Gypsy, my friend from the hard-regime cell told me that one of his friends was curious about Jesus. Mikhail was about thirty-five, with tattoos all over his body. He had been convicted of killing his wife, whom he had tied to some concrete and dumped at sea. But under interrogation he had broken down and confessed. Here in camp he was troubled by his crime, plagued with guilt and remorse.

"I belong to the devil," Mikhail admitted soberly.

"The devil may own your past," I argued, "but he doesn't

control your future. When you turn to Jesus, God will give you a new future and a new plan for your life.''

Mikhail sobbed like a baby, dropped to his knees, and asked God to give him a new life. It was a thrilling moment as I witnessed the remarkable transformation.

''Thank you Valeri, thank you,'' he repeated.

In the excitement of the moment, the time for me to check in had become long overdue, and it was already about 11 p.m. Captain Verona met me on my way to the office.

''What are you doing out so late?'' he asked, somewhat amused.

It was a clear night and stars twinkled in my defence. ''I was just out for a stroll breathing the fresh night air,'' I said gallantly.

My remark caused him to chuckle. ''Well, let me invite you to breathe some air in the punishment cell.''

I was awarded twenty-four hours in the punishment cells, but as I recalled the events leading up to it, I praised God. It had all been worthwhile.

In Captain Verona's absence it was Vadim's duty to check me off in the camp office.

''It's Prisoner Barinov. I'm here to tell you that I haven't run away.''

Vadim nodded, not bothering to pick up the file. He just grinned at me. We had met frequently in this fashion so a rapport had developed between us and I had been praying for him.

Today the office was empty. ''Yes, I'm in charge of the labour camp today,'' Vadim declared. ''Any special requests?''

''Only one,'' I replied.

Vadim understood and we didn't pursue the point. We were both prisoners and the concept of freedom was too painful to discuss.

About twenty-one, tall, intelligent and skilful in the ways

of camp life, Vadim had engineered himself into a coveted position: a desk job in the administration block.

With time on our hands, Vadim expounded his theories of philosophy and life. His mother, of whom he was proud, had a mathematics degree, but he also told of his father's criminal record. Vadim spoke like a fascist, with deeply-held convictions.

"Do you want some tea?" he asked.

"Sure," I grinned. It was an amusing scene. Two prisoners of the Soviet Gulag sipping tea, engaged in intellectual pursuits. But I had to be careful, as it was possible that Vadim could be a traitor.

Vadim opened a drawer and for the next few moments proceeded to twist a Rubik cube in dizzying combinations. "It's driving me crazy," he confessed. "I just can't work it out. Something like life, isn't it?" he said with a grin, looking up at me.

Vadim confided in me that he had written an article summarising his philosophy, and he offered it to me. "Read it quickly," he said. Even though Lobanov and Verona were out of the office, the other camp officers could walk through the door at any moment.

In this rambling mixture of fascism, nihilism and folk theology, Vadim acknowledged an anonymous deity. Life was absurd and meaningless, but maybe someone was waiting round the corner with a pack of cards that could tell the future.

"What do you think," Vadim cut into my thoughts as I skimmed the last page.

"Interesting," I sighed, stroking my chin. "but I met two fascists in the KGB prison who had exhausted this idea. Even they agreed that it didn't really work."

We discussed fascism as an opposition movement to communism for a few minutes, and then I asserted, "But I believe in a greater truth."

Vadim's eyes widened. "What do you mean?"

"God," I stated.

"I don't believe in God," Vadim shot back.

"But do you believe in justice, truth and love?" I asked.

Vadim fidgeted, nodding his head slowly.

"That's God," I explained.

"Now I understand why Lobanov calls you Public Enemy Number One," Vadim chuckled.

"It's a revolutionary idea," I continued, "but there's greater power in God than in the communist revolution."

Vadim's questions came in quick succession and in the intensity of the moment, the truth found a foothold in his heart. The Rubik cube lay untouched on the table beside him.

"Valeri, I want to believe," Vadim whispered.

Like a deer edging cautiously towards the riverbank, Vadim stepped nearer the kingdom of heaven.

Shortly afterwards, Vadim was transferred from the administration office and placed in charge of the camp library. One informer told us that he had heard Verona remark that, "Vadim spends too much time with the Christian preacher."

Vadim and I became close friends and over the next few weeks I watched an astounding transformation in his life as he set off as a pilgrim on the road to find truth, justice and love. He became fascinated with the idea that God could heal our sick bodies, and when some months later his mother visited him in camp and he learned that she had a severe headache, he insisted on praying with her. Within half an hour she had made a remarkable recovery and questioned him closely on his new wave of beliefs.

"What are we going to do with you?" Lobanov said, perplexed at the thought of devising new forms of punishment. "You'll never leave camp alive if you carry on spreading these ideas!" he thundered.

Zinchenko, the camp commandant, joined the debate, and eventually it was decided that I should be sent back to the work force assembling net bags for sale in local towns.

There were three shifts: 8 a.m. to 4 p.m. with a short lunchbreak, 4 p.m. to midnight, and midnight until 8 a.m. These schedules lasted about a month each followed by a move to the next time slot and so forth.

The nets were produced on the second floor of a brick building about twenty-five metres long and ten metres wide. There was no proper ceiling, merely a plastic covering giving a tent-like appearance. The plastic was old and tatty, and rain dripped on us. In summer, we caught the raging heat of the sun, causing several prisoners to faint. In winter, we could barely sit on the wooden benches without shivering from cold.

The front rows nearest the toilet were occupied by the lower ranks of prisoners. In keeping with camp custom, the place was actually run by prisoners while the camp authorities maintained a general oversight.

Sitting eight to ten on a bench, three or four hundred people would cram into the hall on each shift. It was hard to believe that so many people could squeeze into a hall that size. The stench from the toilet combined with the dust from the nets was overpowering, and many prisoners became ill from inhaling this dust, coughing violently.

The tough guys sat at the back of the hall smoking and talking among themselves while their "slaves" and "homosexuals" did all the work. With clockwork regularity they would pounce, stealing completed bags so that they would meet the otherwise unattainable production quota. The workers handed over their nets, the gang bosses collected the money, and the camp paid out. That was the way the game was played.

The more I thought about it, the more outrageous it seemed. What a great opportunity it would be to preach to a large company of people. Yet another captive audience. And so I put Lobanov's warning aside. This was too good a chance to miss.

It was a daring plan, and I soon found some co-conspirators with the audacity it required. The first step was to get rid of the guard. This was achieved by offering him cigarettes and tins of meat. Gypsy and other gang leaders assured him that they would take charge of the group in his absence.

With the guard out of sight, Gypsy stepped back into the hall and yelled out, "Who wants to spend the afternoon sewing nets, boys?" This was greeted with a chorus of boos and hisses. "OK, who wants to hear Valeri speak about Jesus?" A few hands were raised, and there was a murmur of "Anything but nets!"

"Tell some jokes!" someone called out.

Lev, one of the gang leaders with a scar running down the side of his face, was not amused. He had been instrumental in setting up the meeting and he wasn't going to have his plans upstaged. "Who said that?" Lev called out sharply and stepped in the direction from which the voice came.

A tall gangly youth stood up, holding his hands in the air, pleading, "No, no, I was only joking. Let's hear Valeri tell us about Jesus. We're desperate to hear about Jesus, aren't we comrades?" He looked round imploringly, seeking support.

Confirmation spread, "Yes, we want to know about Jesus!" There was no doubt that these people were curious about God. A watchman was posted at the window and I was summoned to the front.

Without waiting another second, I began, "Comrades . . ."

21

THE POWER OF LOVE

These clandestine encounters proved phenomenally successful. Carried along by the enthusiastic support of my audience, I sometimes found myself preaching for two hours without a break. I knew it couldn't last, but I had decided to take it to the limit.

When I was arrested there wouldn't be time to return to the barracks. I always wore extra clothing so that I would be kept warm in the punishment cell. I kept waiting to hear my name called. Any moment now, I thought . . .

Then finally, one rainy afternoon, "Prisoner Barinov, report to the main desk."

Zinchenko was furious. "You'll never learn," he swore.

Cell No. 10 was freezing cold, and I was glad of my extra clothing. There were three others in the cell, and although we had never met before, one of them asked me, "The holy one?" I nodded my head.

Late one night, with the wind rattling our window, we huddled under our blankets. "Valeri," one of the prisoners called out softly, "are you awake?" I raised my head, and he continued, "Do you know the Christian's prayer?"

As usual the cell was bathed in a dull glow from the bulb fixed over the door. Wrapped in a faded grey blanket, all I could see were two eyes twinkling in the shadows.

"The Christian's prayer," I mulled over the request.

"Yes, it talks about God being our Father. I never had a father," he said wistfully.

I nodded my head.

"Say it for me, Valeri, say this prayer for me," his voice was sober and sincere.

In the silence of the night, with the shadows falling softly on the wall, I repeated the prayer that I had learned as a child. The words reminded me of the carefree years with Mama in the Pioneer Camp:

Our Father,
Who is in heaven,
Blessed and holy is your name,
May your kingdom come
May your will be done
On earth as it is in heaven.
Give us this day our daily bread,
Forgive us our sins
For we have forgiven those who sinned against us,
Don't allow us to be tempted,
But rescue us from evil.

The cold had driven a quiver into my voice, but the words took on a power and presence of their own as they hung gently in the air. We lay awake in the dark, listening to the howling wind outside, watching the shadows dancing on the wall, reliving precious memories.

It was hard to believe that one year had passed since I had arrived at labour camp. It would be Easter in a few weeks, and my mind recalled the extraordinary way in which we had celebrated the death and resurrection of Jesus last year with Easter eggs and cakes.

How different this Easter was to be. I had a cold that didn't get better, and a painful cough which seemed to tear my insides apart. I felt tight pains around my chest as I sneezed and shivered.

All the time my temperature was rising, and for two weeks I had a fever and was delirious. The cell seemed to spin round in a whirl, and my legs were too weak to stand.

Once again, Machine and I were captives together. My cellmates pleaded with the guards to call a doctor. At first their requests went unheeded. Then Zhora came to check me. After studying the thermometer and seeing the precarious situation I was in, he tossed some headache tablets into the cell.

"This is all you need," he said casually.

But Machine and the others pleaded with him to send a doctor.

"Don't argue with me," he warned, slamming the door.

Every time a guard went past, my cellmates called for a doctor, and eventually their diligence was rewarded. The "doctor" was dressed in military uniform, and when pressed, admitted that he was a soldier first and a doctor second. He, too, prescribed pain-killers. "No, this man does not need hospital treatment," was his verdict.

My cellmates collected some wooden planks and made a makeshift bed, insisting that I sleep on it. Despite this kind gesture, I could feel a cold breeze creep through a gap in the planks.

A few nights later, my fever rose yet higher. Machine banged on the door, yelling through the hatchway. He had learned that the doctor was visiting the punishment zone. "Bring the doctor here, Valeri needs him," he cried.

Zhora opened the door to our cell and demanded an explanation. Despite my condition, the doctor wouldn't examine me and Zhora couldn't help. His chilling words were delivered in a curt, business-like manner: "The administration has ordered the doctor to stay away from Prisoner Barinov."

"Let us break your hand, and you'll be in hospital," Machine suggested, when I had regained consciousness.

"That's not God's way," I told him, coughing violently.

"But they want to kill you, Valeri," he said, with a note of alarm in his voice. "Zhora has vowed that you will rot in here."

"God knows, God knows," was all I could muster.

My frail body became a magnet for all the prison insects. I was too weak to resist them, so Machine and the others picked the fleas and bugs from my flesh. The toilet was another torment. Without water or privacy, it was the last humiliation. I would lapse into unconsciousness, delirious and deranged.

On the worst nights, my cellmates would huddle close to me to preserve my body heat. I could feel my life flowing out of my body, and for two weeks, I balanced between life and death. The only words I could feebly whisper were, "Jesus! Jesus! Jesus!"

Desperately weak, I crossed the line. "God will deliver me from this place today," I announced. Machine and the others stared at me in disbelief. Was I hallucinating? Did I mean that death would be the ultimate release? I began to sift through the blankets and clothes, handing back whatever had been loaned to me during the worst moments of my illness.

Around 3 p.m. the cell door opened, and a guard told me to report to the camp "medicine point". Zinchenko had apparently been monitoring my situation, and somewhere in the bureaucratic jungle a decision had been taken. Hospitalisation!

"How did you know this was going to happen?" Machine asked, incredulously.

"I had a vision," I replied calmly.

"I should have taken bets on it. I'd be a rich man now," Machine remarked, an inveterate gambler.

A Jewish friend of mine, Alex Zelichenok, had been hospitalised one week before me, but had returned to camp on the day I left for hospital. He was an older man who had become very dear to me. We would quote Psalms to each other, and share the God of Israel together, usually in English, much to the annoyance of the guards. Alex's wife, Galina would sometimes accompany Tanya on the 2,000-km journey from Leningrad, and they became good friends.

Alex and I had crossed en route, and Galina visited Alex a few days later. Through their meeting, news of my plight reached the West. In a strong physical way, I sensed the prayers of God's people. It was an exhilarating feeling to know that all over the world, people were sharing my ordeal.

From the medicine point I was bundled into the back of a lorry with twenty-five other patients from various labour camps in the region. As we jolted towards the hospital, I introduced myself as a Christian to my neighbour, a defector from the Red Army in Afghanistan.

This drew an immediate response. "We had a preacher just like you in our camp," he said. "He was also from Leningrad."

"What was his name?" I asked.

"I don't know," he replied. "Everyone called him " 'the holy one'."

I marvelled at the wisdom of God. Instead of putting us together, we had been put in separate camps so that we could bring light to the darkness around us.

The staff at the hospital were local people who probably had little idea about conditions in labour camp. Here the rooms were clean, the food was an improvement, and most significantly, we were treated like ordinary people.

After registration, I was led into an ante-room where a tall bearded doctor conducted the interview. I had contracted pneumonia and pleurisy, and malnutrition was also diagnosed. The doctor stared curiously at the notes. "I see you've been under psychiatric treatment," he commented diplomatically.

"Yes, special psychiatric treatment by the KGB," I said pointedly.

The doctor winked knowingly. He scribbled something on my card and said, "I don't think we can improve on KGB techniques, so you won't need any further psychiatric treatment here."

That evening we were given chicken to eat. You could actually chew on the flesh, unlike the strange bony lumps which appeared from time to time in camp soup. I was given vitamins and penicillin, and began to feel better immediately.

As I was finishing dinner, I felt a hand on my shoulder. It was Yevgeny. His arm was still in a sling, but he was grinning, and I remembered how I had prayed that he would be hospitalised.

Yevgeny confirmed that hospital facilities were superb. "I would have died in that camp," Yevgeny said confidently. "Please take my advice. Break your arm. That's the only way you'll survive your sentence. You know they want to kill you."

I grinned and shook my head. "Valeri, it's best, believe me. Join the company."

Yevgeny turned his head and I followed his gaze around the room where the inmates were finishing dinner. I was surprised at how many left arms there were in slings.

"I only have one choice, and that is to follow Jesus," I told Yevgeny.

"Yes, I know," he said in a subdued tone. "But Valeri, if you change your mind, call me and I'll be the first to help you. You know what I mean?" he implored.

The guard on duty in the hospital looked strangely familiar. I recognised him as a friend of old Yura Taikov, called Nikolai. He had clashed with Lobanov and been transferred from our camp to the hospital. Yura once told me that Nikolai's mother had been a Christian, and that a sense of justice and fair play had been instilled into him as a child. On one occasion Nikolai had saved Yura from a beating, and it was evident that he wasn't going to have a promising career in this profession.

Nikolai led me into an alcove along the corridor and looked over his shoulder to see if we were alone. "Valeri, be careful," he whispered.

He saw my eyes widen in surprise, and then added, "We were expecting you. The hospital administration received a call yesterday. We were told to patch you up and send you back to camp as quickly as possible."

Our meeting ended abruptly, and I was left wondering what God was saying to me. I resolved to receive the medical treatment on offer, but to trust God for the healing of my body.

As each hour passed, I felt energy and strength flow into my limbs. After one week I attempted simple exercises, and soon after that Nikolai showed me an inner compound where I could jog without interference during the afternoon.

Within ten days, God had restored my health. Even my hair, which had fallen out, began to grow again. The doctors were impressed with the transformation.

It was customary for hard-regime prisoners to work as orderlies, and these hardened criminals were recognised by a stripe on their sleeves. Surprisingly, the "stripers" were the most interested in Jesus, and many of them asked me to write down scripture verses for them as they had never seen a Bible. In return, they arranged for me to receive extra portions of food.

One of the stripers was an elderly Tartar of the Muslim faith. "I am also religious like you," he told me. "You call your God Jesus, and we call ours Allah. As the saying goes, 'All roads lead to the Kremlin.' "

We established a genuine friendship and enjoyed several intense discussions together. "Christianity has its own doctrine and rituals," I explained to the Tartar, "but there's a difference between religion and Jesus. Jesus is a real person and through him you can find new life. When you believe in Jesus, you feel as if you've been born a second time.

"Actually, I'm not a religious person," I confided in him. "Religion can be a covering that in fact keeps you from God."

The Tartar confessed that he had killed a man in camp who had betrayed him. "The traitor deserved his fate, but I still feel guilty."

We talked about forgiveness, and gradually, like a child, he seemed to receive faith into his heart and began to pray to Jesus. The transformation was striking, and even the guards asked what had brought about the change.

"Jesus!" he declared boldly.

The hospital ward was a twisting corridor with rooms leading off it, each of them locked and bolted, but with a barred window above the door. One night the Tartar announced that I would be speaking about Jesus, and for over an hour I stood on a chair and spoke through the window to everyone else in our ward. This provoked numerous questions, and whenever I met anyone after that, the talk inevitably turned to discussions about the faith.

While in hospital, I also met Old Pasha, a "lifer", first arrested during Stalin's regime and now over sixty years old. "I don't agree with you, but I admire your courage and zeal," he said.

We made an odd couple, the lifer and the Christian rock musician. But I think he felt at ease with me because he identified with my outspokenness. He hated all politicians and the administration hated him because he spoke out fearlessly. "I've got nothing to lose. They locked up my body in prison years ago and threw away the key. But they can't lock up my mind."

One day he turned to me and said, "Why does God punish the Russian people?"

I likened Russia to Israel. "God allowed disaster to fall because they rejected the Messiah."

The old man found this hard to comprehend. "But Russia is a religious country," he argued.

"Worshipping icons can detract you from recognising the one true God," I explained. "Some priests have kept this treasure hidden from the people, disguising the truth with a complex book of rules and rituals. To discover the truth you must come as a child to God and experience freedom in Jesus."

"I'll write to you," Old Pasha said, clasping my hand tightly with the warmth of a father to a son.

"I'll wait for your letter," I replied. The friendships

formed in prison forged a bond that could not be forgotten and I knew that a letter would await me should I return to Leningrad.

Without warning one Tuesday morning after breakfast about a month after I had arrived at the hospital, an orderly gave me this message: "Prisoner Barinov, report to the duty officer." I was led directly to the quarantine section and handed back the squalid prison clothes. Somehow the very uniform evoked the camp atmosphere and shedding the soft linen hospital clothes was like leaving a part of our life behind.

If I had thought I was forgotten in Camp No. 27, I was in for a rude surprise. "Barinov!" Captain Zhora greeted me with a laugh. "We've kept cell number seven reserved for you in the punishment block."

My expression must have spoken a million words. Zhora patiently explained the situation, delighting in every nuance. "You see, when you left for the hospital you were serving a fifteen-day sentence, and there are still six days to run." He could control himself no longer and broke out in a loud guffaw.

"We never forget," he said, ordering me forward with a tap on the back.

It was raining hard, and I arrived at the cells dripping wet. My boots were cardboard-thin, and my socks were sodden.

Back in the cells, three faces turn to gaze at me. Nowhere to run to, nowhere to turn. Time, so much time. But this is my mission, my territory. I remember the Tartar, and Old Pasha back at the hospital, and their words ring in my ears like the chimes of freedom.

This trumpet must never be silent.

After six days of dry bread and cold soup, Group Eleven welcomed me back to camp with the customary fruit, food and drinks.

"Did you hear about Alex?" Yura Taikov asked me. Yura

himself was shortly to leave the camp to spend the rest of his sentence in exile.

Yura went on to tell me the sad news about my dear friend, Alex Zelichenok. As he had received permission to be transferred from our camp to another, his wife Galina arrived to accompany him because of his ill health. But the administration sent him with common criminals and so he was severely beaten. He had been hospitalised, and Galina feared he would not survive.

"The godless Soviet system must not be allowed to get away with this," I said. "We must pray for Alex and Galina."

Yura was equally concerned, but sceptical. "Valeri," he said with deep sincerity, "what good can it do to repeat some words of prayer? How do you know this reaches any further than the ceiling?"

"Prayer is the weapon we must use," I exclaimed with total conviction. "You see, we don't fight against the administration, but against the kingdom of evil, the sinister forces behind the structures that exist.

"These people aren't the real enemy, but have fallen victim to a greater evil. The greatest resistance that we can bring against men such as Zhora is the power of love. When they persecute us, we must love them. If we can do this, their resistance will crumble."

"I'd like to believe you, Valeri," Yura said slowly, "but I just don't know how this can be possible."

I shook my head, understanding his dilemma. "With God all things are possible. We can't do it alone."

I realised that these were merely words. The test would come when we were face to face with men like Zhora.

"Valeri!" Yura yelled, "I almost forgot."

"What is it?" I asked.

Yura chuckled and slapped me on the back. He told me that while I was in hospital, a new batch of prisoners had arrived in camp, and among them was a musician named

Sergei Markov. He had heard "The Trumpet Call" broadcast over the BBC and "Voice of America" and was astonished to hear that I was imprisoned in the same camp.

Under cover of darkness, I evaded the guards and arrived at his barrack hut around midnight.

Sergei was young and highly intelligent. "Economic crimes" had led him to jail, while his collaborators avoided prison. For Sergei it was particularly frustrating, as he lived in the region and yet was prohibited from stepping outside the camp. Our musical interest founded an immediate relationship between us.

I shared a secret with Sergei: that I had been composing a follow-up concept album while in labour camp. I could tell that he was excited, and I began to hum a few of the melody lines to him, improvising the bass line, guitar licks, and the synthesiser's moody images.

"Maybe we will be able to play together? Jailhouse rock!" I said with a smile.

"You mean a concert here in camp?" Sergei's jaw dropped in surprise at the outrageous suggestion. "You've got to be joking!"

"Just pray," I told Sergei.

Sergei reacted immediately, "But Valeri, I can't pray. I'm not a Christian."

Over the next few weeks we hung out together. Sergei's mind had a childlike openness, and blessed with such an attitude, it was easy for him to absorb new ideas and I watched faith grow in his heart. When he questioned me about God, I replied, "Try God. Pray, and see if he answers."

22

GULAG SERENADE

The criminal subculture operated an effective underground network in camp. A city within a city. At the right price and with the right connections you could get almost anything.

One gang used the facilities of the technical workshop to produce a variety of items that were smuggled out of camp and sold in the local town. These were mostly pens, lighters, rings, and similar objects for quick sale. Brass fillings for teeth were always popular, despite the acute shortage of qualified dentists. Tattoos were also in demand among the prisoners.

Once an imitation gun was produced in camp. "With an assembly-line in fake revolvers, we could stage a mass break-out," someone joked.

But it wasn't a joke, and a few weeks later a real gun was made and smuggled out to be sold on the black market.

I was never under threat from the gang bosses who said I was on "a mission from God", and although it always prompted a chuckle there was a degree of seriousness about their tone.

Sergei Markov and I hung out with Vadim in the camp library. Sometimes the back room was used to negotiate a deal, and one evening I walked in on Tomas, one of the gang bosses, bargaining with someone from Group Twelve who travelled out of the camp. He was holding five or six watches in his hand while the other convict counted out a bunch of notes.

I had seen too much. It wouldn't have taken a child long to work out what was going on. I decided not to assume any disguise. I bowed my head, held my hands up, and walked backwards out of the room.

Vadim immediately understood that something was wrong, but it didn't always pay to get involved.

A few minutes later, the door opened and the Group Twelve leader made a hasty exit. Tomas peered round the door and called me in. We stared at each other for a few seconds. Tomas broke the silence. "Are you OK?" he asked.

"Praise God, I'm fine," I replied.

Tomas eyed me carefully. "Weren't you in the cells and then hospitalised?"

"That's right, but my God healed me," I nodded.

"Valeri," Tomas faltered, "look after yourself. We wouldn't want anything to happen to you."

Tomas gave meaning to his cryptic words: "You have a message for our people. A message they must hear."

I relaxed, grateful that the back room business was over with. "Yes," I said, "I believe that God will make it possible for this trumpet call to cry out to our people, and to people all over this world. Maybe."

"Maybe," he agreed.

A few days later I saw Tomas at breakfast and we arranged to meet that evening at the library. "I've got something for you," he said enigmatically.

Tomas pointed to the back room and I followed him. "Making good use of the Party's paper," he said with a grin and pulled a crumpled issue of *Pravda* from his pocket.

Tomas unwrapped the package with great care. "There's only one person in camp who could use this," he said proudly. I couldn't imagine what it was going to be.

In his hands he held a carefully crafted cross.

My face registered surprise. "Thank you Tomas, thank you," I repeated.

I received it joyfully as a sign of God's abiding presence during the final six months in camp. Although the enemy would hurl poison arrows at me, I would not be harmed. Tomas refused to accept any payment for the cross. Instead, he asked me to write out some "words of Jesus", and I agreed.

I was careful to tuck the cross under my clothes, but on close inspection, it was visible.

The shop in camp was run by an elderly woman who lived locally. A few days later, I stopped to buy some chocolates, and as I reached into my pocket, the cross swung free. Her eyes widened in surprise and she cautioned me in a whisper, "Why do you wear a cross? It's bad for you. You'll have trouble, my son."

"No, no, it's all right. I'm a Christian."

But she wagged her finger disapprovingly at me. In a low voice she recounted an incident that happened in 1982. "There was a man like you, a holy one, and he carried a cross despite repeated warnings. One night the guards beat him mercilessly and crucified him on one of the posts. They actually nailed him to the post. He was hospitalised for a very long time, and after that, I don't know what happened to him."

The woman's deep brown eyes looked imploringly at me, "Please, my son, don't wear the cross."

"I know that I am a marked man, but my safety lies in obeying God." I explained.

A new officer, Captain Pushkin, had arrived in camp. Young and intelligent, he played strictly by the rules with a no-nonsense approach. Pushkin's first few days were eventful, and the gamblers in camp were taking bets on how long he would last.

Captain Pushkin was patrolling the camp one night when he saw the lights on in the kitchen block. Thinking some of the convicts had broken in to steal food, he was surprised to stumble on an extensive bootlegging operation. The network was an open secret, run by hard-regime prisoners who paid the guards to keep silent.

Pushkin immediately arrested everyone, forcing Lobanov

and Zinchenko to take a stand by extending their sentences. The camp administration were concerned that the gang would lead a revolt, and doubled the guard in the punishment zone.

The gang leaders were ruthless men with nothing to lose, and a contract was put out to get Pushkin. One evening the library went quiet as he walked in. He paused in front of me and called out, "What is it?"

His gaze had fallen on the cross around my neck.

"What is it?" he repeated.

"It's a cross," I replied calmly.

"Remove it now," he ordered. "This is forbidden by Soviet law."

I pleaded with him for permission to wear the cross but he was adamant. "No!" It was emphatic and beyond debate.

He received the offending item with a shake of his head, turned on his heel and left the room.

I had committed an offence for which I could be punished severely. One week later I was summoned to Captain Pushkin's office. Predictably, it was clean, neat and orderly. Without preliminaries, Pushkin began, "So, Barinov, you believe in God?"

"Yes," I replied simply.

He smiled, "It's funny to find someone like you in the twentieth century. You believers are like dinosaurs. You belong to the prehistoric age."

I sensed that Pushkin wasn't merely mocking Christians, but sincerely believed the truth of what he was saying. When I realised that he disliked religious people, he was surprised to hear that I was not religious.

"No, I believe that Jesus brings freedom. Even here in labour camp, I have experienced freedom of the spirit."

"But how can intelligent people believe in something they have never seen?" Pushkin insisted.

"But can you see electricity?" I asked him pointedly.

"No, I agree, but we can experience the effect of that power."

"You can experience the power of God," I smiled.

Two hours had passed. "I'm pleased that we talked," Pushkin said.

I couldn't be sure that I wasn't being manipulated, but there was a growing conviction in my heart that Pushkin was genuinely seeking the way of truth. I prayed for him continually.

Three days later a guard ordered me to follow him. "Captain Pushkin wants you in his office. Hurry up!"

Pushkin acknowledged the salute my escort gave him, but when the door was closed, he relaxed. "Take a seat," he said, pointing to a chair in front of his desk.

"Do you want some tea?"

This spontaneous question, although quite natural between friends, seemed to startle both of us. Pushkin was aware that I was running a risk by being with him. Only traitors and informers formed such liaisons, and our cosy chat could have serious repercussions.

Pushkin took some papers out of his desk drawer and spread them out. "If anyone interrupts us, we'll need a cover for our dangerous words," he said, amused at his own ingenuity.

The labour camp captain leaned forward, with a steaming cup of tea at his elbow. "Now Valeri, let's talk about Jesus!"

Pushkin called me a third time to his office. This time he was less talkative, and I could tell that he had something on his mind. He reached under his desk and pulled the bottom drawer open.

He looked up at me and said, "Valeri, I'm sorry I took your cross away and threw it in the rubbish. It was a terrible thing to do. It was the action of a blind man. Over these last few days I feel as though I have caught a glimpse of God through what you have told me. I know that you truly believe in Jesus, and I want to give you something."

With that, Pushkin pulled a large heavy cross out of his

drawer and handed it to me. "Please accept this as a gift
for the one I destroyed."

Stunned and deeply moved by this gesture, I knew I could
not accept the cross. To Pushkin's surprise, I declined his
offer, and the cross lay on the desk between us.

"Why won't you take the cross, Valeri?" he said
dolefully. "Are you angry with me?"

"Not at all," I said quickly. "No! When you took the
cross away, I took that to be a symbolic gesture that God
would also take me away from labour camp. I know that
the camp administration are plotting against me, but I now
believe they will be unable to hold me here.

"I am confident that I will be released when my sentence
is over," I declared. "No, I'm not angry, in fact I want to
thank you for playing a part in this."

Pushkin returned the cross uncertainly to his drawer. Then
he brought out another package and said with a prophetic
ring of truth in his words, "I brought this food for you.
Eat! You must be strong, and the struggle isn't over."

Sergei was shaking. "I can't believe it. I can't believe this
is happening."

We stood side by side at the morning assembly where
prisoners lined up to hear camp news. A list of names for
the punishment block was read out.

Then another announcement confirmed that a historic
event was to take place in two weeks time. A concert!

Our names were among the six or seven performers taking
part. The news sent a buzz through the crowd. "A concert?
What did he say? What kind of concert? Is this some kind
of joke?"

Through the prison network, we had been able to obtain
a trumpet, a bass drum, and a homemade guitar. Sergei had
learned of a few other musicians in camp and we had secretly
rehearsed the popular *Varyak March*, the story of a
battleship sunk during the war. In an outrageous move, we
had sneaked a meeting with Zinchenko, and performed it

for him. Somewhat dumbfounded, Zinchenko found himself agreeing to this ragged bunch of musicians playing for the camp drill and organising a concert.

The news spread like wildfire. I saw Machine that night at dinner and he grabbed my arm. "What's all this about a concert?"

"It's true, we're going to organise a concert," I replied.

"You're crazy," he said, thinking I was hiding something from him.

I could hardly believe it myself. But the duty officer confirmed it the next morning. Only God's intervention made this possible, and I told that to everyone who asked.

The concert was held at the assembly point, and was an unprecedented moment in the life of the camp. The guards wandered around non-plussed and were caught up in the excitement of the moment. In the punishment zone, the convicts crowded round the cell windows as the music wafted across the courtyard. Even Zinchenko and the other camp chiefs attended for a few minutes.

My songs combined old nostalgic folk tunes, Beatles numbers, and a rhythmic Hebrew rag called "Jerusalem". I sang a few Christian songs ending with the "Prisoner Song". There wasn't a single person listening who couldn't identify with the lament of a captive.

Before leaving the stage I told everyone that by popular demand, the final item was to be "The Christian's Prayer".

To my surprise, the men listened in silence, overwhelmed by the occasion and the power of the words. As we walked off the stage to thunderous applause, Sergei turned to me. "It's a miracle!" he said emotionally.

All around people congratulated us. For a few minutes we had brought a moment of hope into the despair of camp life.

Snake, and a long-timer called Mickey who was inside for armed robbery tapped me on the shoulder. "I didn't know you were a rock singer," Mickey said.

Before I could answer, Snake butted in, "His music has

been broadcast on the BBC and Voice of America, yes
indeed,'' he said proudly.

Mickey's eyes widened in amazement. It was all the
endorsement that was needed. Snake and Mickey were
music enthusiasts, and I promised them copies of "The
Trumpet Call''. In a wild moment we began to make plans
for meeting up in Leningrad and arranging further concerts.
Snake envisaged himself as an entrepreneurial concert
promoter.

"We could make a lot of money," he said excitedly. It
was like talking about launching a rocket from our labour
camp, but it was hard not to get swept along with the
enthusiasm of the moment.

With childlike wonderment we began to make plans but
gradually the reality of our plight hit home. We weren't in
Leningrad, we were in labour camp. But no one said
anything to break the spell.

Snake stopped abruptly, and his eyes flickered. "Valeri,"
he said "that prayer you closed the concert with . . ." his
voice tailed off uncertainly.

"It's the prayer Jesus taught his disciples," I explained.

"Could you write the words down for me?" he asked.

Mickey interrupted, "That prayer was really powerful.
It reminded me of something my mother taught us, but that
was such a long time ago and so much has happened in my
life since then." His head dropped down. "That prayer left
me in tears. Could you write the words down for me also?"

Snake turned to him and snapped, "Wait a minute, I
asked Valeri first."

"Hey, I can write the words down for both of you," I
grinned.

"That's not the point," Snake said, disgruntled. "You
see, I don't want you to give the words to anyone else, only
me," he said uneasily.

Snake saw a flicker of understanding in my eyes. A piece
of paper materialised in one hand and a gold-capped pen
in the other. "I'll share the profits with you," he said

sheepishly. "Everyone wants a copy, and they're all coming to me because they know I'm a fixer."

"Profits?" I questioned. "Look Snake, thanks for the offer but I can't sell the prayer. It's not right."

"But Valeri," he coaxed, "we could really clean up."

"No," I said firmly, "I'd like to help you, but not this way."

"But Valeri, I really do want the prayer for myself."

I promised both Snake and Mickey that I would have copies for them the next day, praying that the words would have a powerful impact on their lives.

Snake was right. The prayer had caused a stir, and not only among the prisoners. Two days later I was on a work assignment with Sergei Markov carrying supplies to the kitchen when Viktor, a new guard aged about twenty-two, beckoned to me.

"Weren't you the singer from the concert?" he asked. "What was that prayer you used at the end of the show?"

"It's a prayer that Christians say," I explained.

"Are you a real Christian, a believer?" he emphasised every word. "Or merely a Christian in name?"

"I am a Christian believer," I confirmed. "In fact, I am imprisoned here for my Christian activity."

Viktor was startled. "No, no, there must be some mistake. You wouldn't be sentenced for such a thing. But I'm curious that people can believe in Christianity when you can't prove that there is a God."

"On the contrary," I answered, and crouching down I drew a circle on the ground with a stick. "Assume that this is the total knowledge a man can possess."

Viktor nodded, and I continued, "Do you have access to this total knowledge?" He grinned and shook his head. "Who knows everything?" he laughed.

"Then how much knowledge would you claim to possess?" We agreed that a smaller circle within the full circle would be more realistic.

"In your life you say you have no experience of God, but

what about in the total knowledge and experience outside of your own? If you don't claim to know what happens in the area of knowledge outside of your own, then how do you know that God does not exist?"

Viktor grinned and scratched his head. "I guess this does prove at least the possibility of God's existence. I could tell that Viktor was struck by our conversation, and I was impressed by his sincerity. It was clear that God had already begun to work in his heart as he thought about these questions.

I always found it easy to pray wherever I was, and as I returned to the job of unloading gunny sacks, I immediately prayed for Viktor.

Oleg, one of the convicts, nudged Sergei in the ribs as he heard me praying. "What's the matter with him? Is he crazy?"

"He believes in God and he's praying to Jesus," he commented.

Oleg rolled his eyes upwards. "Then he is crazy."

"Why is he crazy because he believes in Jesus?" Sergei said. "I also believe in Jesus." I smiled to hear Sergei go on to explain to Oleg the steps that had led him to faith in God.

I knocked lightly on Captain Pushkin's door. I heard him call out and stepped inside. Pushkin was by the window talking with another officer. He looked at me sternly so that his colleague would suspect nothing and said, "Wait there. I'll deal with you in a minute." I bowed my head in a suitably subservient manner.

A few minutes later the officer left the office briskly. Pushkin yelled, "Now then Barinov, what's all this I've been hearing about you?" When I stepped into the room, I saw that he welcomed me with a smile.

He beckoned me forward and spoke in a hushed voice, "I've only got a few minutes, but I wanted to warn you that Lobanov and the others are furious about the concert. They are angry with Zinchenko for giving you permission to perform.''

He went on, ''They are planning to add five years to your sentence so that you won't be able to leave in three months' time.'' Pushkin stared at my face, which didn't register any dramatic emotion. ''Did you hear what I said?''

''Yes, I did,'' I replied, ''but how can their plots change the will of God?''

''No, you don't understand,'' Pushkin went on, still staring at me. ''They are collecting false documents to frame you. With Andropov's new law they can add an extra five years to your sentence on evidence from someone like Captain Zhora. They can do anything they like. Who's going to stop them?''

At that moment the door opened and another officer strolled in. Pushkin assumed an authoritative air and pointed angrily at the door. ''Out!'' he shouted, ''And don't forget my warning!''

In fact, his warning stirred me deeply. Time was running out. I believed that my safety lay in obeying God, rather than staying one step ahead of Lobanov's conspiracies. Soon my belief would be put to the test.

Three months. Ninety days. I imagined the moment when I would hold Tanya in my arms again and stroke her cheek, when I would pick up Zhanna and Marina, one on each arm, and collapse in a joyous embrace. I couldn't wait. But the KGB trap had been set. I asked to see Zinchenko, and waited outside his office in the hour allocated for prisoners' enquiries. He spoke to me uneasily, as the concert affair had put him under intense pressure.

''Yes, what is it?'' he said sharply.

''Sir, I have three months left here in camp . . .''

''Yes, yes, I know,'' he interrupted, ''so what, I can't do anything.''

I knew at that moment that he was aware of the plot to extend my term. I continued, ''But prisoners with three months left in camp are given permission to grow their hair.

I'm asking for permission from you, sir. Will you let me grow my hair?''

I could almost see Zinchenko's brain whirring as he debated the complex issue. If he said yes, then it would soon become visually obvious to the whole of camp that I would be leaving in three months. If he said no, then the sinister intrigue would have a public face.

Zinchenko stammered and lost his temper. "I can't be bothered with such matters. No, no, I can't give you permission."

I questioned why not, and he shouted, "I don't have to answer to you. Remember I'm the boss." Zinchenko called for the guard and terminated our encounter.

I felt that I had gained the advantage. By forbidding me to grow my hair, their conspiracy had become public. They had lost the initiative.

What should I do next? It was my move.

Stay low. Keep out of sight. Don't try anything risky. It sounded right. Yes, that's what I would do. Stay out of sight. Become the invisible man.

And then late one night, Vadim, Sergei Markov and I were talking about faith.

"Valeri, will you baptise me?" Sergei said quietly.

I could feel my insides rumble.

Vadim peered at me and said in a husky whisper, "And me. Valeri, will you baptise me also?"

I had been informed on and sentenced to the punishment block the last time baptisms had been planned. If the KGB could catch me red-handed conducting baptisms here in camp I would be giving them all the necessary evidence for them to lock me up and throw away the key.

I looked at Sergei and Vadim, marvelling at the transformation God had done in their lives. Lord, what should I do? In a flash, the answer was clear.

Trust me!

I smiled at them both and heard myself say "Yes, I'll baptise you. Let's make a plan!"

23

DANCING IN THE DRAGON'S JAW

Lobanov leaned back in his chair staring into space with his hands behind his head. His eyes looked bloodshot and his tousled, greasy hair fell across his forehead. A table lamp on his desk was switched on, although his room was bathed in sunlight.

I stood unperturbed in front of him. I understood the rules, I had played the game before.

"She's a pretty woman." His words were issued without warning. His gaze finally came to rest on me. "Red hair. They're supposed to have fiery tempers, or so the saying goes."

I recognised what his opening gambit would be.

"Does she?" he said, sounding genuinely curious.

I expressed bafflement.

"Your wife, the redhead, does she have a fiery temper?" Lobanov had made his move. It was important to stay one step ahead to beat the dealer.

My face showed the anguish that Lobanov had hoped to see. I watched his lips quiver with a smile of accomplishment. The target was in his sights.

I played the game. "Well yes, she does have a temper, that's right."

Lobanov opened a drawer and shuffled around until he found a matchbox. He leaned across the desk and began to pick his teeth. I was right, he had been drinking. I could smell his breath from where I stood.

"Shame," Lobanov muttered. "Shame." He stared at me

and scowled, shaking his head. "She's going through hell for you."

I felt the blow in the pit of my stomach, but I didn't let on. I just stared back at him.

"And those girls of yours," his words slurred slightly, "they're really pretty."

There it was again. An ache inside. A smashing blow that came hurtling down.

"Don't you care what happens to your family? What kind of a man are you?" he spat the words out contemptuously.

I started to pray within my spirit. This was my only defence.

The blows came fast and furious. Lobanov had obviously received recent information from Leningrad about my family. Twisting the knife with the expert skill of an experienced interrogator, Lobanov spelled out in graphic detail the humiliation facing my family.

"They'll be ruined," he said sympathetically. "And all for nothing. That's the real tragedy."

Then he laughed a lowdown cackle deep within his throat. "And no one cares. If only you knew that. You resist, but it's all in vain," he said, drawing out the words.

"God knows everything," I replied. "My life is in his hands."

Lobanov slammed his hand on the desk. "Don't you understand? We can do anything we want with you. I heard you wanted to grow your hair."

"That's right," I replied. "My sentence ends in a few weeks."

"You'll stay here until we've finished with you," Lobanov said with finality. "Do you know the law of the labour camp?"

I nodded, and in response, Lobanov bunched his fist and shook it at me. "This is everything."

But Lobanov had tired of his game, pressed a button beneath his desk to call the guard, and terminated the interrogation. The whole time he eyed me closely, picking his teeth and spitting on the floor.

"God bless you," I said as I turned towards the door.

Infuriated by my remark, Lobanov cursed me. "Don't think you're going to get away, Barinov," his voice boomed out across the room. "Remember Moshinsky!"

Moshinsky had believed that if the Party Boss knew how the camps were run everything would change, and so he drafted an appeal to the Kremlin. However, a traitor had handed his appeal over to Captain Verona, negotiating his own exchange. Two days later Moshinsky was caught in the showers and subjected to a brutal sexual assault. He was then held in the cells and continually abused by some of the homosexual prisoners from the hard regime. This went on for over two weeks, until Moshinsky was released from the cells as a broken man.

Lobanov watched my face for a reaction. Just the sound of Moshinsky's name was enough to sting.

The back room in the library was used by fences and dealers. Why shouldn't it be used for Jesus? With some wine, we could even celebrate the Lord's supper after the baptisms.

"Viktor can get us some wine," said Vadim, "but he wants to see you."

I met Viktor behind the barracks. He pretended to search me, and he made me stand with my legs apart and my hands up.

"What is it Viktor? Do you want us to pay for the wine?" I knew we only had a few minutes together.

Viktor shook his head vehemently. "Of course not, don't be absurd." Then he blurted out, "Valeri, don't baptise them without me!"

I didn't know what to do. Was it a trick? He appeared to have a great interest in Jesus. Vadim had sought me out to answer some of the questions Viktor had asked. What was baptism of the Spirit? Was it possible to lose our salvation? Was it possible never to sin again?

I said to Viktor, "You live in freedom. You can go

anywhere you like, to any town, and be baptised. Why do you want to be baptised here?"

"I have met some priests," Viktor confessed, "who are priests only by profession. They keep God hidden from people. But I have watched you and I know that you are a real Christian."

I felt privileged and humbled by Viktor's words. He was running an extraordinary risk, and I was surprised by his bravery. I decided to baptise him by his desire for faith.

The next few days were spent in prayer and fasting. If something went wrong, I knew I would not leave this camp and see Tanya and the girls again. Not for a very long time.

Zinchenko's office on the first floor of the administrative block had a commanding view of the woods behind the camp. It was rumoured that he took long walks in the woods, seeking the tranquillity which evaded him in the turbulence of camp life.

I had lain awake for much of the previous night, wondering what the tactics would be, plotting a strategy, determined to be strong. But now, strangely devoid of anxiety, I strode into the room knowing that God was my only shelter, my only peace.

"I'm an inspector from the Police Procurator's Office in Leningrad," Zinchenko's visitor explained in a city accent. He was tall, neatly dressed, and in his mid-twenties.

The inspector confirmed with Zinchenko that the interrogation would take the entire day, and Zinchenko waved his hands expansively, putting all facilities at his guest's disposal. "Let me know if there's anything else you need," he said, collecting a few of his own papers in a slim brown file and closed the door behind him gently.

The inspector got down to business. He looked like a career officer who would play by the rules. His smart black attaché case bulged with papers, files, documents. I was obviously a "high priority" criminal.

As we traced the criminal trail of Valeri Barinov, using

KGB Bureau notes, transcripts from the trial and interviews with witnesses inside camp, it became clear from the investigator's remarks that his brief was to compile sufficient evidence to secure a second conviction.

The morning passed without incident.

Skimming a report detailed by Captain Zhora, the inspector mused, "This case is puzzling."

"It's not that puzzling," I said slowly.

"What do you mean?" the inspector asked.

"The State hates Christians," I continued. "My only crime is that I'm a Christian. That is why I am threatened with an additional sentence even though my time is nearly up."

The inspector paused, reflecting on the mass of documentation on the case. "I just can't believe the accusations you make against the State. After all, everyone claims to be innocent," he said.

"But sir, you have read my documents. You have all the evidence there in front of you," I said quietly.

"Then if what you claim is true, the entire Soviet judiciary system and institutions such as these corrective re-education camps have been a waste of time," he exclaimed, clearly troubled.

"Re-education camps?" I cried. "We receive a criminal education here. Good people come here to be corrupted."

The inspector shook his head and was silent. "There must be something to warrant your criminal record," he continued.

The inspector confirmed that the orders had come from high up. That meant the KGB in Leningrad. All that was required was to rubber stamp the evidence. But where was the evidence? What was he going to tell Zinchenko? Far more importantly, what was he going to tell the KGB General back in Leningrad?

I began to pray. The inspector shuffled through the documents once more. The most damaging evidence was a note indicating that I had been interned in the punishment cell. "Why were you in the hard regime? There's no reason listed on the charge sheet. By law you should have signed this and it should have been countersigned by the commanding officer."

It was 4.30 p.m. and time was running out. Briefly, I tried to explain the laws of the labour camp. Rather, the lack of them. Yes, I had been dumped in the hard regime without reason.

"I know they want to kill me," I continued. "Extending my sentence is part of the plan."

The inspector leaned across the desk. "Do you realise what's happened? Your punishment in the hard regime could probably be used to extend your sentence by an additional five years. Captain Zhora would testify against you. But the document is unsigned. Without your signature it is worthless."

The inspector rose to switch on the light in Zinchenko's office. This movement heralded the change to follow. "I'm going to complete your documents and authenticate them with the Leningrad Procuracy's seal. This means that nobody will be able to alter the file or add anything to it."

The procedure was undertaken with professional skill. Each document was sealed and initialled by the inspector, and a final form placed at the front of the file noted that it contained thirty-seven pages. The inspector signed the document, and pressed the seal of the Leningrad Procuracy on the top right hand corner.

In a court of law, this document compiled within the final half hour of the business day would be my protection from a second sentence. But would it really serve as protection here in "Bloody Special" Camp No. 27?

It had been a long day. The inspector was staying overnight in the local town and flying back to Leningrad in the morning. As though reading my thoughts, he said, "It'll be your turn soon. You'll be on the way back to Leningrad. Just be careful during these last few days in camp. Do you know what I mean?"

"Yes," I said, "I know what you mean."

The inspector shook my hand and reached for the door. As an afterthought he said softly to me, "Perhaps God sent me to you?"

The second investigation was conducted in a casual manner by a KGB officer from Leningrad who wore a patch over one eye. Merely a formality that required my signature on the document that lay on the table between us.

"I'll have to notify the authorities of your refusal to assist with this investigation," he declared.

I shrugged my shoulders. "Do whatever you have to do."

The official sighed. "You're making life very difficult for yourself. You've only got a few weeks left in camp. Don't make waves. Don't you want to get out?"

Never stated, always implied, the judgement could be lifted with a stroke of a pen. His pen, my signature. But I won't sign.

"Do you believe?" I said gently to Sergei as he knelt in an attitude of prayer.

Sergei's eyes revealed the secrets of his heart as he looked up at me. There was a flicker of emotion in his voice as he whispered, "Yes, I do believe."

I made the sign of the cross and the secret ceremony commenced. "Sergei, because of your faith, I baptise you in the name of the Father, Son, and Holy Spirit."

The cascade of holy water made Sergei flinch as it crashed down on his naked frame. The water trickled down his body and into the drain in the corner.

Bathed in warm candlelight, the ante-room to the showers behind the library was strangely transformed as we experienced the presence of God with us. I felt a tingle in my heart. Sergei shook the water out of his hair and reached for a towel.

Smiling, Viktor quickly unbuttoned his uniform and knelt on the cold concrete floor. As I baptised him, I knew that he would never forget these moments in the quietness of our makeshift sanctuary.

Vadim was last, and as the jets of water raced down his body, he declared, "Praise God! Praise God!"

While Vadim was drying himself and dressing, we quickly moved the candles to a central location and spread a mat on the floor. Viktor placed the wine and some fresh bread beside the candles, and we huddled close to share communion together.

Emotions were running high as we ate the bread and drank the wine which had been provided by the guard, now our brother in the family of God. Smiles marked our coming together with a joyousness that I have rarely experienced.

Viktor unpacked another cardboard box. Fruit and chocolates. The celebrations continued for a few more minutes as we clasped hands together and prayed the Lord's Prayer.

It would be difficult meeting Viktor in the morning and having to refrain from charging after him in the camp street. He had to leave us to prepare for the early morning shift, but Vadim, Sergei and myself stayed behind for another hour.

But with Zhora on duty, anything could happen. Finally we locked the library door and climbed out of the rear window, cautiously setting off to our barracks.

It had been an extraordinary, unbelievable moment in our lives.

"You have to sign these documents," Lobanov said abruptly. "It's all to do with the end of your sentence. It ends in a few days. You know that of course?"

"Yes, I will leave camp soon," I replied, but he hadn't really heard me.

Like a magician Lobanov flashed the papers past me, placed them face down on his desk and covered them with his left palm. With his right hand he shoved a blank piece of paper over to me and said curtly, "Sign it."

Lobanov's hair was rumpled and he looked tired. Cigarette butts littered the floor of his office. "Show me the other documents," I said confidently.

Lobanov looked up at me. I could see the rage building up in his eyes, "You don't believe me?"

"If I can't read the documents, I won't sign this blank piece of paper," I replied.

Lobanov bunched his fist and glared at me. But I stood my ground, locked for an instant in this jangled war of nerves. Lobanov was the first to break.

Perhaps he had promised to trick me into signing some false document intended to frame me. "You will die in here!" he yelled, and shouted for the guard. "Take him away," he snarled.

Lobanov's fury erupted and he hurled abuse at me. He looked on the verge of bounding across to hit me.

"You will die here!" Lobanov repeated his threat as the door slammed shut behind me.

24

FINAL HOURS

I had dreamt of these moments a million times or more. I could almost taste the fresh air of freedom, feel the warm embrace of Tanya and my girls.

I didn't need a calendar. My inner clock had been set. It was September 3rd. Tomorrow, I would walk free. And yet danger overshadowed every footstep I took.

Evening roll call for the last time. Borodin . . . Zamyatin . . . Popov . . . punishment block, fifteen days. A groan went up from the crowd, and Captain Verona scowled at this expression of comradeship.

No one paid attention to the monotonous notices which followed. And then the release list. Nobody moved. Not a sound. It seemed as though life itself had stopped. Just the names.

Yevshenko . . . Marchenko . . . Yakhimovich . . . Zakharov . . . Vedeneyev . . . Golubyatnikov . . . Andzhaparidze . . .

There must have been twenty names. Every time a name was announced, there was a gasp. From the front. From the side. There next to me.

Barinov!

Finally!

Astonishingly, a ripple of applause erupted after my name.

Someone cheered. It seemed as though the entire camp were rejoicing. It was common knowledge that I had been threatened with extra time.

I smiled, with the joy of triumph in my heart. "Jesus, I praise you, you really are the victor!"

Captain Zhora paced restlessly at the front. "Dismiss, dismiss, that's all," he yelled, driving us away like a flock of pigeons.

Vadim signalled, holding up two fingers. I understood and winked back. So, two hours later, tea and choice foods materialised as guests arrived to say farewell.

"You don't know me, but I've heard about you," said a gaunt figure, hand outstretched, "Give my love to Leningrad." And then as an afterthought, he said proudly, "I've got God's Book for this week."

The New Testament was still around, passed regularly from hand to hand. It could never be stopped. You can arrest a man and jail his body, but how do you imprison an idea?

Vadim, Sergei, Machine, Snake, Mickey, Gypsy. It was hard to say goodbye. We had shared the bitter cup together. We could never forget.

The next morning was a cool grey autumn day. I was allowed to shower, and to wear my civilian clothes. They were loose and baggy.

Zhora caught my eye as I stood in the reception area. The atmosphere was tense. A document signed by Zinchenko allowed me to walk to the main gate where my personal items and internal passport, confiscated at Murmansk two and a half years ago, were handed back. I stared at them as though they belonged to a stranger.

The duty officer pointed me to the "box" located at the main gate. One final humiliation.

As I walked, I turned back to peer at the camp. The marshy swamp, the barracks where the rats prowled, the cells with water running down the walls. And the faces, the haunted, doomed eyes of witnesses tramping through the cold wilderness. The scene was caught, as by a photographer's lens, frozen in time, from some forgotten far country.

A guard opened the box, and I stepped inside, a tiny wooden hut where I sat huddled with two others. No one said a word. Then the other two were summoned, transferred by van to another prison.

But I was going to walk free. I knew. Jesus had told me.

An hour passed.

I rattle the door.

"What is it?"

"It's me. I'm still here."

Silence.

"If there's a woman outside with red hair, tell her I'm still in here. She's waiting for me."

Silence.

Another hour passes.

The rollercoaster of emotions. I pray aloud.

I will lift my eyes to the hills . . .

It's after 11 a.m., four hours after I arrived at the reception area. Without warning, the door opens and I'm tossed my own coat. Tanya must have brought it with her. It hangs loosely on my shrunken frame.

A hand points the way. It's now quite warm in the midday sun. I press my palm against the gate, ensuring that my fingerprints remain.

There she is, red hair blowing gently in the breeze. Tender eyes express relief when I appear, as if from nowhere. My arms go round her and she clings to me. It's exactly how I knew it would be.

I made it. I'm outside the gates. I'm with Tanya.

But we're not alone.

A green-grey Moskvich saloon car was parked at the gates, driver ready, engine running. A lieutenant leaned against the vehicle puffing on a cigarette.

"Barinov." Not a question, more a command. "Get in," he said, gesturing to the car's open door.

"Not this time," I called back. "Now I'm free. Why should I listen to you?"

The officer looked stern. "Take a look at those prison

gates. One wrong move and you'll be back so fast your feet won't hit the ground.'' He pointed to the car. ''I've got orders to escort you to the railway station. We've got tickets reserved for you.''

Tanya interrupted. ''But my luggage is back at the hotel in Uktah.''

''No problem,'' the officer replied. ''Give me your room number and we'll send your belongings on to you. But I must put you on the train.''

Tanya gripped my hand. The KGB were sending us a telegram to get on the train. Perhaps they had negotiated an ''accident'' further down the track?

In a flash, the officer gripped my arm and moved me towards the car. ''Let it be,'' Tanya whispered, as we were shoved on to the back seat. Tanya sat huddled next to me, holding my hand. I gave her a peck on the cheek and she smiled.

Ten minutes later the driver braked sharply, pulled up outside the railway station and we were hustled out. There were no tickets. ''Buy them on the train,'' the officer insisted, as the train pulled in.

''But why the rush? Why can't I take the next train?'' I argued.

''Don't give us any trouble,''the lieutenant replied, urging us across the platform. Tanya climbed aboard, and I followed. The officer slammed the carriage door shut and yelled his farewell speech, ''Obey what we tell you, or we'll throw you in prison again.''

As the train picked up speed we prayed for guidance. Both of us felt that to stay on the train would be playing into the hands of the KGB.

''Let's find the conductor,'' I said to Tanya. He was in the next carriage, a tall man with a full bushy beard.

''I am a Christian,'' I declared. ''The KGB put me in prison and I was released today.''

He stared at me and nodded. Could he possibly understand just what we had gone through? ''Christian?''

he said, pulling the edge of his beard. "Hmm, that's interesting."

"Tell me," I asked, "where does the train stop next? Is it soon?"

"Next stop, hmm," the conductor repeated my question thoughtfully. "Not for a few hours, I'd say. Let me check the timetable for you."

A few hours. Anything could happen. The inspector held on to the window rail and tried to peer out. Trees and bushes went charging past.

I stared at Tanya. She felt it too. The track led straight ahead, no bends or curves in its path. Tanya turned to me and stuttered incredulously, "The train is slowing down."

Within minutes the train had stopped. The conductor peered at the signals ahead. "Can't understand what's happening up there."

Tanya and I stared at the door. "Could we get off here?"

The conductor looked non-plussed. "Certainly!" he replied, scratching his head. "Just be careful. There isn't a platform and you're in the middle of nowhere."

"That's all right," I said as I jumped out and helped Tanya step down.

It really was the middle of nowhere. Pine trees and railway track were all there was, and like children we held hands and tripped along the track delighting in our dance of release. This was the first burst of freedom I had experienced in two and a half years. The energy of our joy kept us going, and Tanya produced some chocolate and two apples from her bag.

This was the first chance I'd had to talk to Tanya and catch up on news about the girls and our friends. About eight kilometres down the track towards Uktah, we hit a small provincial station at Yarega. The station was deserted, but I recognised the area. Group Twelve used to drive through it from the camp on the way to chop trees.

We followed the dirt track until we saw a bus stop, and within half an hour, the bus pulled in. Tanya and I stood to one side as a few passengers disembarked. I recognised the second man to step down. He had helped me obtain the Easter eggs, and his brother worked as a driver for the camp.

"Hello, Valeri," he said, taken by surprise. "What are you doing here?"

"I'm free," I replied. But I couldn't contain the disappointment I felt. "Why didn't you help us in camp? Why didn't you bring us scriptures?"

I could see he was startled. "But Valeri . . ." the excuses rolled off his tongue.

For a dazzling second, I felt as though I could look inside his soul and feel the fear pounding in his heart. For that instant, he came to symbolise the Christian church, asleep, bound, afraid, peeping through the window, hiding behind the door.

I was imprisoned, but free. He walked everywhere he wanted, but was imprisoned by fear.

The bus pulled out and wound its way along the track. Yarega is a small town, and the people we encountered had a richness and purity, arranging their lives in an uncomplicated mode. During our brief moment there, I felt a deep affection for this hidden country and its simple folk.

In Uktah, we slipped discreetly into the hotel and recovered Tanya's luggage. As we climbed down the creaky, wooden stairs and headed for the main reception to return the room key, I noticed a military officer enter the hotel. "He's come for your luggage," I whispered to Tanya.

"Where are the people from Room 717?" the militiaman called out to the hotel clerk.

"Perhaps you came for me? I am Valeri Barinov," I called out to the officer.

His expression changed and he looked serious. "Why aren't you on the train? You must be on the train!"

We knew that this officer was merely following orders, but like all bureaucrats, when the situation changed he became perturbed and didn't know what to do.

"Why did you leave the train? That route would have taken you direct to Leningrad," the officer charged.

I smiled at him and said nonchalantly, "No, you're mistaken. That route would have led me direct to prison."

He stared at Tanya and me, uncertain as to what his next move should be. I resolved the issue by seizing the initiative. Tanya handed back the key and paid her bill. Together we crossed the hotel's foyer, our every move watched by a confused military officer and an uncertain hotel clerk.

What a strange sight this couple must have been. I walked like a criminal, my eyes darting from side to side, alert for any sudden move. By my side, Tanya walked like a lady, her head held high, her eyes bold and courageous.

It was getting dark and the town wasn't safe, so we jumped in a taxi to the airport. I didn't turn back to see if the officer was still at the hotel and we weren't followed.

The airport at Uktah was like any provincial depot. There were lots of people milling around, but no one knew what was happening. The young dark-haired girl at the counter informed us that the Leningrad flight had departed several hours ago.

"When is the next flight to Leningrad?" I asked, trying not to sound alarmed.

She pondered for a moment and then replied somewhat uncertainly, "Tomorrow." She smiled courteously and then added cheerfully, "Probably."

"Thank you," I said, struggling to hide the growing concern. I realised that it wasn't her fault. This was how the system operated in our land.

"When does the next plane leave?" I asked her, on the spur of the moment.

The girl checked her watch and said brightly, "Ten minutes."

I watched her for an instant, recognising the signals. "Probably," we said together, chuckling.

Tanya hurriedly counted out forty-eight roubles and

handed them over the counter. The girl had followed the transaction and reached out for two airline tickets.

"Oh, where's the flight going?" I added curiously.

"Moscow," the airline clerk replied.

"Thanks!" I called out as we raced across the terminal building. The plane was on the concourse with its passengers all on board as Tanya and I strode breathlessly on to the aircraft. We found two seats together near the rear of the plane and sank down.

Within minutes of clicking our safety belts into place, the engines started up and the "No Smoking" sign appeared.

We were airborne.

I reached out and took Tanya's hand. "We've been so busy I forgot to tell you that I love you."

Her eyes twinkled and she rubbed my palm against her cheek. "It's been the longest day of my life," she said with a sigh.

I peered through the window. There was nothing to see except the profound darkness of the night. Both Tanya and I were relaxed and calm.

We had got away.

Polkova airport in Moscow was deserted. The next flight out was not until the morning, and we couldn't be sure of getting on it. There was nothing to do but wait.

Weary and exhausted, we collapsed on the nearest bench that would accommodate our prostrate forms. Tanya was unwell, suffering from high blood pressure, so we prayed together for healing and then settled down to sleep. It was clear that Tanya had matured spiritually during my time in prison. In the morning she awoke feeling no discomfort and we were able to book tickets on the second flight out to Leningrad. We tried to sleep on the long journey across the country.

Leningrad. I looked down at my hometown as the plane descended. It seemed that nothing had changed, as though I had never been away. As we stepped from the plane I felt a surge of energy flow through me.

But I couldn't wait to get home and we took a taxi from the airport. The driver was a young lad dressed in a trendy denim jacket, obviously obtained from a foreigner. Observing my short haircut and gaunt appearance he assumed that I had been "inside". When he learned that I had been imprisoned for Christian rock music, he shouted, "Not 'Trumpet Cry'?"

I laughed, "You mean 'The Trumpet Call'."

He looked flabbergasted. "You mean you're the guy who recorded and sang 'The Trumpet Call'?" He spun round to catch a better glimpse of me. With only one hand on the wheel, the car zigzagged, swerving recklessly as it hurtled along.

"Look out. We're going to hit that car!" Tanya shrieked.

The kid spun round and calmly turned the wheel to avoid a head-on collision. The journey home was a series of nail-biting near misses as he questioned me about "The Trumpet Call". When we reached Khudozhnikov Prospekt where we lived, I invited the driver into our home, "I'll give you a copy of 'The Trumpet Call'."

He grinned, "No thanks, I've already got a copy. In fact, I've been giving copies to all my friends."

The key in the door. The narrow hallway. Panthera, my faithful dog, stared cautiously, circling the intruder. Could it be him?

Suddenly, Panthera pounced, leapt, almost knocking me over, her black tail lashing the air furiously. She went wild and charged through the apartment in a frenzy. As I hugged Tanya, Panthera forced her way between us, showering me with affection, slurping my face with her long wet tongue.

A figure rushed from the living room and embraced me tightly.

Amidst the tears and flowing long brown hair, I recognised my cousin Valya.

"Valeri, thank God you're safe," she sighed.

Tanya's mother appeared and kissed me on both cheeks.

"Sit down, I'll get some tea," she said. "You must be hungry."

"Where are the girls?" I enquired.

Tanya's mother checked the clock. "They're still at school," she remarked. "They will be home soon."

Tanya and I settled down on the sofa, her mother served tea and cakes that she had baked to celebrate my homecoming. There was so much to do, so much to catch up on, but I wasn't in a hurry, curiously at peace.

Tanya handed me a photo album and I flipped through it. I stared at these beautiful young women. "Which one is Zhanna?" I asked. I could not believe that they had changed so much.

Then Tanya opened a drawer and pulled out bundles of postcards and letters that had arrived from around the world. London. New York. Paris. Amsterdam. Frankfurt. Dublin. Brussels.

"I knew that people were praying for us and thinking of us," she said softly. "Somehow that gave me strength to carry on."

I could tell that the family had struggled without me and that things had been hard.

As I flicked through the mail, a tall young girl with dark hair cascading down her back appeared at the door. I couldn't imagine who this could be as she walked into the room and came over to me.

"Zhanna!" I stammered.

At that same instant a second, slim, beautiful girl entered the room. She was even taller than the first young lady.

"Marina?" I gasped in shock.

I had left them as girls, and while I was in prison they had grown up into mature young women, aware and attracted by the fashions of this world. I thanked God that they had not succumbed to the corruption and temptations of life.

Zhanna and Marina were collectively responsible for the storming of my memory banks. Both girls fell on top of me, their hands locked around my neck, hugging and kissing me.

It was a moment beyond words.

"Never leave us again, Daddy," Zhanna whispered amidst the tears and the laughter.

We were such a close family, and our lives had been locked together, sharing every experience. But Jesus came first. Zhanna and Marina understood and supported my struggle for faith and freedom, and within that understanding, we would find grace together.

"No, I'll never leave you again," I replied, and I knew it would always be this way.

25

TELEVISION EXCLUSIVE

September 6th, 1987! I was home!

Like a child in a sweet shop, I wanted to taste everything
– all at once! I had two and a half years of living to catch
up with, but I was weary from the journey, and slept a
straight nine hours that night.

The next morning, Tanya surprised me with a jar of
Nescafé. It had been so long since I had tasted strong, black
coffee. The pungent aroma confirmed that I hadn't been
dreaming.

Tanya said she'd cook some fried chicken, but I didn't
want her to leave my side. And so we ate food prepared by
Tanya's Mama and Valya.

Friends phoned continually during the day to welcome
me home. Some time that afternoon a husky male voice said,
"Barinov?"

"Yes," I answered, "it is me."

"Turn on the television in half an hour," the voice
instructed.

"What do you mean?"

"Just watch the television," the voice said confidently.

"Who are you?" I asked the mystery caller.

"You know who I am," the voice said and hung up the
phone.

Tanya had been staring suspiciously throughout the
encounter. "Who was that?" she asked.

"Probably the KGB," I pondered. "They wanted me to

watch television,'' I explained, finding it difficult to disguise the surprise in my voice.

We soon found out why the Secret Police had alerted us. The television programme entitled *Pharisee* accused Bible smuggling operations of dealing with pornography and other vile publications. Juxtaposed with this was footage shot at my trial, carefully edited so that I was shown to be an unreliable witness. The film also included the "confessions" of Sergei Timokhin, my friend and "collaborator".

All through the film, friends rang to alert me of its screening. "Thanks, I knew it was going to be shown," I told the callers, one of whom was George. "You knew?" George asked incredulously. "Then why didn't you tell me?"

We took the phone off the hook and watched the rest without interruption. The phone rang again as soon as we replaced the receiver. It was Lita, one of the girls we knew from the Moonwalk Club. "Valeri, it's you! I'm so glad you're home. You won't believe it, but there's been an amazing film on TV!"

There was no food in the house, so I volunteered to walk to the corner to see what was available. As I stood in the queue to buy fish, brussels sprouts and potatoes, two men in their thirties stared at me.

"What happened to your hair?" the first man said. "You were on TV just now, weren't you?" the other one called out.

Soon a crowd had gathered. Someone said, "Is it him? He looks so thin. I'd heard he wasn't coming home."

I explained what had happened, and immediately there were expressions of sympathy.

"Communist mafia!" someone yelled after I had finished speaking, and everyone laughed.

Two weeks after that, the film was repeated on television. I was impressed with the project and discussed it at length with Tanya and our friends.

Someone had obviously paid close attention to detail and orchestrated the preview to coincide with my release from camp. The same authority must have had access to the television network's programme scheduling. As all media were controlled by the State, this wasn't hard to achieve. But who could have engineered such an operation? There were no prizes for the answer to that question.

The film made a remarkable impact in Leningrad, and wherever I went, people recognised me and shouted their congratulations. "We heard your music on the BBC," one teenager in torn jeans and a punk hair style told me on the subway. "Don't let them beat you down," he said, touching my arm in sympathy.

One old lady stared at me in the street. "Aren't you the Christian whose trial was shown on TV?"

"Yes, it's me," I grinned, "I'm the guilty man."

She smiled and held out her hands. "Let me give you a hug." Then she said, "I hope God keeps you on this path, my son." Tears formed in her eyes and it was clear that she had lost loved ones in the Gulag. "I fear that they will hunt you down," she sighed.

But I smiled and tried to cheer her, "Don't worry about me. I belong to Jesus."

"But you don't know these wicked people," she remarked. "They'll do anything to get you."

"But Jesus has the victory over the devil," I told her confidently.

The next few months were spent relaxing at home, lying in Tanya's arms, holding Zhanna and Marina close. Every time they walked out of the room, I felt restless and uneasy, waiting for the moment when I would see them again.

Some nights I couldn't sleep, and after tossing and turning I would take Panthera for a walk. Usually the streets were deserted, peaceful and serene. Everything seemed so normal, but to me even these everyday occurrences took on special significance. It had been so long since I had lived normally.

It was just like old times. Friends called in, some brought tapes of new singers. In three years styles had changed so much. To my delight, Zhanna and Marina were modern teenagers who loved the new rhythms. They learned the words to Sting's song "Russians love their children too." Although they didn't understand all the lyrics it was great fun.

I jogged every day, exercised regularly, and over the next few weeks I could feel myself growing strong. My strength wasn't the only thing that was growing. My hair, which had fallen out in clumps and had been trimmed to a bristle, was soon down to my neck.

It was like being given a new life, like being born again. I even looked different.

Several days were spent in monastic-style communion with God. I couldn't name the day or the exact moment, but a feeling had grown and been confirmed. I knew what had to be done.

It was just after seven in the evening when the doorbell rang. "That'll be Zhanna and Marina," Tanya said, going to the door. Then I heard her call, "Valeri!" Her voice was heavy with emotion, and I knew something was wrong.

It was the police. No explanation was offered as I was bundled into the back of a police car and driven to Police Station No. 14. The duty officer refused to volunteer any explanation for my arrest but filled out the warrant card and I was shuffled into the cells.

Forty-eight days had passed since I had been released from camp. By 2 a.m. the dingy cell was full of thieves, prostitutes and criminals arrested that night.

One drunk tugged my sleeve and began to tell me his sad story. After he lost his wife, his children had married and moved away, and he lived alone. In despair, he had turned to drink and had frequently been picked up by the police. "But this time," he complained, "I wasn't doing anything. Why did they arrest me? What am I living for? What am I doing here?"

I placed my arm around his shoulder and spoke quietly, "I know why you are here." His eyes bulged as he stared at me. "You are here to meet me," I exclaimed.

Slowly I explained that the presence of Jesus in his life could help him overcome his loneliness and despair. I handed him my address and asked him to visit me.

The next morning, as mysteriously as I had entered the cells, I was released. "No charges," the duty officer at the front desk told me, "You're free to go."

The incident clarified my thinking. I couldn't remain silent. I had to tell everyone about Jesus. This was my mission. A few days later I wrote an appeal to General Secretary Mikhail Gorbachev requesting permission to continue my work, using rock music to share the life-changing message of Jesus with young people. I concluded my appeal with the words, "Please grant me permission to preach the Gospel or allow our family to leave the country so that I can live for Jesus' glory and share this message all over the world."

I gave copies to friends from Britain and was encouraged to learn that those who had campaigned for my release were standing with me in this new venture of faith.

Towards the end of the year, I visited my old adversary, Mr Kirov of the Council for Religious Affairs. I explained to his receptionist that I was "Valeri Barinov of 'The Trumpet Call'."

Suddenly his door opened wide, "Oh, 'Trumpet Call'? Come in, come in.

"You look thin," he said with a chuckle.

Seated in a comfortable leather chair, Kirov reviewed his guest. "So you're going to have a rest now?" he said, sounding cheerful.

I responded with equal optimism, "No, no, I've had a long rest. Two and a half years of rest. Now I want to work."

Kirov jerked forward in his chair. "No! No! Please don't! Please don't!" Kirov sounded alarmed and urged me to consider my family's welfare.

We discussed my options and the risks that I ran by continuing to work among young people. "I don't want to leave Leningrad," I told Kirov, "but I must fulfil my mission." He reflected on my dilemma and then said, "Do you know where the 'big house' is? That's the best place to discuss the subject," Kirov answered confidently.

At their headquarters on Voinov Street, the KGB were unprepared and the interview was dismissive. All they could suggest was that I consult the Ovir (emigration office) who in turn confirmed that it was impossible to leave the country without a personal invitation from a blood relative.

The underground communications network in Leningrad had spread the news that I was still alive and back from camp. Every day someone new called in to see me.

Sergei was a thin, gaunt, long-haired hippie I dubbed "Lennon" because of his resemblance to our favourite Beatle. He was an Orthodox believer who understood that icons and rituals didn't hold any magic power. I gave him a Bible and over the next few weeks we spent a lot of time together.

Café Saigon on Nevsky Prospekt was popular among the city's street people and we took to hanging out with the punks, hippies and dropouts. Within a few weeks we had gained a following of about three hundred people, many experiencing the power of God in their lives. But meeting together proved problematic.

For a few weeks, we met in Gatchinar, a half hour train ride away from Leningrad where an active church opened its doors to us. The meetings were extraordinary as old women shared hymn books with punk rockers.

But tensions within the church and pressure from the authorities closed that door. We suspected that the group had been infiltrated by informers and some of the leaders of our "unofficial church" were being watched and followed. "Lennon" summed up the situation, "This is God's work. Nothing is going to stop us now!"

The gypsy congregation moved from street to street with Café Saigon serving as the cockpit of communication.

After observing several empty church buildings, I visited

Kirov trying to obtain permission for our group to meet in one of them. This turned out to be a lost cause.

Early in March, Jubilee Campaign in Britain told me that they had succeeded in sending a copy of my appeal to Mrs Thatcher, and that they had received assurances that she would raise my case during her meetings in the Kremlin. I knew that the telephone was bugged, and it was difficult to speak freely on an open line.

When I told Tanya the news, we both chuckled with laughter. How would our telephone "bug" file this conversation in his report to the KGB? Meanwhile, other contacts in the West tried to dissuade us from leaving Leningrad. This puzzled us for a while, but we decided to follow God's direction rather than the advice of men.

Gorbachev's doctrine of glasnost was creating widespread speculation throughout the world. Inside the country we learnt of the changes through personal experience.

The British Prime Minister's visit was phenomenal. By all accounts, the openness surrounding her visit was unprecedented in the history of the Soviet Union.

However, for the duration of her visit, our activities were severely curtailed, and padlocks were placed on the doors of the hall where we usually met with our unofficial church of young people.

About ten days after Mrs Thatcher left Moscow, I was called to the emigration office. In a complete U-turn, they told me that if I wanted to, I could pack my suitcase and leave the USSR the following day.

"But I haven't got an invitation," I stammered.

"That's all right," the Ovir inspector told me. "Just fill in these forms and return them. We'll do the rest, and you'll be on your way to Israel."

"But I don't want to go to Israel," I argued, "I want to go to Britain."

"Just take the documents and fill them in," he said in exasperation. I left the office deep in thought. This was clearly a political decision: the British Prime Minister's intervention had resulted in a change of policy regarding my case. But did I really want to leave my homeland?

What I wanted was to fulfil my mission. I wanted to tell the world about Jesus. This was the trumpet call that I had been entrusted with.

On the spur of the moment, I decided to catch the overnight express to Moscow and seek help from the Baptist Organisation there.

Alexei Bychkov, the denomination's General Secretary, greeted me warmly in the old tradition with a kiss on both cheeks. "What are you doing here?" he said jovially. "You should be in the West." From this remark I understood that he knew a lot about me even though we had never met.

When I explained that the emigration office told me that I could leave immediately, Rev Bychkov said, "Yes, go, go."

His response took my by surprise. "But that's why I wanted to talk with you," I explained. "We are Russians, yes?"

"Yes," Rev Bychkov replied.

"Then where is it best to work?" I posed the question that had been preying on my mind.

Bychkov squirmed in his chair. He then began a rambling discussion about the dangers of operating outside official structures. He would be unable to assist me in obtaining permission to register our group of young people. He had one reply to all my questions.

"Go!"

I found it difficult to understand why the leader of the Baptists wanted me out of the country.

Bychkov checked his watch. "One thirty!" he exclaimed, rising to his feet and taking my arm. "Come with me, let's get something to eat."

As we walked to the dining room, I spotted Rev Letuyenka, the Baptist President, standing near the entrance to the hall. I had met him previously in Leningrad and we had clashed over the medium of modern music. "Rock music is from the devil," he had said dismissively.

Abruptly, Bychkov excused himself for a moment and I found myself alone with Rev Letuyenka. "Greetings from Leningrad," I called out to him. To my surprise, he walked away without saying a word.

As I waited for Bychkov's return, a tall well-built man appeared and ushered me into his office. He told me his name and embraced me warmly. "Valeri," he said, "Oh, it's so good to see you! When you were in prison, I prayed regularly for you."

Then he said quietly, "Do you want some Bibles? Could you use them in your work?"

"Bibles?" I repeated the word. Despite all the news reports, Bibles were still hard to find. "Yes please!"

"How many would you like?" he asked.

"How many have you got?" I countered. "I'll take them all."

We arranged a secret rendezvous and my new friend smuggled the Bibles out of the Baptist centre for me. I knew that everyone at the Café Saigon would want one.

Bychkov called my name, and I slipped out to meet him. The dining hall was crowded, but I was given an honoured place at the top table and we were served a generous portion of borsch.

Bychkov turned to me and said, "Valeri, you know who sat in this chair before you? Billy Graham, as well as many other famous Christians from the West." Bychkov repeated other well-known names and related some personal backstage incidents indicating that he knew these celebrities intimately.

But I didn't consider this an honour. I was in prison when Billy Graham visited the Soviet Union, and I found it hard to understand how such people could come to our country and remain silent about the persecution of their brothers and sisters. Perhaps he spoke privately, but I considered such moves to be powerless gestures. I was disappointed that he appeared to make no effort to signal his public support for the persecuted Church.

As I sat with Bychkov at the dining table, I became uneasy, not wanting to remain in this privileged position any longer. I perceived it to be the place of people who had compromised this godless system.

I preferred to be among lowly, ordinary people.

I left the Baptist headquarters in some confusion and headed back to Leningrad. As the overnight express hurtled through the night I prayed, *Jesus, what should I do*?

I considered going underground in order to carry on the work of our group. Many Christian leaders had been forced to live this way, hunted from house to house, rarely seeing their families.

I had been approached by a mysterious group who claimed to have a secret recording studio in the mountains. Did I want to record a follow-up album to "The Trumpet Call"? But the deal, shrouded in secrecy, didn't work out. Yet another door had been slammed shut.

When the train pulled into Leningrad around 9 a.m. I found the house empty. The girls were at school and Tanya was at work. Weary from the journey and tired from yet another sleepless night, I tried to rest but tossed and turned. I got out of bed and paced the floor, a prison habit that I had been unable to shake off.

An hour later, I sank on to the bed exhausted. Once again, I prayed, *Jesus, what should I do*?

Every door seemed to be closing. Yet in my heart I felt a compulsion to continue sharing my experiences with young people, not just in our own country, but throughout the world.

I fell into a deep sleep and experienced a vivid dream.

In the dream, I saw an Orthodox priest moving among the people in the Baptist Church. This was highly unusual, as denominations didn't mingle. I called out to the priest, and he came over to me immediately because I was the only one in the church who called for him. I knelt before him and said, "Please pray for me. I want God's blessing on my life." The priest placed his hand on my head and said,

"In the name of the Father, the Son, and the Holy Spirit."
As he did that, I experienced a great blessing of God flow
through me.

I awoke immediately and recalled every detail. Only
fifteen minutes had passed. But I couldn't understand the
dream.

Why did you bless me, Lord? I had prayed to ask the way
ahead, but was still uncertain about the future.

I suddenly realised that the front doorbell had been
ringing, and hurried to open the door. It was the postman
with a registered package for me. I ripped off the brown
manilla covering and stared at the contents, hardly believing
my eyes.

The package was from the British Embassy in Moscow.
It contained a personal invitation from my friend in Britain,
issued through the British Foreign Office.

My throat felt dry and parched. A tight band had formed
around my chest, and I breathed in short spurts.

In the solitude of my apartment I lifted my hands to
heaven, recalling the vision. Instantly I felt God's blessing
flowing through me, just as it had in the dream.

This was the way!

I mailed Bibles to my friends in labour camp. It seemed such
a great distance away, like a planet dangling in deep space.
But when Yura Taikov and Alex Zelichenok visited me, I
knew that labour camp had not been a hallucination.

One evening a tall haggard man rang my doorbell. I knew
immediately that he was from the camps. He had that
haunted look of a man who had travelled to the moon. But
he smiled kindly and his eyes were alive. I realised that he
was the Christian that I had heard about from the other
prisoners. We prayed together and I told him how pleased
I was that we were held in separate camps.

Viktor, the guard, also visited me and together we went
to some of the meetings at Café Saigon.

The emigration papers and documents from the British

Embassy were kept neatly folded in the sideboard drawer.

That summer, I travelled to several towns and cities all across the country. Without an itinerary or money, I moved as God prompted me. Everywhere I observed the amazing fruit of "The Trumpet Call" broadcasts. When I arrived in one town with no contacts, God led me to take a taxi from the airport to the town.

"Do you know any Christians?" I quizzed the taxi driver when he asked me where I was heading.

"Not really," he replied, "but my brother is a Christian."

When the driver learned that I was the creator of "The Trumpet Call", he swung the vehicle over to the side of the road and we talked for an hour. This led to a series of meetings in clubs, bars, and halls where many people followed us round asking to know more about God.

In one city we held an open air meeting that lasted for three hours and was attended by hundreds of people.

In one town, about six people from the KGB joined a group of young people who had come to listen to me and I was able to share my views about Gorbachev. I said that he was a special man brought by God on to the stage of history. I drew attention to the birthmark on his forehead and explained prophecies from the Bible about the Kremlin, Lenin and Gorbachev.

In Moldavia, I met many gifted musicians and together we organised a Christian Rock Festival. The KGB tried to stop us and closed all entry roads leading to the park where the event was to be staged.

The festival went ahead and was a phenomenal success, attracting more than a thousand young people, hippies, punk rockers, heavy-metal fans and other dropouts.

About sixty people were arrested and held in custody for a few hours. Many local Christians lived in fear of the KGB, but I exhorted them to be courageous.

This missionary tour was a remarkable odyssey as I criss-crossed the country. My new-found friends would collect money for me and drop me at the airport. In the terminal building, I prayed, *Lord, where should I go next*? Sometimes I had just enough money to buy a ticket on to the next destination.

I returned to Leningrad at the end of that summer. While I had been away, Lennon and the others had kept in contact with the group of young people we called the gypsy church. We were still dogged by the same problem. We had nowhere to meet together to pray and sing.

After witnessing some astonishing open air meetings on my journey, the idea of holding a public meeting in Leningrad was compelling. We found ourselves working at an extraordinary moment in Leningrad's history.

The meeting was scheduled for Friday, October 3rd outside the Museum of Atheism, an orange building on the busy Nevsky Prospekt. The museum was formerly Kazansky Cathedral, but now stood desolate, glorified only in its desecration.

I asked our friends from the music group Winter Garden to play, and as a crowd gathered I moved to the front and preached the Gospel, intent on restoring God's Spirit within the Museum of Atheism.

The meeting was so successful that we returned the following night, assisted by active Christians from several different churches.

The open air meetings continued whenever possible until the inevitable happened. I was arrested, held overnight, and fined fifty roubles. Some people questioned the wisdom of these open air meetings and were dismayed by the fine. But I argued, "We must force glasnost to its limits to prove that it works. Anyway, I'm happy to pay the fine," I said, addressing the issue directly. "It's only fifty roubles. If we hired a hall for meetings, it would cost us three hundred roubles. Brothers, it's cheaper this way!"

Lennon and I still visited Café Saigon. Whenever we announced a meeting, the place was packed out. Teenagers with mohican haircuts, leather jackets and torn jeans told us they were hooked on drugs and homemade booze. Girls

with pink eyebrows no older than seventeen who sold sex
in the doorways and the back seats of cars told us they
wanted to slam the door on the past. Boys with homemade
switchblades told terrifying tales of crime and violence as
they asked if Jesus could really change their lives.

"We're bored. We've got nothing to live for. We have
no hope." This plea was heard wherever we went. The
message was simple. If you trust Jesus, he will radically
transform your life.

Flick-knives were tossed to the front and drugs flushed
down the toilet as conviction swept the group.

Lennon emerged as a gifted leader with pastoral insight
who was trusted by everyone; he supported the decision that
had been taken regarding our departure, as did all the others.

Although I believed that God was directing our family
to leave Leningrad, I couldn't understand what this would
really mean.

Leaving Leningrad!

Leaving my hometown, my friends, the gypsy church and
the ministry that God had given me among Leningrad's
street people. I wasn't leaving for a holiday in the West.
I knew that the spiritual warfare might be more intense but
I had to obey God. Several prophecies had confirmed this
dramatic move leading us away. It was clear that I could
help our people more by leaving. Now the moment had come
to act on the conviction that God had placed in our hearts.

26

RAINBOW'S EDGE

When Tanya's Mama died, the final block to us leaving Leningrad was lifted.

Zhanna and Marina did not want their teenage romances to be broken up, but they acknowledged that their first allegiance was to Jesus.

But the saddest farewell was reserved for Panthera, who would be unable to travel to the West with us. She had become part of our lives, and the house seemed empty without her.

The night before we left Leningrad, I preached my last message. Coincidentally, our meeting was arranged soon after the annual celebrations of the Communist Revolution. "We in Leningrad have been celebrating seventy years of the Soviet system, but we are about to see the end of the godless empire." It was an emotional time as we celebrated communion and baptised several young people who had come to faith in Christ. "I'm not leaving you behind," I explained, "but I'll be able to serve you best by continuing our work in the West."

The authorities played a cat-and-mouse game until the end. Although a political decision taken in Moscow had granted us permission to leave, we were hassled everywhere. We were prevented till the last moment from collecting airline tickets to London that had been provided by friends from the British Campaign group.

The airport was crowded with friends, who gave us a raucous send-off with songs and prayers. It seemed that all of Leningrad had turned out to say one last goodbye.

Sergei Timokhin was there, and clasped my hand tight.

George, my childhood friend, threw his arms around my neck. "Send me your address! I'll try to visit you," he said impetuously. My cousin Slavik embraced me. "For Holy Russia!" he said emotionally, and kissed me on both cheeks.

Valya stepped forward and clutched me tightly. I could hardly believe that once we were like tramps on the street with nowhere to run.

Her eyes were wet as we embraced one last time. "I'll never forget," she whispered amidst the tears.

"Neither will I," I said and kissed her tenderly.

I had already said goodbye to Aunt Tamara, who was unable to make the journey to the airport.

Someone grabbed me from behind and tossed me like a ball in the air. The KGB men with their cameras clicked away, documenting our parting scenes for the KGB files.

It was hard saying goodbye to Lennon and the others. "I'll never forget our gypsy church," I said. "You'll always be on my mind, but the world must be our mission field."

"Don't worry, Valeri, we'll continue your work," he assured me.

The final farewell was an emotional reunion with many whose lives we had touched in passing.

Zhanna and Marina had their own friends who lined up to say goodbye. Leaving Leningrad was a traumatic experience for Tanya, who feared the uncertainty of the West.

I couldn't believe that this moment had come. The sea of smiling faces seemed like a movie's final scene.

It had been snowing, and we stepped from the airport bus on to a carpet of white to reach the silver jet parked on the runway.

In my mind's eye, I saw a bald haggard man sitting in a prison cell, who prophesied that I would leave for the West when snow was on the ground. "Praise you, my Jesus!" I said aloud, as the cold night wind cut through me like a knife.

I looked up at the plane, shining in the night, illuminated by a lone spotlight from the tower. The British Airways sign reassured me. I was pleased that our flight out of Russia was not to be on an infamous Aeroflot aircraft. "One of God's little jokes," I whispered to Tanya.

Inside the plane, I peered through the cabin window. Down below us, a worker with a giant shovel swept the snow away from the enormous wheels of the plane.

He paused for a moment to peer up at the aircraft and then went back to his task on the ground.

But in that fleeting instant, I saw the faces of our poor Russian people reflected in his haunted image. I had seen that look all across our land. Everyone looked as if they had lost something, as though they needed something.

"Goodbye, my friend, God bless you!" I whispered as the labourer slipped from view.

Goodbye my poor Russian people. Goodbye KGB, perhaps one day you will understand how Jesus led me away and helped me cross the red barbed-wire.

As we were lifted into the night sky above Leningrad I reflected on the extraordinary events that had led to this precious moment.

Beside me, Tanya held my hand tight.

My heart felt heavy as I sensed the spiritual oppression that had fallen like a shadow across the land. God's special gift to man was the river of life, but the godless Soviet system stood against this stream by stealing God from our people. These bandits spread communism like poison all over the world. Those who tried to reveal the truth were hunted down like animals. How could people be so blind as to believe these lies?

But even the KGB couldn't chain the hearts of the Russian people.

A young stewardess welcomed us on board and asked if we wanted a drink. "You can have wine or cognac. Anything you like," she said in a foreign accent.

"How much is it?" I asked. I only had a few kopeks in my pocket, as we had spent our money on gifts for friends in Britain.

"No, no, the drinks are free," the British Airways stewardess replied with a smile straight out of charm school.

"Free? Why?" I asked, perplexed. She explained that the aircraft's cooling system had developed a problem and the captain had ordered free drinks for everyone to compensate for the discomfort that some passengers might experience.

Immediately, I understood that we had reached freedom. This would never happen inside the Soviet Union.

Tanya requested a glass of wine, and I ordered cognac. Together we raised our glasses and toasted our new life in freedom.

The British Airways 707 soared through the sky. But for me, time had stopped.

I found myself praying for the KGB, for Katchkin, my investigator, and Starkov in the KGB headquarters in Leningrad, Captain Zhora, Lobanov and Zinchenko in the labour camp.

They tried to kill me, but I escaped.

Adrift in a labyrinth of prisons, labour camps and psychiatric hospitals, a virtual kingdom of evil, I became a prisoner of Jesus. Captured by his love, I could never be free of my bonds. My guards were the captives, imprisoned and chained by the lies and deception that had come to rule over them.

The labour camp was like a small country on some remote island. A town without law and order, an island drifting off the coast of hell.

I hadn't known if I would ever return alive from the camp. I had seen many broken bodies adrift in anonymous space.

But I dared to live, to resist the terror that I had witnessed. Yet some things I wanted to forget. To shut my eyes and banish the image from my mind. But like a demon in the night, the darkness of the netherworld was lit by a flare out of hell. I was condemned never to forget.

Tanya's frozen smile, fading in the distance, growing dim and faint, like some old sepia photograph. The train pulling out of a station, figures huddled on the platform. Hands waving, and then a blur.

Zhanna and Marina, my babes in arms, who grew tall and beautiful while I was sewing nets and pulling lice and bugs and fleas from my body.

The pain of separation between a man and his family, the wound that cuts the deepest. Memories became the gifts I cherished. Standing alone, naked, I hid them deep in my heart.

But many others shared my experiences. Vladimir Bukovsky, who trod the treacherous path before me, estimated that almost a third of the Soviet population has passed through the camps. Bukovsky built a castle inside his cell, every detail, from the foundations, floors, walls, staircases, secret passages right up to the pointed roofs and turrets. Sharansky also withstood every assault and remained a tower of strength.

For me there was no doubt that the power of Jesus kept me alive.

Like a bullet blazing out of the midnight sky, the silver bird circled London's Heathrow airport. The lights of the city twinkled below us, a trillion glittering stars in a dazzling cavalcade of shining streets and neon boulevards.

Beside me, Tanya's grip on my hand tightened. I gave her a little squeeze. Zhanna and Marina leaned over the back of their seats. "Daddy, Daddy, we've arrived," they squealed excitedly.

"Ladies and gentlemen, we are approaching London's Heathrow Airport," a friendly voice announced. "Please extinguish your cigarettes and fasten your safety belts."

My heart seemed to reach bursting point, overflowing with a profound sacrifice of praise.

I didn't know what would happen in the next few days. What did the future hold?

Only one thing mattered as we took our first few steps in freedom.

My Jesus!

POSTSCRIPT

In 1989 the Barinov family moved to Bognor Regis, West Sussex and are members of a local parish Church. In 1990, Zhanna married her Russian boyfriend, Maxim, in Chichester.

Valeri has plans to record new albums and is preparing for an international "Jesus March" which includes a visit to the Soviet Union.

Jubilee Campaign worked for Valeri's release, and also worked with the Women's Campaign for Soviet Jewry to free Alex Zelichenok who is now in Israel.

If you would like to help others like Valeri Barinov and Alex Zelichenok, please write to: Jubilee Campaign, P.O. Box 80, Cobham, Surrey KT11 2BQ.

THE BOOK OF THE DUN COW

Walter Wangerin

A strange and magical story set in the time when the sun turned around the earth and animals could speak. Chaunticleer the Rooster rules over a more or less peaceable kingdom, but what the animals do not know is that they are the keepers of Wyrm, monster of Evil, long imprisoned beneath the earth. And Wyrm is breaking free.

"A beautifully written fantasy . . . in which there is adventure and humour, betrayal and despair. But most of all there is hope."

Washington Post

WHICH ONE'S CLIFF?

Cliff Richard

A sparkling new edition of Cliff's autobiography, bringing his story right up to date. Sixteen pages of original colour photographs, together with a few shots from the archives, a complete discography, and a new chapter, give a fascinating account of over thirty years at the top of showbusiness.

"An excellent book, frank, funny and engaging."

The Baptist Times

THE ARCHON CONSPIRACY

Dave Hunt

Computer genius Ken Inman's life-long goal to contact highly-evolved intelligences explodes into reality . . . leaving him face-to-face with the seemingly all-powerful Archons who promise a New Age of international peace and prosperity. But is their benevolent promise all that it appears to be?

In a race against time, journalist Carla Bertelli goes behind the scenes and uncovers a plot more sinister than she ever imagined. Intrigue and suspense follow as the reality of spiritual warfare in unleashed.

LIFE MEANS WHAT?

J John

What is life all about?

Is there anything beyond the here and now?

Happiness is elusive in the modern world. Fear, anxiety and loneliness are hallmarks of our society. Where is the cure? Wealth and possessions do not supply it, any more than fame, brilliance or good looks.

Where else can we look? To God?